Primer
On
Sexual Harassment

ACKNOWLEDGMENTS

The law firm of Seyfarth, Shaw, Fairweather & Geraldson, devoted substantial resources to the research and preparation of this book. Without the assistance of Seyfarth Shaw this book could not have been published. The authors gratefully acknowledge the law firm's support and encouragement.

We especially wish to express our gratitude to the labor and employment lawyers at Seyfarth Shaw who drafted chapters for this book, including: Anita Barondes, Washington, D.C., James R. Beyer, Chicago, Robert E. Buch, Los Angeles, Christopher E. Cobey, San Francisco, Deborah A. Folloni, Washington, D.C., Georgeanne Henshaw, Los Angeles, Keith A. Hunsaker, Jr., Los Angeles, David D. Marshall, Los Angeles, Gerald Pauling, Chicago, Kaiulani Poderick, Los Angeles, Lawrence P. Postol, Washington, D.C., Krista Schoenheider Kaplan, Chicago, Ray Schoonhoven, Chicago, Keith M. Sherman, San Francisco, Kenneth D. Sulzer, Los Angeles, and Helen K. Whatley, Chicago.

We would also like to thank Kelly J. Koelker of Paul, Hastings, Janofsky & Walker, Atlanta, for drafting the chapter on Claims by Third Parties.

We also acknowledge the great assistance of the many paralegal and support staff personnel of Seyfarth Shaw who devoted untold hours to this project, including Thomas D. Brown, Mahlon McLean, Loretta Peller, Rosemarie A. Ahmed, Carolyn Hennings, Le'Kisch Laidley, NaDari Taylor, Paul Fronczek, and Jeff Holley.

and pernicious effects of harassment, and the means by which to prevent and correct it. We hope that this book will prove helpful to employment professionals in their efforts to keep the workplace free of harassment and the human and economic costs associated with it.

Barbara T. Lindemann

PREFACE

The Civil Rights marches of the 1960s and the passage of the Civil Rights Act of 1964 were major turning points in the struggle to afford people equal employment opportunities. In *Employment Discrimination Law*, by Barbara Lindemann Schlei and Paul Grossman, we codified and explained the legal developments spawned by that Act. *Employment Discrimination Law* benefited from the contributions of dozens of experienced employment lawyers. Now about to be issued in its third edition, *Employment Discrimination Law* has come to be viewed as the "Bible" in its field, largely because it provides the employment professional with a readable description of what the law requires and why.

The widespread recognition that harassment was one of the evils addressed by employment discrimination law did not come until much later, in the 1980s. In our new book, *Sexual Harassment in Employment Law*, by Barbara Lindemann and David Kadue, we have addressed the developing law of employment-related harassment. In *Sexual Harassment in Employment Law*, we again attempted to divide the material into categories in order to make the law sensible in light of our everyday experiences. This effort was again enhanced by the contributions of experienced lawyers from across the country.

While *Sexual Harassment in Employment Law* focuses heavily on the needs of the legal specialist, this *Primer on Sexual Harassment* addresses the need to make the law of sexual harassment plain to nonlawyers. This book will help improve the work environment to the extent that it educates people about the nature

DEDICATION

To George, Frayda, Adam, Elizabeth, Helen, Charlotte,
George, and Sloan Lindemann

B.T.L.

To Martha, Arnold, and Marjorie Kadue

D.D.K.

Copyright © 1992
The Bureau of National Affairs, Inc.

Library of Congress Cataloging-in-Publication Data

Lindemann, Barbara, 1935–
   Primer on sexual harassment / Barbara Lindemann, David D. Kadue.
     p. cm.
   Includes bibliographical references and index.
   ISBN 0-87179-764-X
   1. Sexual harassment of women—Law and legislation—United
States. 2. Sex discrimination in employment—Law and legislation—
United States. I. Kadue, David D. II. Title.
KF3467.L55 1992
344.73'014133—dc20
[347.30414133]   92-25748
                                                               CIP

Authorization to photocopy items for internal or personal use, or
the internal or personal use of specific clients, is granted by BNA
Books for libraries and other users registered with the Copyright
Clearance Center (CCC) Transactional Reporting Service, provided
that $0.50 per page is paid directly to CCC, 27 Congress St., Salem,
MA 01970. 0-87179-764-X/92/$0 + .50.

Published by BNA Books
1250 23rd St. N.W., Washington, D.C. 20037

Printed in the United States of America
International Standard Book Number: 0-87179-764-X

PRIMER ON SEXUAL HARASSMENT

Barbara Lindemann
David D. Kadue

Seyfarth, Shaw, Fairweather & Geraldson

The Bureau of National Affairs, Inc., Washington, D.C.

CONTENTS

INTRODUCTION

This book is written primarily for human resource professionals and others who need or want to explore the legal aspects of sexual harassment in employment. Courts in recent years have firmly established that sexual harassment is unlawful under any of the several different laws that forbid discrimination in employment on the basis of sex. Chief among these laws are Title VII of the Civil Rights Act of 1964 as amended (Title VII) and the fair employment practices (FEP) statutes of various states. Title VII makes it an "unlawful employment practice for an employer . . . to fail or refuse to hire or to discharge any individual, or otherwise to discriminate against any individual with respect to his compensation, terms, conditions, or privileges of employment, because of such individual's race, color, religion, *sex*, or national origin" (emphasis added).

Sexual harassment in employment is simply one form of sex discrimination. Narrowly defined, sexual harassment is a demand that a subordinate grant sexual favors in order to get or keep a job benefit. More broadly defined, sexual harassment includes any situation in which a significant unwanted condition is imposed on a person's employment because of that person's sex. The behaviors that constitute sexual harassment fall into three basic categories: sexual advances; gender-based animosity, where people are hostile to an employee because of that employee's sex; and a sexually charged workplace, featuring sexually oriented behavior or material.

This book describes various court decisions to help explain exactly what words and actions transcend the normal travails

1

of a workplace and become so severe or so pervasive that they constitute illegal harassment. If the facts of a case seem extraordinarily specific, please understand that they are presented not to offend, but to show exactly what kind of behavior has been found unlawful.

To make a person's employment miserable because of his or her race, color, national origin, sex, religion, age, or disability is both illegal and mean. This book addresses only what is unlawful. Certain behavior may not rise to the level of a violation of the law, yet it still may be undesirable workplace conduct. An employer may wish to foster an employment environment that sets a higher standard for conduct among employees than that which violates the law. Indeed, much of what the law would call "sexual harassment" would never occur if employees behaved decently toward others who share their work environment and did not use power to make the lives of others miserable—a misery often endured out of economic necessity.

Sexual harassment almost always involves the harassment of women by men. We therefore generally refer to the victim of sexual harassment as "she" and the alleged harasser as "he."

Various studies have reported that 50 to 80 percent of women have experienced sexual harassment on the job, and that harassment may be the most widespread problem facing American women at work. The forms of harassment reported, with the percentage of women reporting them, include rape (1 percent), pressure for sexual favors (10 percent), pressure for unwanted dates (20 percent), deliberate touching, pinching, or leaning over (25 percent), and sexual remarks, teasing, jokes and questions, and the display of unwanted sexual materials (35 percent).

The studies suggest other important characteristics of sexual harassment at work:

- Men and women, as classes, tend to differ in their tolerance of certain forms of sexually related conduct, with many men accepting certain conduct that offends many women. Some courts now view charges of sexual harassment made by women from the viewpoint of the "reasonable woman."

- Sexual harassment occurs in all work settings, the office as well as the factory.
- Sexual harassment tends to occur most often in "gender hierarchies" in which men hold power over women, either as their organizational superiors or because the women are present in small numbers in a traditionally male job or workplace.
- Women who are most vulnerable economically are the most vulnerable to sexual harassment.
- Victims of sexual harassment often remain silent, even while suffering physically, economically, and psychologically, in order to avoid reprisal or embarrassment.
- Sexual harassment creates significant productivity costs for the employers of harassed employees and for the economy as a whole.

Sexual harassment litigation has increased dramatically since the early 1980s. It occurs in several different forums and pursuant to various common-law theories and statutory schemes. Those suing in court are called "plaintiffs," those bringing charges before the EEOC are called "charging parties," those bringing charges before state FEP agencies are sometimes called "claimants," and we have chosen to use the term "complainant" to cover all of these situations.

Courts have developed two basic theories of liability for sexual harassment. One theory is called "quid pro quo." Quid pro quo cases typically involve an allegation that the complainant has suffered some job detriment (been denied a raise, lost a promotion, been fired) because of her reaction to a sexual advance. Questions in quid pro quo cases often focus on whether advances occurred, whether they were welcome, and on the employer's motivation for imposing a job detriment. These and other quid pro quo issues are discussed in Chapter 2.

The other theory of liability, "hostile environment," typically involves an allegation that the complainant is being treated in a hostile manner because of her sex. Hostile environment cases often involve an "intangible job detriment." One common hostile environment issue involves the degree of harassment a woman must suffer: whether the harassment is significant enough to alter a condition of employment. Another common hostile environment issue is whether the employer is responsible for the unwelcome conduct. These and other hostile environment issues are discussed in Chapter 3.

Both quid pro quo and hostile environment harassment may affect third parties—people who are not the direct targets of harassment but are still affected by it. Sexual favoritism in the workplace may adversely affect people who are not themselves directly involved in the favoritism. In a situation where a female subordinate gains a job benefit, a more qualified third party may have a claim of sex discrimination. Further, sexual activities or displays—pornographic posters, sexual horseplay, or sexual graffiti—may be welcome to most of the work force and still be highly offensive to others. Claims by such "indirect victims" or "third-party victims" are discussed in Chapter 4.

Sexual harassment often is alleged to be so unbearable that it caused the complainant to quit her job. Under these circumstances the law permits a complainant to sue as if she had formally been fired. "Constructive discharge" cases are discussed in Chapter 5.

Another common issue arising in sexual harassment cases is retaliation. The law protects individuals who suffer an adverse job action because they have protested unlawful discrimination, have filed a charge of employment discrimination, or have supported such a filing by another person. The law on retaliation is discussed in Chapter 6.

Most employment discrimination lawsuits have been filed under Title VII. This trend is likely to continue. Under the Civil Rights Act of 1991, Title VII suits are no longer limited to trials before judges in which the only available remedies are essentially back pay, reinstatement, and attorney's fees. Title VII cases may now be heard by juries, and prevailing plaintiffs may be awarded additional damages for emotional distress. In egregious cases, punitive damages are also available. These new damages are subject to maximum amounts, which vary from $50,000 to $300,000, depending on the size of the employer. The effects of the Civil Rights Act of 1991 on sexual harassment litigation are summarized in Appendix 5.

State FEP statutes, discussed in Chapter 7, exist in virtually every state and often provide for the unlimited relief that is still unavailable under Title VII.

Sexual harassment complainants have also relied on other sources of legal protection. Foremost among these are common-law actions, which are discussed in Chapter 11. Common-law actions provide for jury trials and unlimited damages. Public employees have the additional source of certain statutory and constitutional protections, which are discussed in Chapter 8.

Still other sources of possible relief for sexual harassment complainants can be found in unemployment compensation statutes (Chapter 9), workers' compensation statutes (Chapter 10), criminal statutes (Chapter 12), and laws governing workplaces that are organized by unions (Chapter 13).

Employers must take reasonable steps to prevent and correct sexual harassment. Chapters 14, 15, and 16 discuss the issues relating to that duty. A checklist for an in-house audit of a company antisexual harassment policy is provided in Appendix 6.

The Equal Employment Opportunity Commission (EEOC) is the federal agency that interprets and helps to enforce Title VII. It has issued persuasive sets of guidelines on sexual harassment (Appendices 1–3). The EEOC has the duty to investigate federal discrimination charges by sexual harassment complainants. Chapter 17 describes the EEOC's investigation process.

Sexual harassment cases raise important litigation issues, some that are common to all cases of employment discrimination and some that are unique. The last part of the book discusses the defense litigation strategy (Chapter 18), insurance coverage considerations (Chapter 19), evidence and discovery issues (Chapter 20), remedies (Chapter 21), and settlement (Chapter 22).

The defenses in sexual harassment litigation are both factual and legal. They include the complainant's failure to file a timely complaint and to exhaust administrative remedies (Chapter 17), the complainant's failure to abide by an agreement to arbitrate (Chapter 13), and potential constitutional restrictions on the government's ability to forbid certain verbal forms of sexual harassment. Defenses also include the complainant's failure to invoke the employer's internal grievance procedure, the welcome nature of the conduct complained of, the employer's nondiscriminatory reasons for its challenged employment decisions (Chapters 2 and 3), the employer's prompt remedial action (Chapter 16), the complainant's failure to mitigate damages, "unclean hands," and other defenses (Chapter 21).

Part I

Theories of Liability Under Employment Discrimination Statutes

1

CHARACTERISTICS OF SEXUAL HARASSMENT IN THE WORKPLACE

I. THEORIES OF LIABILITY

A. Conduct That Constitutes Sexual Harassment

Sexual harassment can be best understood by looking at the kind of conduct involved. Sexual harassment usually involves one or more of three basic kinds of behavior:

(1) unwelcome sexual advances,
(2) gender-based animosity (hostile conduct based on the victim's gender), and
(3) sexually charged workplace behaviors (conduct that is offensive on the basis of gender to persons who are not necessarily the targets of the conduct).

Sexual harassment is unlawful sex discrimination under either of two legal theories: "quid pro quo" and "hostile environment." All three forms of behavior mentioned above may constitute a hostile environment; only unwelcome sexual advances are an essential part of a claim of quid pro quo harassment.

9

B. Quid Pro Quo Harassment

Perhaps the most vivid example of sexual harassment in employment is the supervisor who uses supervisory power to pressure a subordinate employee to grant sexual favors. The illicit exchange of job benefits for sexual favors has been given the name "quid pro quo" (see Chapter 2).

C. Hostile Environment Harassment

Unwelcome sex-based conduct can constitute unlawful sex discrimination even without a tangible job loss, if it creates a "hostile environment." In this form of harassment, an employee's supervisor, co-workers, or even nonemployees engage in conduct that offends the employee because of the employee's gender. The conduct usually involves a series of incidents rather than a single episode, and may consist of unwelcome sexual advances. More often, the conduct reflects hostility rather than sexual interest. In many cases, this conduct reflects and stems from the same kinds of prejudice and stereotypical thinking that has led to abusive conduct directed at racial and ethnic groups. Thus, a sexually hostile environment is "sexual" not because it necessarily involves sexual activity, but because the victim is an object of harassment as the result of her gender (see Chapter 3).

D. Quid Pro Quo and Hostile Environment Harassment Compared

The essence of a quid pro quo claim is a "play or pay," "put out or get out" bargain by which an individual must choose between forgoing job benefits or submitting to sexual demands.

The essence of a hostile environment is that an individual must endure a work environment that, while not necessarily causing any economic loss, causes psychological or emotional harm or otherwise unreasonably interferes with the individual's job performance.

Notwithstanding their differing characteristics, quid pro quo and hostile environment situations overlap and often converge. Victims of quid pro quo harassment often suffer a hostile environment. Similarly, victims of hostile environments often suffer the job losses associated with quid pro quo harassment. A hostile environment may drive employees off the job, demoralize or upset them to the extent that they are fired for absenteeism or unsatisfactory work, or cause them to complain about the harassment and risk retaliatory discharge.

II. LEGAL RECOGNITION OF SEXUAL HARASSMENT AS SEX DISCRIMINATION

Title VII does not mention sexual harassment; nor is there any mention of sexual harassment in the legislative history of Title VII. Indeed, the very term "sexual harassment" was not in common use before 1975. For this and other reasons, it was not until 1976 that any court recognized sexual harassment as a form of unlawful sex discrimination. It was 1986 before the Supreme Court, in *Meritor Savings Bank v. Vinson*, finally established that sexual harassment constitutes sex discrimination in employment even if the harassment does not cause a direct financial injury.

In retrospect, the great question posed by the judicial history of sexual harassment is not how it came to be regarded as a form of discrimination, but why for so long it was treated differently from other forms of discriminatory conduct. In most respects, the legal concepts surrounding sexual harassment can be shown to be a form of sex discrimination under the same basic rules that are applied in other employment discrimination cases.

Sex discrimination cases, like employment discrimination cases generally, are analyzed under either a "disparate treatment" or an "adverse impact" theory. Disparate treatment occurs if a woman is intentionally treated differently from a man because of her gender. An employer engages in disparate treatment if it refuses to consider women for employment, pays a woman less than a man for the same work, or discharges a woman for an offense for which men are not discharged. Disparate treatment cases often involve the issue of the employer's intent: whether the employer was motivated in making an employment decision on the basis of a nondiscriminatory reason. The assertion of a nondiscriminatory reason might be unpersuasive if the reason has not been applied uniformly. For example, if an employer seeks to justify its failure to hire women by claiming that it requires that all employees be six feet tall, that justification is not credible if it turns out that the employer still hires male applicants who are not six feet tall.

An adverse impact occurs if a facially neutral employment practice disproportionately disadvantages women, as opposed to men, and if the practice is not justified by "business necessity" (a notoriously ill-defined term). For example, a requirement that all employees be six feet tall would have an adverse impact on women because proportionally more women than men are less than six feet tall. That height requirement would be unlawfully discriminatory unless it is a business necessity, as with, perhaps, a basketball team. Practices found to have had an adverse impact on minorities have included a general intelligence test or a high-school diploma requirement that disqualifies substantially more blacks than whites and that cannot be shown to predict successful job performance.

A. Quid Pro Quo Cases

An analogy illustrates how easily quid pro quo harassment fits within traditional notions of disparate treatment. Suppose that, in addition to the normal duties of the job, female clerks— but not male clerks—are required to take the boss's children to school, pick up his laundry, balance his checkbook, and do his grocery shopping. There is nothing inherently improper in hiring an employee, male or female, to perform these tasks, even though they are admittedly personal in nature. When, however, they are assigned on the basis of gender, sex discrimination has occurred. Moreover, if a woman objects to these assignments because of their discriminatory nature, any resulting reprisal would be unlawful retaliation (see Chapter 6).

The analysis is exactly the same where the personal tasks are sexual in nature, except that it would be superfluous to require proof that the assignment had been made on the basis of sex, because only a woman can perform sexual tasks for a heterosexual man. Harassment of men by heterosexual women stands on the same footing; so, too, does homosexual harassment. Only in the case of harassment by a truly bisexual supervisor is there a theoretical absence of disparate treatment. Moreover, the disparate treatment is always clearly intentional. The employer is liable for this conduct to the extent that the supervisor accomplishes discriminatory acts by using the employer's authority to grant or deny an employment benefit.

Despite the force of this reasoning, many courts initially objected to recognizing quid pro quo harassment as sex discrimination. These courts reasoned that quid pro quo harassment simply reflects a conflict between personalities rather than discrimination on the basis of gender; that quid pro quo harassment is based on sexual attractiveness, not gender; that the employer cannot be liable for quid pro quo harassment, because an individual's sexual advances were not truly employment-related unless an employment policy authorized them; that recognizing quid pro quo harassment as employment discrimination would open the legal floodgates to a deluge of litigation presumably not intended by Congress; and that there is no mention of sexual harassment in the legislative history of either Title VII or its amendments.

An additional factor that may have inhibited the recognition of sexual harassment as employment discrimination is the same fear of false reporting that once led to women being limited in their testimony in the prosecution of rape cases. Reinforcing this fear is the fact that labeling conduct as sexual harassment often has greater personal consequences for the accused than does a finding of some other type of discrimination.

The 1977 federal appellate court decision in *Barnes v. Costle* was one of the first to hold that quid pro quo harassment is sex discrimination. Paulette Barnes, who worked in a federal agency's equal employment opportunity division, claimed that she lost her job because she rejected repeated requests of her male boss for sexual favors. The lower court rejected her sex discrimination claim, reasoning that even if the boss's conduct was inexcusable, it was not based on Barnes' sex, but rather involved their personal relationship.

The appellate court reversed, holding that the harassment was based on gender, because the male boss would not have sought sexual favors from a male in Barnes' position: but for her gender, Barnes never would have been subjected to sexual demands as the price for keeping her job.

Barnes v. Costle thus established that the sex-based assignment of duties, sexual or otherwise, constitutes unlawful sex discrimination where the employer, through its supervisors, enforces the assignment by threat of discharge or other adverse economic consequence. The case did not address whether Title VII would also be violated by sex-based disparate treatment that had no economic impact.

In 1980, the EEOC issued its Guidelines on Discrimination Because of Sex (EEOC Guidelines). The EEOC Guidelines are not binding on courts but have persuasive weight as the official view of the EEOC, which is charged with administering Title VII. One subpart of the EEOC Guidelines, addressing sexual harassment, states that quid pro quo sexual harassment is sex discrimination in violation of Title VII, and that an individual's response to unwelcome conduct of a sexual nature may not lawfully be made the basis of any adverse employment decision (Appendix 1, EEOC Guidelines §1604.11(a)).

B. Hostile Environment Cases

The EEOC Guidelines also state that unwelcome sexual conduct violates Title VII whenever it "has the purpose or effect of unreasonably interfering with an individual's work performance or creating an intimidating, hostile, or offensive working environment." When the EEOC Guidelines were adopted, no court yet had held that a sexually hostile environment was unlawful in the absence of any specific job loss. Now, however, that principle is well established.

Most hostile environment cases present situations that, like quid pro quo cases, involve disparate treatment based on an employee's gender, because the employee is subjected to offensive, hostile, or intimidating behavior to which men are not subjected. Unlike quid pro quo cases, hostile environment cases are not limited to incidents of sexual advances, but may consist wholly of other forms of conduct, such as conduct reflecting gender-based animosity or constituting a sexually charged workplace.

1. Sexual Advances. In one common situation, a female employee is subjected to unwelcome sexual advances, innuendo, touching, and propositions by a male employee who may or may not be her supervisor. The conduct, which would not necessarily be considered undesirable by all women, continues, although she makes it clear that it is unwelcome to her. The woman may or may not eventually submit. She suffers emotional distress and finds it difficult to do her job. She may or may not resign.

When this conduct is not an isolated act of an individual employee and is so pervasive that the employer knew or should have known of it, it is attributable to the employer. In that event the conduct is little different from the typical quid pro quo case in which an employee is fired for rebuffing the boss's advance: the detriment she suffers, while solely emotional and psychological, is no less real than a specific job detriment. Her working conditions differ from those of her male colleagues, and she would not have suffered the disparate treatment but for her sex. Her tolerance of an adverse condition based on her sex has been made part of the employment bargain.

2. Gender-Based Animosity. In another common situation, a woman employee, often in a traditionally male-dominated occupation (*e.g.*, truck driving) or workplace (*e.g.*, a coal mine), is subjected to scorn, ridicule, and verbal abuse from males who resent her presence. The behavior consists of gestures, words, or conduct that may or may not be sexual in content. If the conduct is sexual, that fact may suffice to prove that the conduct is because of the victim's sex, but the conduct may be based on sex even if it has no specifically sexual content.

3. Sexually Charged Workplace. In a third situation, a woman's workplace features open displays of pornographic posters, calendars, and graffiti, or pervasive incidents of sexual horseplay or sexual favoritism. This conduct, even if not directed specifically toward the woman, may create a hostile work environment for her, or for women employees in general.

III. *MERITOR SAVINGS BANK v. VINSON*

The Supreme Court decided the leading sexual harassment case, *Meritor Savings Bank v. Vinson* (*Meritor*), in 1986. Mechelle Vinson was hired by Meritor Savings Bank as a teller trainee, and over the course of four years she worked her way up to assistant branch manager. Her supervisor, Sidney Taylor, was the manager of the branch where she worked. Vinson was discharged when she failed to return to work after her sick leave expired. She then sued Taylor and the bank, claiming that she had been subjected to sexual harassment by Taylor while on the job.

Vinson testified that, at Taylor's suggestion, they had had sexual relations 40 to 50 times. She said she agreed to do so out of fear of losing her job. She also claimed that Taylor had fondled her and exposed himself to her at work. Vinson never reported Taylor to his supervisors, assertedly because of her fear of him. Taylor completely denied Vinson's accusations. The bank, citing the absence of any complaint by Vinson, claimed ignorance of any improper conduct by Taylor.

The trial court ruled that if Vinson and Taylor did have an intimate relationship, it was voluntary and had nothing to do with her employment at the bank. Hence, said the court, Vinson was not the victim of sex discrimination. Even if Taylor's conduct was discriminatory, the bank had no notice of the conduct and could not be held liable for it.

Taylor and the bank argued to the Supreme Court that even if Vinson had been sexually harassed, she had no claim under Title VII because she had suffered no tangible loss of an economic character. The Supreme Court rejected this argument, ruling that discrimination because of sex violates Title VII even if it affects only the psychological aspects of employment. The Court cautioned, however, that this kind of unwelcome conduct violates Title VII only if it is "severe or pervasive"; trivial offenses do not count.

The Supreme Court also rejected the defense argument that no liability could exist, given the trial court's finding that Vinson's submission to Taylor's advances had been voluntary. The

Supreme Court held that voluntariness is not determinative. The correct question was whether Vinson, by her conduct, had indicated that the sexual advances were unwelcome. The Court acknowledged that the answer would turn on difficult decisions about the credibility of witnesses, which would require the fact finder to consider all of the circumstances, including any evidence that the alleged victim dressed in a sexually provocative manner or spoke at work about her personal sexual fantasies.

The Court also ruled that although an employer is not automatically liable for a supervisor's misdeeds in a hostile environment case, the employer's ignorance and the alleged victim's failure to complain do not necessarily insulate the employer from liability. The lower courts were left to grapple with the proper standard for employer liability in such cases.

IV. HARASSMENT FOR REASONS OTHER THAN SEX

A. Overview

Much of the law of sexual harassment was drawn from the law of harassment on the basis of race, national origin, and religion. Each of those forms of illegal discrimination can poison a working environment in equal measure: a sexually hostile environment can be a barrier to equality for women in the workplace just as racial harassment can be a barrier to equality for blacks.

Two characteristics of sexual harassment distinguish it from harassment on other protected bases. First, sexual harassment frequently consists of sexual advances, which often are welcome and socially useful for fostering relationships between men and women. By contrast, nonsexual forms of harassment, such as racial epithets, inherently lack social value.

Second, the term "sex" is ambiguous, in that it describes not only a basis protected by statute, but also an activity. To the extent that "sexual" harassment consists of hostile activities directed at an individual because of gender, sexual harassment analytically resembles harassment based upon any other protected class. The resemblance is much weaker, however, when sexual harassment is of the quid pro quo variety, for then the discrimination results from an *activity* (rejection of sexual advances) rather than directly from a *status* (being a woman).

Notwithstanding these differences, the law on nonsexual harassment helps one to understand sexual harassment. First, sexual harassment sometimes occurs in combination with other types of prohibited harassment, such as racial harassment. The facts that support a harassment claim based on race or other grounds can contribute toward a showing of the "pervasiveness" element of a hostile environment sexual harassment claim (*Hicks v. Gates Rubber Co.*).

In addition, because a finding of harassment of any kind involves an analysis of severity, repetition, and response or knowledge of the employer, a discussion of nonsexual harassment helps to provide a better sense of where one draws the line in sexually hostile environment cases.

B. Race, Color, and National Origin

Rogers v. EEOC was the first federal appellate case to consider whether Title VII prohibits harassment even if it causes no tangible job detriment. Josephine Chavez, an optometrist's assistant, claimed that her employer segregated patients by race so that Chavez could not serve white patients. The trial court ruled against Chavez, reasoning that she had suffered no harm that Title VII prohibited. The appellate court, however, thought otherwise. It held that psychological as well as economic employment benefits are entitled to statutory protection. The phrase "terms, conditions or privileges of employment" in Title VII thus includes an employee's emotional and psychological stability.

Since *Rogers*, courts have evaluated hostile environment cases by focusing on the gravity *and* the frequency of the offensive conduct. A steady barrage of mean-spirited, racial comments is unlawful race discrimination. Title VII does not, however, prohibit racial comments that are merely accidental, sporadic, or part of casual conversation. In *Davis v. Monsanto Chemical Co.*, black workers complained of racial slurs, derogatory racial graffiti on bathroom walls, restrictions on lunchroom use, and spitting on time cards. The court concluded that the conduct was not sufficiently pervasive to alter the complainants' conditions of employment, because racial epithets were directed only once at the complainants, and because the employer acted quickly to correct any abusive situation reported.

Yet even isolated acts, if sufficiently severe, can create a racially hostile environment. In *Vance v. Southern Bell Telephone & Telegraph Co.*, a black complainant twice found a noose hanging from the light fixture above her work station and found that some of her work had been sabotaged. The court, ruling for the complainant, stressed the gravity of the incidents. In *DeGrace v. Rumsfeld*, a civilian fire fighter feared reporting to work after receiving threatening notes from his co-workers. One note read, "Hey boy get your Black ass out before you don't have one," and another warned, "Nigger, If we end up having a fire, you'll be staying in it and getting a lot blacker." The fire fighter eventually was discharged for excessive absenteeism. Ruling for the discharged fire fighter, the court held that an employer cannot justify the discharge of an employee on the basis of absenteeism caused by racial harassment for which the employer was responsible.

Racial harassment often takes the form of racist language. In *Walker v. Ford Motor Co.*, the complainant proved a racially hostile environment with proof that the defendants called the complainant a "dumb nigger," referred to poorly repaired cars as "nigger-rigged," and referred to the salesman with the lowest sales volume as "the black ass." The court rejected the employer's argument that because racial slurs were common in the relevant geographic area, they were not intended to carry racial overtones.

Racial harassment need not be racial in content: it may consist of pranks and other forms of hazing. The question in such cases is whether the circumstantial evidence is strong enough to prove racial motivation. In *Vaughn v. Pool Offshore Co.*, however, the hazing of a black oil rig worker—by greasing his genitals, dousing him with cold water and ammonia, and pouring hot coffee in his pocket—was not found to be racial harassment since nearly all rig workers, including the white supervisors, had been victims of similar pranks at one time or another.

C. Religion

In *Young v. Southwestern Savings & Loan Association*, the employer held a monthly staff meeting that began with a short religious talk and prayer delivered by a Christian minister. When the employer insisted that the complainant, an atheist, attend the religious portion of the meeting, she resigned and was found to have suffered a "constructive discharge" (see Chapter 5).

A religiously hostile environment can take the form of comments that disparage an employee's religious views, or meanness to employees because of their religion. Complainants must show that the harassment was severe or pervasive. In *Shapiro v. Holiday Inns*, where the complainant could point to only a few examples of anti-Semitic remarks, and where she admitted that the remarks had no real effect on her, they did not constitute actionable harassment.

To hold the employer responsible for religious harassment, complainants must establish that the employer had actual or constructive knowledge of the harassment and failed to take prompt and adequate remedial action. In *Weiss v. United States*, the employer was found to have had such knowledge because of the complainant's internal complaints and his EEOC charges.

D. Age

Claims of age-based harassment by an employee of at least 40 years of age can be brought under the Age Discrimination in Employment Act (ADEA), which closely resembles Title VII. In *Young v. Will County Department of Public Aid*, the court, assuming that the ADEA protects older employees from a hostile work environment, adopted the same analytical approach followed in sexual harassment cases.

E. Disability

The Americans With Disabilities Act of 1990 (ADA) prohibits employment discrimination against qualified individuals with disabilities. Because the ADA is modeled after Title VII, it prohibits harassment based on an individual's disability. Harassment on the basis of disability also is prohibited under state FEP statutes and under statutes applicable to certain federal and state contractors.

2

QUID PRO QUO HARASSMENT

I. ANALYZING QUID PRO QUO CLAIMS

Quid pro quo harassment is a form of sex discrimination. The essence of the quid pro quo theory of sexual harassment is that someone with the authority to control employment opportunities, such as promotions or salary increases, tries to get a subordinate employee to grant sexual favors in order to obtain or retain that employment opportunity.

The typical quid pro quo case is analyzed as a matter of disparate treatment (see Chapter 1, section II.). The question for a court, a jury, or a human resources director investigating an allegation, is whether the denial of a job benefit was motivated by a nondiscriminatory reason, such as the complainant's relative qualifications, or by a forbidden reason, such as the complainant's rejection of her supervisor's sexual advances.

Courts have identified the following elements that a complainant must prove to establish liability for quid pro quo harassment:

(1) the complainant is a member of a protected group (see section II. below);

(2) the complainant was subjected to unwelcome sexual advances (see section III. below);

(3) the complainant suffered an adverse employment action (see section IV. below);

22

(4) (a) the sexual advance was because of the complainant's gender, and (b) the complainant's reaction to the sexual advance affected a tangible aspect of her job (see section V. below); and

(5) the employer is responsible (see section VI. below).

II. MEMBERSHIP IN A PROTECTED CLASS

The first "element"—membership in a protected class— will be present in every case, because everyone is either male or female. The only reason for including this element is to identify precisely what the alleged basis is, and what it is not, particularly since prohibited factors other than sex may also be the basis for the harassment. It is important to clarify what is claimed—for example, whether the claim involves the complainant's sex, age, race, or national origin.

III. UNWELCOME SEXUAL ADVANCES

A. The Advance Must Be "Sexual"

The EEOC Guidelines describe sexual harassment as involving unwelcome "sexual advances, requests for sexual favors, and other verbal or physical conduct of a sexual nature" (Appendix 1, EEOC Guidelines §1604.11(a)). Usually the sexual nature of the request is plain—a supervisor demands that a subordinate employee provide sexual favors to get or keep a job benefit.

But the complainant need not prove an express demand for sexual favors. In *Boyd v. James S. Hayes Living Health Care Agency*, a supervisor was held to have engaged in quid pro quo harassment during an out-of-town business trip when he invited the complainant to his hotel room, gave her wine, turned on a pornographic movie, touched her shoulder, and offered her sexually explicit magazines.

Whether conduct is sexual in nature is judged by an objective standard. Behavior interpreted by the complainant as sexual may not result in a finding of sexual harassment if another motive is established. In *Jackson-Colley v. Army Corps of Engineers,* the court found that the defendant's gawking was actually an eye problem, that his groin-scratching stemmed from a medical condition, that his gifts and encouragement did not imply requests for sexual favors, and that his excessive use of vulgar language had been aimed at all employees without regard to their sex. In *Chamberlin v. 101 Realty,* the boss invited the complainant to meet customers of the firm at his house and to have lunch at the beach. The court concluded that these invitations were not sexual advances, but rather social invitations extended to an employee by a supervisor. Other conduct in the *Chamberlin* case, however, did constitute sexual advances, even though it was not explicit. That conduct included telling the complainant that she had a good body, telling her that she looked good in tight jeans, and taking her hand and saying, "My women are special. I like to put them on a pedestal."

The EEOC has reached conclusions similar to those of the courts. The fact that a male supervisor invites a female employee to lunch or dinner is not sufficient to constitute sexual harassment; it is a common practice for supervisors and their employees to dine together for business or social purposes. It was a different matter, however, where the unwelcome conduct toward female employees consisted of pushing them against the wall, placing arms around them, buttoning their blouses, and stating that a complainant's curly hair looked like a sheep before warning her that she might "get rammed" (EEOC Dec. 81-18).

B. The Advance Must Be Unwelcome

The Supreme Court in *Meritor* stated that the essential element "of any sexual harassment claim is that the alleged sexual advances were 'unwelcome.' " Unwelcome conduct is conduct that the employee did not solicit or incite and that the employee regards as undesirable or offensive.

The "unwelcome" requirement is a special feature of sexual harassment law. Usually, harassment is inherently unwelcome. For example, harassment based on race or national origin is presumably offensive and unwelcome to whomever it is directed. Sexual advances differ in that, although they are potentially offensive, they may reflect a friendly, romantic interest in the recipient and often are welcome, or at least not offensive.

It often is hard to tell what sexual advance is invited, what is uninvited-but-welcome, what is offensive-but-tolerated, and what is flatly rejected. Even so, one must distinguish welcome from unwelcome conduct, because a consensual sexual relationship does not amount to discrimination against either of the participants in the relationship.

Cases involving sexual advances can be understood best by analyzing them according to the nature of the complainant's response to the sexual advance:

(1) outright rejection,
(2) initial rejection and later acceptance,
(3) initial acceptance and later rejection,
(4) ambiguous conduct,
(5) coerced submission, and
(6) welcome acceptance.

1. Outright Rejection. Did the complainant immediately say no? Contemporaneous expressions of rejection strongly suggest that a sexual advance was unwelcome (Appendix 3, Policy Guidance on Sexual Harassment §A.).

How immediate and how clearly stated must the rejection be? The court in *Lipsett v. University of Puerto Rico* emphasized that the alleged harasser who makes what he believes to be innocent or invited overtures (that she has a "great figure" or "nice legs") must be sensitive to signals from the woman that his comments are unwelcome. The woman in those circumstances may have to make those signals clear. These signals were found to be clear where the complainant informed her supervisor that she was interested only in a business relationship and left the room (*Jones v. Wesco Invs.*). The complainant need not always confront the harasser directly to show that his conduct was unwelcome (*Zowayyed v. Lowen Co.;* EEOC Dec. 84-1); consistent rejection of sexual advances may be enough to establish their unwelcomeness.

2. Initial Rejection and Later Acceptance. An initial rejection does not necessarily prove that later sexual advances are unwelcome. In *Trautvetter v. Quick,* Patsy Trautvetter, a second-grade school teacher, had, over a period of weeks, rejected several sexual and social invitations from John Quick, her principal, but she never told him that his conduct was inappropriate until after she finally had sexual intercourse with him in a motel. The trial court concluded that the complainant eventually accepted and even invited the principal's sexual advances, even if she did so with the secret feeling that she was pressured to comply.

3. Initial Acceptance Followed by Later Rejection—The "Soured Romance." Special problems arise when a consensual sexual relationship comes to an end. The complainant's prior consent is obviously relevant to the question of unwelcomeness, but it does not bar a claim of later harassment, as shown by the following examples:

- A complainant prevailed on a claim that she was denied a promotion because of negative input by a supervisor she had formerly dated (*Boddy v. Dean*).
- A court held that legal protection is not withdrawn merely because the complainant once had a consensual sexual relationship with the alleged harasser (*Babcock v. Frank*).
- An employee who terminated a relationship with her supervisor prevailed on a claim that the supervisor attempted to force her to submit to further sexual advances by withholding performance evaluations and salary reviews (*Shrout v. Black Clawson Co.*).

The complainant's prior consent does, however, complicate the complainant's proof. The EEOC has stated that where the complainant previously has consented to the relationship, she "must clearly notify the harasser that his conduct is no longer welcome." Her failure to complain of conduct that was once welcome would indicate that the "continued conduct is, in fact, welcome." (Appendix 3, Policy Guidance on Sexual Harassment §A.).

One court has said that a supervisor should report to upper management the termination of any consensual sexual relationship with his subordinate to ensure that work-related factors alone are considered in later decisions affecting the subordinate's job (*Williams v. Civiletti*).

4. Ambiguous Response. The complainant, because of politeness, indecision, or fear, may fail to express an outright rejection. In *Kouri v. Liberian Services*, the court rejected a sexual harassment claim because the complainant had failed to show that her supervisor's attentions were unwelcome to her. Although she did not like his frequent friendly notes, his practice of escorting her to the bathroom and to her car, and his visits to her at home and in the hospital, she never made any realistic effort to cut it off. Her elaborate schemes to let the supervisor know in a subtle way that she was happily married were hopelessly indirect actions that delivered a weak message. The test here is the extent to which the complainant manifested that the sexual advances were unwelcome.

5. Coerced Submission. One paradoxical aspect of sexual harassment law is that a complainant may prevail even if she submits to sexual advances, so long as the sexual advances were unwelcome and the complainant has a credible explanation for why she submitted. In a "coerced submission" case, the complainant submits to unwelcome sexual advances under duress. The duress can be physical:

- The complainant was drugged and then raped (*Gilardi v. Schroeder*).
- A sheriff allegedly raped a dispatcher (*Moylan v. Maries County*).

The duress also can be economic:

- The complainant may "reasonably perceive" that protest will prompt dismissal, especially when sexual overtures are made by the owner of the firm (*Chamberlin v. 101 Realty*).
- The harasser knew the complainant needed her job to make house payments and exploited her financial need

by demanding sexual favors (*Phillips v. Smalley Maintenance Servs.*).

- The complainant allegedly was coerced into sexual conduct by her supervisor's job-related threats (*Babcock v. Frank*).

Voluntary participation in sexual conduct can be consistent with unwelcome advances. As the Supreme Court made clear in *Meritor*, the correct inquiry is not whether actual participation in sexual intercourse was voluntary; instead, one must ask if the complainant by her conduct indicated that the alleged sexual advances were unwelcome. The *Meritor* Court thus refused to reject the sexual harassment claim of a woman who had voluntarily had sexual intercourse 40 to 50 times with her alleged harasser.

Thus, acquiescence in sexual conduct does not necessarily mean that the conduct is welcome:

- The complainant's voluntary actions, such as going to her supervisor's hotel room or accepting a ride in his car, did not prevent a finding that she was offended by his touching and his sexually explicit movie and magazines (*Boyd v. James S. Hayes Living Health Care Agency*).
- A lower court erred in rejecting the quid pro quo claim of a coal company employee where she had finally relented to her supervisor's multiple demands for sex because she "felt pushed" and thought "this will get him off my back" (*Westmoreland Coal Co. v. West Virginia Human Rights Comm'n*).

Acquiescence without fear of any adverse consequences, however, obviously would defeat a claim of unwelcomeness.

A complainant who submits to sexual advances because of coercion often does not protest the sexual advances. Experts have testified that reticence about complaining and a diminished sense of self-worth are common in cases of sexual harassment. Silence in the face of harassment, however, requires an examination of why the victim did not complain, in order to determine whether the harasser's conduct was welcome or unwelcome.

6. Advances Found Welcome. Although the complainant must prove that a sexual advance was unwelcome, as a practical matter the employer may need to show that the advances were in fact welcome. Typically this proof consists of evidence that the complainant invited the advances. In one case, the court found that the complainant induced the sexual advances by inviting her supervisor to discuss opportunities for promotion during a meeting she had proposed in a bar. It was there that he had placed his arm around her and stated that if she was really interested in becoming a co-manager, "there was a motel across the street" (*Highlander v. KFC Nat'l Mgmt. Co.*). In another case finding no unwelcomeness, the complainant admitted to voluntarily having sexual intercourse with her boss on a hundred occasions over three years until she was fired after she and the boss were discovered together by his wife. The court cited the complainant's failure to complain and her gift of a pen-and-pencil set to her boss just days before the surprise visit by his wife (*Jensen v. Kellings Fine Foods*).

C. Objective Versus Subjective Standard

The Supreme Court in *Meritor* suggested that deciding whether sexual advances were unwelcome requires the use of an objective standard rather than consideration of the complainant's subjective secret feelings. One can assess welcomeness by seeing if the complainant, by her conduct, indicated that the advances were unwelcome. Complainants' allegations of unwelcomeness have been rejected where:

- after the alleged harassment occurred, the complainant visited her harasser at the hospital and at his brother's home, and allowed him to enter her house alone at night (*Sardigal v. St. Louis Nat'l Stockyards Co.*);
- the complainant continued to accept rides from the alleged harasser even after an alleged sexual assault (*Christoforou v. Ryder Truck Rental*); and
- the complainant continued to invite her supervisor to dinner and flirted with him after the complained-of incident, which involved a kiss and a proposition (*Reichman v. Bureau of Affirmative Action*).

An objective standard may differ depending on whether it adopts a "male" or "female" perspective, or whether the perspective of the alleged harasser or that of the complainant is used in assessing unwelcomeness.

D. Proof of Unwelcome Sexual Advance

Sometimes the proof that a sexual advance has taken place and that it has been rejected is direct, such as where a supervisor, after the complainant rebuffed his advance, told her over the plant's public address system that "you'd better be nice to me," "your fate is in my hands," and "revenge is the name of the game" (*Sparks v. Pilot Freight Carriers*).

Usually, however, there will be no direct evidence, other than the complainant's testimony, that the supervisor made any advance. This testimony alone can prove her case, but must be seen in light of the evidence that supports or undermines it. As the Supreme Court noted in *Meritor:* "The question of whether particular conduct was indeed unwelcome presents difficult problems of proof and turns largely on credibility determinations committed to the trier of fact." Thus, "in a case of alleged sexual harassment which involves close questions of credibility and subjective interpretation, the existence of corroborative evidence or the lack thereof is likely to be crucial." Some courts have admitted corroborating evidence in the form of testimony that an alleged harasser used his supervisory power to sexually exploit other female subordinates, and that the alleged harasser was a self-described womanizer (*Toscano v. Nimmo*).

When confronted with conflicting evidence as to welcomeness, one must look at the totality of circumstances, evaluating each situation on a case-by-case basis (Appendix 1, EEOC Guidelines §1604.11(b)). An inquiry into "welcomeness" may properly consider the complainant's contemporaneous clothing, conduct, and speech (*Meritor Sav. Bank v. Vinson*). The inquiry does not extend, however, to the entirety of the complainant's sexual history. Courts and the EEOC take the view that evidence concerning a complainant's general character and past behavior toward others has limited, if any, probative value (*Swentek v. USAir; Katz v. Dole*; see Chapter 20).

The most probative evidence offered to show welcomeness is the complainant's conduct toward the alleged harasser. Evidence of whether specific conduct was unwelcome will consist in large part of how the complainant reacted to the initial sexual advance. The complainant's report of harassment to the employer, soon after it occurred, while not required, can be very important.

Where a complainant has failed to prove unwelcomeness, it usually is because the complainant was found to have invited or encouraged the advances or to have failed to make it known that the sexual advances were unwelcome.

IV. ADVERSE EMPLOYMENT ACTION

In the classic quid pro quo case, the complainant must prove that because of her rejection of sexual advances she suffered some tangible, "pocketbook" injury to her job. That injury might be loss of the job, denial of a promotion or pay raise, denial of training, or failure of the employer to recall the complainant after a layoff.

Courts have rejected quid pro quo claims in the absence of a clear economic loss (*Trautvetter v. Quick*; *Jones v. Flagship Int'l*). In one case, the court rejected a quid pro quo claim based on a failure to promote because the employer eventually granted the promotion and gave the complainant a pay increase, retroactive to the date that the raise was first sought (*Walker v. Sullair Corp.*).

V. THE CAUSAL CONNECTION BETWEEN THE ADVERSE EMPLOYMENT ACTION AND THE COMPLAINANT'S GENDER

In a sex discrimination case involving a discharge it is not enough for the complainant to prove that she is female and that she was fired. She must also show that she was fired *because* she is female. If the claim is based on sexual advances, the complainant must prove that she was fired because she rejected sexual advances that were made because she is a woman.

Thus, in a quid pro quo case, unlike a typical disparate treatment case, the job detriment does not occur directly because of the complainant's gender, but because of her reaction to a sexual advance that in turn was based on her gender. The causal connection thus has two prongs: (1) that because of the complainant's sex she was subjected to a sexual advance, and (2) that either (a) because of her negative reaction to the sexual advance she was subjected to a tangible job detriment, or (b) because of her tolerance of the sexual advance she avoided a tangible job loss or gained a job advantage.

A. On the Basis of Sex

1. The "But For" Test. Courts now uniformly find quid pro quo harassment to be discrimination on the basis of sex: conditioning employment opportunities upon sexual services is discriminating on the basis of gender. In *Chamberlin v. 101 Realty,* because the supervisor did not make sexual advances to male employees, the court found that but for her sex, Katherine Chamberlin would not have been subjected to sexual harassment (see also *Barnes v. Costle,* discussed in Chapter 1, section II.A.).

In the typical case, in which a male supervisor makes sexual overtures to a female worker, it is obvious that the supervisor does not treat male employees in the same fashion. It therefore will be simple for the complainant to prove that, but for her sex, she would not have been subjected to sexual harassment.

Female supervisors who use their power to exact sexual favors from male subordinates similarly are harassing their subordinates on the basis of gender (*Huebschen v. Department of Health & Social Serv.*).

2. Homosexual Advances. Quid pro quo harassment by a homosexual supervisor of a same-sex subordinate is sex discrimination because it, also, is based on the gender of the victim. A woman who is fired for refusal to submit to a lesbian supervisor is just as fired—and her firing is just as related to her gender—as if the perpetrator were a heterosexual man.

3. The "Bisexual Defense." One academic possibility is the "bisexual defense": an employer theoretically could defeat the "because of sex" element in a quid pro quo case by showing that the harasser treated members of both genders equally as his sexual prey. Thus, the sexual overtures of a bisexual supervisor would not be sex discrimination because they would not reflect differential treatment of either gender. As a practical matter, however, a fact finder could conclude that even a methodically bisexual harasser was acting on the basis of gender with respect to any particular encounter.

B. The Link Between Harassment and the Adverse Employment Action

The complainant must show a causal connection between the unwelcome sexual advance and the adverse employment action by showing that the action resulted from the rejection of the sexual advances, or was avoided only by coerced submission.

The causal connection might be more difficult to show in the case of a soured romance than in the case of an outright rejection. Where the complainant has suffered a job detriment soon after rejecting a swap of sexual favors for job benefits, one might presume, subject to the employer's rebuttal, that a subsequent adverse employment action resulted from sex discrimination. In a soured romance case, by contrast, some courts have presumed that the adverse job action stemmed from the termination of an emotional relationship rather than from the rejection of sexual advances (*Keppler v. Hinsdale Township High School Dist.*). This distinction is unnecessary where, after initial acceptance and later rejection, there is a renewed unwelcome request for sexual favors.

Some relevant factors to consider when deciding whether there is a causal connection are presented below.

1. Lapse of Time. Timing is key to proving a causal connection. In the classic quid pro quo case, rejection of a sexual advance promptly leads to economic retaliation. Thus, a causal connection has been found where:

- The complainant's supervisor speculated about the complainant's sexual needs since her husband had left her, and told her that he would make it easy on her if she would go out with him. A week after she rejected these advances, she was reprimanded for substandard work, transferred to a different position, and fired (*Horn v. Duke Homes*).

- A supervisor became markedly more negative immediately after the complainant rebuffed his sexual overtures during a seminar trip (*Boyd v. James S. Hayes Living Health Care Agency*).

- A supervisor enlisted the help of other management personnel to fire the complainant when she called in sick two weeks after she last rejected his sexual advances (*Sparks v. Pilot Freight Carriers*).

Where a significant time has elapsed between the sexual advance and the adverse employment decision, courts have been reluctant to find a causal connection. Nonetheless, even delays of several months are not necessarily fatal to a claim:

- An interval of ten weeks between the last sexual advance and the discharge does not preclude a finding that the discharge was because of the complainant's rejection of her supervisor's sexual advances, especially where the supervisor was on vacation for a month during that period (*Chamberlin v. 101 Realty*).

- A gap of one year between the sexual advance and the firing did not bar a finding of causal connection (*Tomkins v. Public Serv. Elec. & Gas Co.*).

2. Comparative Evidence. The complainant may establish a causal connection by showing that another female employee who had succumbed to her supervisor's sexual desires received larger pay increases than the complainant and that the complainant, after rebuffing her supervisor's advances, was denied a promotion for which she was qualified (*Spencer v. General Elec. Co.*).

Another relevant factor is whether employees of the opposite gender were afforded opportunities that the complainant was denied, such as allowing male employees to attend the police academy while preventing the complainant from doing so (*Henson v. City of Dundee*).

3. The Alleged Harasser's Involvement in the Adverse Employment Decision. Quid pro quo harassment may be perpetrated only by the employer through someone who has the power to grant or deny the job benefit in question. If the alleged harasser lacks authority to make or influence employment decisions, no quid pro quo case ordinarily is possible. To establish the requisite degree of supervisory authority, the complainant must show that the alleged harasser possessed the apparent or actual authority to execute the relevant employment decision (*Henson v. City of Dundee*), and in fact made or influenced the decision that caused the job detriment. The capacity to recommend or otherwise influence employment decisions may be sufficient (*Miller v. Bank of Am.*). A harasser who has no current supervisory control over a subordinate may still possess the authority to influence employment through a relationship with a new supervisor (*Simmons v. Lyons*). Where a woman who had resisted sexual advances by her manager was fired by another manager, evidence that the harassing manager had influenced the decision to fire the complainant caused the court to find liability for retaliation, even though the harassing manager had not done the firing himself (*Sparks v. Pilot Freight Carriers*). A complainant's discharge did not result from rejection of her supervisor's advances, however, where another manager recommended her discharge over the initial objections of the harassing supervisor (*Dockter v. Rudolf Wolff Futures*).

VI. EMPLOYER RESPONSIBILITY

The EEOC consistently has stated that the employer is automatically liable for supervisory misconduct in quid pro quo cases involving tangible job detriments (Appendix 1, EEOC Guidelines §1604.11(d)). Under this view, which is generally endorsed by courts, where a supervisor exercises employer-delegated authority to make job decisions, the supervisor's actions are charged to the employer without regard to whether the employer knew of the supervisor's discriminatory intent or whether the supervisor had actual authority to discriminate on that basis (*Horn v. Duke Homes*).

VII. EMPLOYER REBUTTAL

A. Disputing Elements of the Complainant's Case

The first line of defense for an employer is to rebut elements of the complainant's case. Thus, the employer may prevent the complainant's recovery by showing that:

- no sexual advances occurred;
- if they did occur, then they were welcomed;
- if unwelcome sexual advances occurred, then no job detriment resulted; or
- the job detriment was not "because of" the rejection of the sexual advances.

Employers most frequently tend to attack the unwelcomeness element.

B. Stating a Legitimate Nondiscriminatory Reason

The employer may also attack the complainant's effort to prove a causal connection between her gender and a job detriment by explaining a legitimate, nondiscriminatory reason for that detriment. The employer will try to show that the adverse employment action was based on legitimate factors and not on the complainant's reaction to any sexual advance. The employer may introduce facts to show that the action resulted from such legitimate considerations as poor work performance, excessive tardiness or absenteeism, insubordination, a violation of company policy, or a lack of available work.

An employer thus may be able to show that even if the complainant did resist sexual advances by a supervisor, her discharge occurred not because of her sex, but because of her insubordination or other work-related shortcomings (*Christoforou v. Ryder Truck Rental*). In one case, the complainant's discharge was found to have resulted from her inability to become proficient as an operator of a personal computer, not as a result of her objections to harassment (*Dockter v. Rudolf Wolff Futures*).

If discrimination was a motivating factor in the decision, liability is established under Title VII as amended by the Civil Rights Act of 1991. Nonetheless, the employer can avoid any back-pay or reinstatement remedy by proving that the same employment decision would have been made even in the absence of the discrimination (see Appendix 5).

VIII. THE COMPLAINANT'S PROOF OF PRETEXT

Where the employer has stated a legitimate, nondiscriminatory reason for its job decision, the complainant may show that the stated reason is really just a "pretext"—a cover-up—for sex discrimination. The issue of whether the stated reason for the adverse employment action was a pretext for sex discrimination is a factual question based largely on the credibility of the witnesses. That factual determination depends on such things as the relative qualifications of competing employees and the complainant's job performance.

Complainants try to prove pretext in various ways:

(1) that the employer failed to follow company procedures in taking the adverse employment action (*Craig v. Y & Y Snacks*);

(2) that although the employer alleged a lack of work, it hired new employees, or failed to lay off other workers, after the complainant's layoff (*Hallquist v. Max Fish Plumbing & Heating Co.*); and

(3) that although the employer has cited excessive absenteeism, (a) the facts recited by the employer are not true (*Boyd v. James S. Hayes Living Health Care Agency*), (b) the complainant's attendance at the time of discharge was no worse than it had been prior to the rejection of sexual advances, when no adverse job action had been taken (*Mays v. Williamson & Sons Janitorial Servs.; Ambrose v. United States Steel Corp.*), or (c) similarly absent employees who did not reject sexual advances were not fired.

The complainant might also claim that the decrease in work performance cited by the employer was itself the result of sexual harassment. For a discussion of that theory of liability, which resembles but is not quite the same as proof of pretext, see Chapter 3, sections IV.E. and VIII.B.

3

HOSTILE ENVIRONMENT HARASSMENT

I. ANALYZING HOSTILE ENVIRONMENT CLAIMS

The 1980 EEOC Guidelines interpret Title VII to prohibit "unwelcome sexual advances, requests for sexual favors, and verbal or physical conduct of a sexual nature" that have "the purpose or effect of unreasonably interfering with an individual's work performance, or creating an intimidating, hostile, or offensive working environment" (Appendix 1, EEOC Guidelines §1604.11(a)).

In 1986, the Supreme Court in *Meritor Savings Bank v. Vinson* unanimously endorsed the EEOC's concept that sexually harassing conduct, if sufficiently severe or pervasive, can alter an employee's working conditions, and thus amount to unlawful sex discrimination, even when no tangible job loss has occurred. The same facts may support both a quid pro quo and a hostile environment case (Appendix 3, Policy Guidance on Sexual Harassment §A.). Nonetheless, a sexually hostile environment has several distinguishing features:

(1) While quid pro quo harassment necessarily involves actions by a supervisor, a hostile environment may result

38

entirely from the actions of co-workers, or even nonemployees.

(2) While the employer's liability is generally automatic in a quid pro quo case, in a hostile environment case employer liability under Title VII is determined on a case-by-case basis, through use of traditional agency principles.

(3) A hostile environment is not limited to sexual advances; it also may involve hostile behavior that is not sexual but that is directed at the complainant because of gender.

(4) A hostile environment is not limited to targeted behavior; it also may involve activity that is not directed at the complainant at all but that nonetheless affects the complainant's job.

(5) Hostile environment harassment, unlike quid pro quo harassment, requires no proof of actual or even threatened economic injury. It is enough to prove that the incidents were either so severe or so pervasive that they effectively changed the complainant's working conditions.

(6) The issues most frequently litigated in hostile environment cases—the amount of harassment an employee is expected to endure in the workplace before it rises to the level of being severe or pervasive, and the employer's accountability for the harassment—are seldom significant in quid pro quo cases.

Courts have identified the following elements that a complainant must prove to establish liability for hostile environment harassment:

(1) that the complainant is a member of a protected group (see section II. below);

(2) that the complainant was subjected to unwelcome sex-based conduct (see section III. below);

(3) that the conduct affected a term or condition of the complainant's employment (see section IV. below);

(4) that the conduct affected the complainant because of the complainant's sex (see section V. below); and

(5) that the employer is responsible (see section VI. below).

These are the factors to consider in reviewing any allegation of a hostile environment. If any one of these elements is not present, then the employer is not liable for sexual harassment. Nonetheless, many employers maintain an even higher standard than the law imposes. This standard will sometimes cause the employer to impose discipline for violation of an antiharassment policy even though no unlawful sexual harassment has occurred.

II. MEMBERSHIP IN A PROTECTED GROUP

Both men and women can bring actions for a hostile environment. Very few environmental harassment claims are made by men, however, perhaps because men are rarely abused in the workplace on account of their sex. Nonetheless, any action predicated on the "maleness" or the "femaleness" of the complainant will satisfy the first element of a hostile environment claim (see Chapter 1, section IV.).

III. UNWELCOME CONDUCT OF A SEX-BASED NATURE

A. Unwelcome Conduct

To establish a hostile environment claim, the complainant must show that the requested conduct was unwelcome. This unwelcomeness element can best be understood by considering the kind of conduct involved.

1. Sexual Advances. Hostile environments can be created by unwelcome sexual advances, even if, unlike quid pro quo harassment, the advances were not offered in return for employment advantages, and even if the harassment was by a co-worker or a nonemployee rather than a supervisor. (For a more detailed discussion of sexual advance cases, see Chapter 2, section III.B.)

2. Gender-Based Animosity. Many hostile environments are created by acts of gender-based animosity that are analogous to harassment based on race or national origin (see Chapter 1, section IV.). The harasser can be a supervisor, a co-worker, or a nonemployee. This hostile behavior often arises when women enter male-dominated jobs (*e.g.,* fire fighter) or workplaces (*e.g.,* oil rigs). Gender-based animosity is actionable because the conduct would not occur *but for* the sex of the complainant.

Behavior motivated by gender-based animosity usually consists of: (1) hostile conduct of a sexual nature, which can be called "gender-baiting," or (2) hostile conduct of a nonsexual nature but based on gender, which can be called "hazing."

a. Gender-Baiting. Like sexual advances, gender-baiting is obviously sex-based conduct, for the behavior explicitly aims at making life unpleasant for women employees because they are women. Gender-baiting can take the form of speech or action. In *Morris v. American National Can Corp.,* Jacquelyn Morris—a machinist and the only female in her department—was anonymously presented with clay replicas and pictures of erect penises, pictures of nude women, a sausage with a note stating "bite me baby," and a sanitary napkin with a reddish substance. She found the words "bitch," "slut," and "whore" written on her desk, and a semen-like substance on her toolbox. Her supervisor said that she had "a nice ass," that he'd "like to have a piece of that," and that she should sit under his desk "because that's where everyone says you do your best work." He also touched her buttocks on several occasions and said "Didn't you get any last night?" and "Do you spit or swallow?"

Morris saw doctors for "nervousness," "sleeplessness," and "an occasional inability to breathe." Two doctors suggested she resign, which she eventually did, citing her physical problems, her feeling that she was not protected at work, and her feeling that no one would help her. The court found both the employer and a supervisor liable for the harassment and for constructive discharge.

In another classic case of gender-baiting, *Hall v. Gus Construction Co.,* three women—Darla Hall, Patty Baxter, and Jeanette Ticknor—were hired to work for a road construction company as "flag persons" in an otherwise all-male environment. Hall and Baxter were single mothers trying to provide for their children. Immediately after their hire they became the target of verbal abuse, incessantly being referred to as "fucking flag girls" by their male co-workers. One of the women was nicknamed "Herpes" after she developed a skin rash from the sun. Another found "Cavern Cunt" and "Blonde Bitch" written in dust on her car. The women repeatedly were asked if they "wanted to fuck" or perform oral sex, and were subjected to unwanted touching of their breasts and thighs. Male crew members mooned and exposed themselves to the women and showed them pictures of naked couples performing oral sex. One crew member held Hall up to the window of a truck cab so that other men could touch her.

   b. Nonsexual Hazing Based on Sex. If offensive conduct is imposed on women because of their gender, the conduct constitutes sex discrimination even if the conduct is not overtly sexual in nature. Nonsexual hazing, no less than explicit gender-baiting, may be used to harass, intimidate, and make life miserable for the victim because she is a woman. Thus, hazing conduct, which may include a variety of conduct such as verbal insults, hostile graffiti, unwelcome touching, and threats of physical violence, can amount to harassment on the basis of sex. In *Hall v. Gus Construction Co.*, there was ample evidence of explicit sex-based conduct, but the court also relied upon offensive conduct that was not sexual in nature but that was directed to the complainants because of their gender. Thus, for example, a male mechanic ignored the women's complaint of a carbon monoxide leak in the exhaust system of the pick-up truck assigned to them, male co-workers urinated in one woman's water bottle and in the gas tank of another woman's car, and the women were denied the use of a truck to drive to town for a bathroom break, so that when they relieved themselves in a ditch the male crew could watch them through surveying equipment. The court held that all of the offensive conduct, even those parts that were nonsexual in content, amounted to harassment based on sex.

   3. Sexually Charged Workplace. Complainants might also have a claim on the basis of conduct that was not directed against them. A sexually hostile environment might exist even in the absence of targeted conduct where (1) promotions and other job benefits are based on sexual favoritism, or (2) management condones sexually offensive language or visual displays.

a. Sexual Favoritism Cases. In the typical sexual favoritism case, supervisors favor subordinates who grant sexual favors, thereby creating an implicit quid pro quo. In *Broderick v. Ruder,* Catherine Broderick, a staff attorney with the Securities and Exchange Commission, cited romantic involvements between supervisors and their subordinates that seemed to explain the accelerated career advancement of those subordinates. One supervisor helped a female subordinate achieve three promotions, a commendation, and two cash awards in one year. Another sexually cooperative female received two promotions, a cash award, and a perfect score in each element of her performance appraisal. The court found that this atmosphere of sexual politics amounted to a hostile environment for Broderick.

b. Sexually Charged Workplace Cultures. A workplace full of sexually explicit posters and reading material (*e.g.,* magazines depicting partially clad or nude women in sexually suggestive poses) may create a hostile environment for women. This is true even though this environment may have existed in the workplace long before the complainant's arrival and might offend only some women. Although the displays may not be directed at any particular woman, a woman nevertheless may be offended and feel demeaned by such materials to the point that her employment is affected.

Visual displays of graffiti or pornography that have been cited in sexual harassment cases include:

- obscene cartoons in a men's bathroom (*Bennett v. Corroon & Black Corp.*);
- a pornographic movie and pornographic magazines (*Boyd v. James S. Hayes Living Health Care Agency*);
- a videotape of rabbits mating shown at a business meeting where the complainant was the only female present (*Kinnally v. Bell of Pa.*);
- a T-shirt worn by the boss stating "I gagged Linda Lovelace" (*Priest v. Rotary*);
- sexually oriented pictures and cartoons in the workplace (*Shrout v. Black Clawson Co.*); and
- sexually oriented drawings or graffiti on pillars and other conspicuous places in the workplace (*Zabkowicz v. West Bend Co.*).

In *Robinson v. Jacksonville Shipyards,* male shipyard workers displayed, on workplace walls, pictures of nude or partially clad women with exposed breasts and pubic areas. Lois Robinson, a shipyard welder, complained about these visual displays as well as verbal harassment consisting of name-calling ("honey," "dear," "baby," "sugar," "sugar-booger," "momma") and comments ("Hey, pussycat, come here and give me a whiff," "I'd like to have some of that," and "I'd like to get in bed with that"). Although the court found harassment on the basis of conduct directed specifically at Robinson, the court's language suggests that, in a male-dominated work environment, sexually offensive visual displays themselves can be inherently discriminatory and can alone create a hostile environment.

4. Proof of Unwelcomeness. In some sexually charged workplaces, proof of unwelcomeness is complicated by the behavior of the complainant that seems to indicate welcomeness but may be just an effort to adjust to the prevailing workplace culture. In *Ukarish v. Magnesium Elektron,* a hostile environment claim failed because the complainant, although subjectively disliking the vulgar language of her male co-workers, appeared to accept it "and joined in it as one of the boys." Similarly, in *Gan v. Kepro Circuit Systems,* a hostile environment claim failed where the complainant herself regularly used vulgar language, initiated sexually oriented conversations with co-workers, asked male employees about their sex lives, and discussed her own marital sexual relations. The court decided that any propositions and sexually suggestive remarks that did occur were prompted by her own sexually oriented conduct.

Nonetheless, participation in *some* sexual conduct does not necessarily show that *all* sexual conduct is welcome. In *Swentek v. USAir,* where the trial court relied on the complainant's use of foul language and sexual innuendo to find that she generally welcomed such comments, the appellate court reversed, holding that her use of such language in a *consensual* setting did not waive her right to complain of *unwelcome* harassment. According to the court, the relevant inquiry is whether the complainant welcomed the particular conduct from the alleged harasser.

All of the circumstances surrounding the alleged hostile environment harassment determine whether it is welcome, including the complainant's:

- "sexually provocative speech or dress" (*Meritor Sav. Bank v. Vinson*);
- participation in sexual horseplay and use of foul language at work (*Ukarish v. Magnesium Elektron*);
- friendly association with the alleged harasser (*Staton v. Maries County*); and
- failure to report alleged incidents of harassment to superiors (*Dockter v. Rudolf Wolff Futures*).

Courts generally have not permitted defendants to explore a complainant's sexual history with persons other than the alleged harasser in an attempt to prove that the sexual conduct was actually welcomed (see Chapter 20).

Conduct that is initially welcome may become unwelcome. The complainant's initial acceptance does not waive the right to complain about later conduct, but the initial acceptance will complicate any attempt to prove unwelcomeness. The EEOC found that no violation occurred where a complainant joined others in making dirty remarks and telling dirty jokes during her first two months on the job, and then failed to give notice that the conduct was no longer welcome. Simply ceasing to participate in the conduct did not show that continuing conduct had become unwelcome (EEOC Dec. 84-1). This situation is analogous to a quid pro quo case in which a romance has gone sour (see Chapter 2, section III.B.3.).

B. The Sex-Based Nature of Conduct

The EEOC Guidelines are potentially misleading, because they imply that unwelcome conduct must be of a "sexual nature" to be actionable (Appendix 1, EEOC Guidelines §1604.11(a)). Actually, the test is whether the offensive conduct is because of the complainant's *gender*. The EEOC, recognizing the ambiguity in its Guidelines, has since made clear that one need not prove sexual activity to prove unlawful harassment (see Appendix 3, Policy Guidance on Sexual Harassment §C.4.).

Courts now generally recognize that offensive gender-based conduct need not be sexual in nature to be actionable as sex discrimination (*McKinney v. Dole,* involving a male supervisor's nonsexual physical aggression against a female employee because of her sex).

IV. EFFECT ON THE COMPLAINANT'S EMPLOYMENT

A. Severe or Pervasive

The Supreme Court in *Meritor* stated that sexual harassment, before it is actionable under Title VII, must be sufficiently severe or pervasive to alter the conditions of the victim's employment and to create a hostile, abusive or intimidating working environment. Accordingly, actionable harassment must be pervasive enough to be distinguishable from the ordinary tribulations of the workplace, such as the sporadic use of abusive language, gender-related stories, and occasional teasing. Telling a single sexually offensive joke does not constitute sexual harassment because it is not severe and it is isolated. An employer may set a higher standard for its own workplace than the law requires, but the law will impose sanctions only where the harassment is so severe or pervasive as to make the workplace hostile, abusive or intimidating.

Conduct creates a hostile environment if the conduct is (1) severe enough to alter the complainant's workplace experience even though the conduct occurred only once or rarely, or (2) pervasive enough to become a defining condition of the workplace. Severity and pervasiveness are inversely related: the more severe incidents are, the less pervasive they need be to create a hostile environment. One rape certainly would be enough to create a hostile environment. One dinner invitation certainly would not be enough. A series of social invitations, continuing even though unwelcome, might be enough.

1. Severity. Some forms of unwelcome sexual conduct are so trivial that, unless pervasive, they are not actionable. Such was the case when a deputy U.S. Marshal was asked out on dates by two of her co-workers (*Robinson v. Thornburgh*).

By contrast, physical incidents may constitute severe harassment even if they occur only once. The EEOC presumes that the unwelcome, intentional touching of "intimate body areas" is sufficiently offensive to alter the conditions of a working environment in violation of Title VII. One incident alone was enough where the harasser rubbed the complainant's breasts and crotch while they were inside a vehicle from which she could not escape (*Barrett v. Omaha Nat'l Bank*).

Severity may be affected by the supervisory status of the person who engages in unwelcome conduct. A supervisor's capacity to create a hostile environment for a subordinate is enhanced by the degree of authority conferred on the supervisor by the employer.

2. Pervasiveness. A hostile environment claim that does not involve "severe" conduct will require a showing of multiple instances of offensive conduct. A finding of pervasiveness may be more likely if instances of harassment are perpetrated by more than one individual. An over-the-road truck driver established a hostile environment claim where her male co-workers exposed their genitals to her, threatened violence, removed the pin that connected her trailer to her tractor, made verbal sexual advances and threats of harm if she reported them, sexually touched her breasts, attempted to drag her into the sleeper compartment of a truck cab, placed a live snake on the floor of her cab, and formed the "37 Club"—a group of 37 male drivers who bet on which man would be first to have sexual intercourse with the complainant (*Llewellyn v. Celanese Corp.*).

B. Standard for Determining Severe or Pervasive Conduct

The severity or pervasiveness of particular offensive conduct is a matter of perspective. Therefore, a threshold concern is the point of view that should be adopted in evaluating the evidence. Because this field of the law is still evolving, there is no one standard accepted by all courts. The most common standards are discussed below.

1. The Objective Standard. Courts generally agree that the fact finder should adopt the objective standpoint of a "reasonable person" to see if incidents were sufficiently severe or pervasive to create a hostile environment. Thus, if the challenged conduct would not substantially affect the work environment of a reasonable person, no actionable sexual harassment has occurred (*Highlander v. KFC Nat'l Mgmt. Co.*).

2. The Subjective Standard. Courts have rejected a subjective standard, which would look only to how the complainant perceived her work environment. A wholly subjective standard would make employers guess at what conduct is acceptable. It would let the complainant alone decide what is acceptable conduct and thus could yield inequitable results by making the law serve as a vehicle for vindicating petty slights suffered by hypersensitive people (*Zabkowicz v. West Bend Co.*).

3. The Dual Objective-Subjective Standard. Several courts have adopted a dual standard by which the fact finder considers, in *objective* terms, the likely effect of the offensive conduct upon a reasonable person, and *also* considers, in *subjective* terms, the actual effect upon the particular complainant. The complainant by this standard must show not only that the work environment of a reasonable person in the same position would have been substantially affected, but that the complainant in fact suffered psychological injury (*Rabidue v. Osceola Ref. Co.*).

Several other courts and the EEOC take the position that no such additional showing of actual psychological harm is required (Appendix 3, Policy Guidance on Sexual Harassment §C.1. n.20).

4. The "Reasonable Woman" Standard. Judges differ concerning whether the objective, reasonable person standard should incorporate what some presume to be gender-based differences in perception. The court in *Rabidue v. Osceola Refining Co.* affirmed a finding that no hostile environment had occurred in a workplace where a male supervisor called women "whores," "cunt," "pussy," and "tits," called the complainant a "fat ass," and said "all that bitch needs is a good lay." The panel majority held that these remarks, and the accompanying workplace display of pictures of nude or semi-nude women, had only a minor effect on the complainant's work environment when considered in the context of a society that condones and commercially exploits written and pictorial erotica at newsstands, on prime-time television, at the cinema, and in other public places.

Critics of the *Rabidue* decision have accused it of really adopting the perspective of a "reasonable male" rather than that of a "reasonable victim." These critics believe that the traditional perspective of the "reasonable person" harbors myths based on male perceptions that some sexual harassment is just harmless kidding around, that women really welcome sexual overtures, that "no" is really a coy way of saying "yes," and that women who complain about sexual advances, far from being reasonable, are overly sensitive or prudish or are too assertive and unable to "get along." The critics further contend that courts sometimes allow these male myths to infect their assessment of the actions of a reasonable person, and thereby bias the formulation of the standard itself and trivialize sexual harassment by assuming that the complained-of conduct is not really serious or harmful.

This kind of thinking has persuaded several courts to hold that the objective standard in a case brought by a female complainant ought to be based on the viewpoint of the reasonable woman (*Ellison v. Brady*).

C. Preexisting Workplace Behavior

Where sexually crude language, pornography, and graffiti have been accepted as part of the workplace prior to the complainant's employment, courts differ on the relevance of workplace cultural norms. The question is whether employment discrimination law forbids only harassment that exceeds the bounds of current social acceptability or forbids all harassment in the workplace, even historically tolerated conduct.

Some courts hold that in determining whether an environment is hostile to a complainant, the court must consider prevailing workplace norms. The *Rabidue* court held that Title VII was not intended to reform the rough-hewn and vulgar conduct found in some work environments. Other courts have agreed, emphasizing the relevance of workplace cultural norms in finding that no hostile environment occurred:

- at a chemical plant where sexually oriented dialogue was "customary plant language" and no worse than it had been before the complainant arrived (*Ukarish v. Magnesium Elektron*);
- at a securities trading house where coarse references to male and female genitalia and to sexual activity were "the language of this marketplace" (*Halpert v. Wertheim & Co.*);
- at a sheriff's department patrol station where a clerk typist complained of a generally offensive atmosphere in which both male and female employees engaged in profanity (*Klink v. Ramsey County*);
- in a factory where the complainant, an inspector, had a separate chain of command from the technicians who created an environment "replete with sexual innuendo, joke telling and general vulgarity" (*Weinsheimer v. Rockwell Int'l Corp.*); and
- in a convention center work environment "permeated by profanity" (*Reynolds v. Atlantic City Convention Ctr.*).

Other courts take a contrary view, holding that the preexisting workplace culture does not excuse or justify an environment hostile to women (*Robinson v. Jacksonville Shipyards*). The EEOC contends that a woman does not forfeit her right to be free from sexual harassment by choosing to work in an atmosphere that has traditionally included vulgar, anti-female language (Appendix 3, Policy Guidance on Sexual Harassment §C.3.).

D. Proof of Severe or Pervasive Harassment

The heart of a hostile environment claim is proof that the incidents of harassment were sufficiently severe or pervasive to alter the conditions of the complainant's employment. In determining whether a black woman was subjected to a *sexually* hostile working environment, courts have considered not only the overtly sexual conduct directed at her, but also (1) sexual conduct directed at *other* female employees, (2) acts that were not sexual but that represented sex-based harassment, and (3) incidents of racial harassment that, combined with the sexually harassing conduct, may have contributed to pervasive harassment (*Hicks v. Gates Rubber Co.*).

E. Unreasonable Interference With Work

A hostile environment may affect more than merely psychological conditions. The EEOC Guidelines expressly endorse the theory that sexual harassment is actionable whenever it unreasonably interferes with "work performance" (see Appendix 1, EEOC Guidelines §1604.11(a)(3)). Under this theory, the employer who is responsible for unreasonable interference with work can also be responsible for the direct consequences of the interference, such as an adverse employment decision that is based on the complainant's absenteeism or other work performance problems that themselves were caused by a sexually hostile environment.

V. CONDUCT AFFECTING THE COMPLAINANT BECAUSE OF GENDER

A. Conduct Based on Sex

To establish a hostile environment claim, the complainant must show that but for her sex, she would not have suffered harassment. This "causal connection" can best be understood by again considering the various kinds of harassment involved.

1. Sexual Advances. A series of unwelcome sexual advances toward a complainant obviously is on the basis of sex. Only in the case of a harasser who approaches members of both sexes equally would the conduct's sexual content not be enough to show conduct on the basis of sex.

2. Gender-Based Animosity. Many varieties of sex-based hostile conduct are, like sexual advances, obviously on the basis of sex. Sexist epithets are an example. The court in *Reynolds v. Atlantic City Convention Center* noted that if the complainant had not been a woman she would not have been called a "douche bag cunt."

Where the hostile treatment is not explicitly sexual, the employer may contend that the hostility results from the complainant's own personality, or that women and men alike received the same hostile treatment. Thus, in *Cline v. General Electric Capital Auto Lease*, where the alleged harasser was generally abusive to subordinates of both sexes and of various racial and ethnic backgrounds, the employer argued that this rough treatment simply reflected the harasser's desire to be a "mother hen" for the good of his department. The court disagreed, however, finding that the harassment of the complainant and other women, which included yelling and pinching, was greater, both quantitatively and qualitatively, than was any harassment of men.

3. Sexually Charged Workplace. In a sexually charged workplace, conduct such as the display of pornographic pictures or graffiti may be directed at no individual in particular. The complainant may still establish the "because of sex" element in these circumstances, however, by showing that the activity by its nature demeans members of one sex and was permitted to continue despite their protests. This evidence implies an intent to discriminate on the basis of sex. Alternatively, tolerance of the activity may be characterized as an employer policy or custom that has an adverse impact on one sex that is not justified by any business necessity (*Robinson v. Jacksonville Shipyards*). For a discussion of the adverse impact theory of liability, see Chapter 1, section III.

Where men and women alike have engaged in vulgar sexual comments and activities, or where the conduct complained of offends men and women equally, the evidence may not support a finding of sex-based conduct. In *Weinsheimer v. Rockwell International Corp.*, the complainant testified that a male co-worker would ask her to "suck him" or "give him head," point to her crotch and say "give me some of that stuff," request an "ice-cube job," and grab at her crotch and breast. The court found a failure to show that the conduct complained of was based on sex, as opposed to "contentiousness and vulgarity" that was gender-neutral. The court stated: "Title VII bars unwelcome harassment based upon sex. It would seem to be stretching the language and aims of the statute were it to now apply *per se* to any argument between coworkers of opposite sex that involves vulgarities or sexual comments."

B. Hostile Environment Claims by Men

The prohibition against sex discrimination clearly protects men as well as women. In *Goluszek v. Smith*, however, the court found that the sexually oriented harassment of the male complainant by other men in a male-dominated environment was not actionable because the harassers did not treat men as inferior because of their sex. The complainant was a sexually inexperienced male who blushed easily. He had always lived with his mother. Although, or perhaps because, the plaintiff was abnormally sensitive to sexual comments, his male co-workers repeatedly questioned his manhood—offering to get him "fucked," asking if he had gotten any oral sex or "pussy," and suggesting that he "get some of that soft pink smelly stuff that's between the legs of women." The shop routine also featured poking the plaintiff in the buttocks with a stick and discussions about "butt fucking in the ass." The plaintiff's employer scoffed at or ignored his complaints about this offensive conduct.

The court found that a woman in the plaintiff's situation would have been subject to pervasive harassment. Nonetheless, by the court's reasoning, the plaintiff, as a male, had no claim because the conduct was not of the type that Title VII was intended to prohibit. The court held that the sexual harassment that is actionable "is the exploitation of a powerful position to impose sexual demands or pressures on an unwilling but less powerful person," where the offender is saying by words or actions that the victim is inferior because of the victim's sex. The court emphasized that the plaintiff, by contrast, was a male in a male-dominated environment and was not subjected to an anti-male environment in the workplace.

C. Harassment Based on Sexual Orientation

Employment discrimination against homosexuals may resemble discrimination on the basis of gender, but courts and the EEOC uniformly have held that Title VII's ban on sex discrimination does not prohibit employment discrimination because of an individual's sexual orientation. Nor does Title VII protect "effeminate" males. Accordingly, harassment of employees solely because of their sexual orientation is not considered to be "because of sex." Homosexual complainants thus are limited to whatever remedies they may have under federal and state constitutions, the common law, state FEP statutes, local ordinances, and executive orders.

In contrast, when the harassment consists of homosexual advances, Title VII forbids the harassment without regard to the sexual orientation of the *complainant*. What is important is the sexual orientation of the *harasser*: he engages in sex discrimination if he makes sexual advances on the basis of the complainant's gender.

D. Harassment on the Basis of Transsexualism

Courts uniformly have held that prohibitions against sex discrimination do not protect individuals who undergo sex-change surgery or announce an intention to undergo sex-change surgery. Thus, a transsexual who had undergone a male-to-female sex-change operation was not discriminated against on the basis of sex where her employer excluded her from company restrooms and fired her because of her transsexualism (*Sommers v. Iowa Civil Rights Comm'n*).

VI. EMPLOYER RESPONSIBILITY

An important issue in hostile environment cases is whether the employer is liable for an individual harasser's conduct. Courts have identified four major grounds for finding employers liable:

(1) automatic liability (sometimes called "strict liability");
(2) harassment within the harasser's actual scope of employment;
(3) harassment within the harasser's apparent authority; and
(4) employer negligence in failing to prevent or remedy the harassment (sometimes called "direct liability").

The first three theories are likely to apply, if at all, only to harassment by supervisors. The fourth theory, by contrast, is based on the employer's failure to exercise control over the workplace, and thus also applies to cases of harassment by co-workers and even to cases of harassment by nonemployees.

A. Harassment by Supervisors

1. Automatic Liability. Courts have imposed automatic employer liability under Title VII when a supervisor has engaged in quid pro quo sexual harassment involving a tangible job detriment (see Chapter 2, section VI.).

The Supreme Court in *Meritor* rejected automatic liability under Title VII, however, in the case of a hostile environment. In a hostile environment, even where a supervisor was the perpetrator, employer liability depends on such factors as the means by which the harassment was effected, whether the employer had notice of the harassment, what opportunity the complainant had to report the harassment, and the employer's response to its knowledge of the harassment.

In *Meritor*, the employer argued that it had an absolute defense to a claim of sexual harassment by its supervisor because the employer knew nothing about it and because the employer had an antiharassment policy and complaint procedure that the complainant had failed to use. The complainant argued that the employer was automatically liable for each act of sexual harassment that its supervisor had committed, regardless of whether the employer knew or should have known about it, because Title VII defines "employer" to include an "agent" of the employer and because the supervisor's knowledge amounts to notice to the employer.

The *Meritor* Court expressly rejected both of these positions, ruling that employer liability is *not* automatic in a hostile environment case, but rather depends on the circumstances. Thus, the employer's knowledge of harassment and the adequacy of its sexual harassment grievance procedure are "plainly relevant" to, though "not necessarily dispositive" of, the issue of employer liability. (For a discussion of automatic liability under state law, see Chapter 7, section II.B.)

2. Scope of Employment. Under agency principles, the employer may be liable for torts that its employees commit while acting within the scope of their employment. This theory of liability rarely applies, since sexual harassment would not be within the scope of a supervisor's duties.

In *Davis v. United States Steel Corp.*, the complainant alleged fifteen months of sexual harassment by her supervisor before she ever notified upper management. Two of the three appellate court judges found no employer liability, because the supervisor's sexual advances were motivated by his own independent purpose, not that of his employer, and because employer liability cannot rest solely on the fact that the advances were made possible, or even more easily accomplished, by virtue of the employment relationship.

The dissenting judge thought that a jury should decide whether the employer was liable on the theory that the employer had delegated supervisory authority to a person who committed acts of harassment "interwoven" with the performance of supervisory duties. The judge reasoned that because sexual harassment at the workplace is foreseeable, a jury could find that the supervisor's sexual harassment was "part and parcel of his supervision" of the complainant.

3. Apparent Authority. An employer can be liable for the tort of an employee that is made possible by the victim's reasonable belief that the employee's conduct was authorized by the employer. The EEOC believes that an employer can be liable under this theory of apparent authority if the employer fails to provide an effective mechanism to correct improper supervisory conduct. The EEOC argues that, absent those mechanisms, employees reasonably may believe that a harassing supervisor's actions will be tolerated or even condoned by upper management: if the employer has not provided an effective avenue to complain, then the supervisor has unchecked, final control over the victim and it is reasonable to impute his abuse of this power to the employer (see Appendix 3, Policy Guidance on Sexual Harassment §D.2.(c)(2)).

Some courts have held that employer liability is also appropriate in hostile environment cases where the supervisor uses or threatens to use his authority to help to create a hostile environment and make the victim reluctant to report it to higher management (*Mitchell v. OsAir*). *Sparks v. Pilot Freight Carriers* illustrates how a supervisor's ability to commit quid pro quo harassment can supply apparent authority to sustain employer liability for hostile environment harassment. In *Sparks*, a trucking company terminal manager had wide discretion over all personnel matters in the terminal. He asked his new billing clerk if she was married, if she had a boyfriend, and if she could become pregnant. As weeks went by, he would rub her shoulders, play with her hair, ask if he could visit her at home with a bottle of wine, and commented "you'd better be nice to me," and "your fate is in my hands." The company's upper management, located in another state, did not know of this conduct until the complainant filed suit. The court held that the employer could be liable for the harassment even though it was beyond the scope of employment, because the supervisor's authority "aided in accomplishing" his harassment.

Application of the *Sparks* apparent agency theory would be doubtful in the absence of explicit threats to misuse supervisorial authority, or in cases where the supervisor lacked power to affect the complainant's tangible job benefits (*Steele v. Off-shore Shipbldg.*).

4. Employer Negligence. Employer liability for a hostile environment generally depends on whether there was employer negligence in supervising the workplace by failing to prevent or remedy sexual harassment. Whether the hostile environment is created by supervisors, by co-workers, or even by nonemployees, the employer will be liable for a sexually hostile environment if the employer (1) knew or should have known of the alleged sexual harassment, and (2) failed to prevent the harassment or take prompt and appropriate corrective action. This theory of direct liability for breach of the duty to prevent and remedy harassment, unlike the previous theories discussed, applies regardless of whether the alleged harasser was a supervisor.

Courts have attached various labels to this theory of employer liability, including negligence, agency by estoppel, and direct liability. Other courts, using no label, have simply required some level of employer knowledge and failure to prevent or remedy known harassment before imposing liability for environmental harassment by a supervisor (*EEOC v. Hacienda Hotel*). Finally, many courts have applied the same standard while using the misleading label of *respondeat superior*. Actually, the doctrine of *respondeat superior* rarely applies in a sexual harassment case, for *respondeat superior* addresses wrongs that the agent believes he is committing to further his employer's business, and such is rarely the case with sexual harassment. When courts use *respondeat superior* as a general label to describe employer liability for sexual harassment (*Henson v. City of Dundee*), they usually are discussing the concept of employer negligence. The elements of this theory are discussed below.

a. Duty to Prevent Harassment. The EEOC Guidelines, many state employment discrimination statutes, and at least one federal court have suggested that employers have an affirmative duty to take reasonable steps to prevent harassment. This duty is especially clear where an employer is aware of previous incidents of harassment and reasonably should have anticipated further harassment (*Paroline v. Unisys Corp.*).

b. Duty to Remedy Harassment. When an employer has set up a proper system to prevent sexual harassment and to provide an appropriate mechanism for remedying any harassment that does occur, the employer is not liable under a negligence theory unless it knew (had *actual* knowledge) or should have known (had *constructive* knowledge) of the harassment, and fails to take prompt corrective action.

Courts will find "actual" employer knowledge where complaints of harassment have been lodged with any representative of the employer who holds a position high enough within the organization that notice to that person constitutes notice to the employer. Some courts have found actual employer knowledge on the basis of reports to low-level supervisors or foremen (*Waltman v. International Paper Co.; Morris v. American Nat'l Can Corp.*), while other courts have held that the employer had no notice where the complainant did not notify management above the level of first-line supervisor (*Ukarish v. Magnesium Elektron*).

Actual employer knowledge of harassment has been found where:

- a police chief saw obscene pictures and photos on the walls of the police department (*Arnold v. City of Seminole*);
- a CEO saw obscene cartoons in the men's room (*Bennett v. Corroon & Black Corp.*); and
- a foreman was present when a crew member picked up the complainant and held her so that other co-workers could touch her (*Hall v. Gus Constr. Co.*).

Knowledge is "constructive"—deemed to exist—where the harassment is so pervasive that the employer, even if it did not know of the conduct, should have known. In *Hall v. Gus Construction Co.* (discussed in section III.A.2.b. of this chapter), the court found that the employer had constructive knowledge that male construction crew members were verbally abusing female traffic controllers because the abuse was so pervasive that the supervisor must have noticed it.

In *Lipsett v. University of Puerto Rico,* the court found sufficient evidence of constructive knowledge where offensive literature was displayed in a rest facility where all members of a medical residency program, including members of management, had their meals, conducted meetings, and checked the bulletin board. In that facility, the complainant's male co-workers had posted on the bulletin board a list of obscene sexual nicknames for all female residents, posted on the wall a sexually explicit drawing of the plaintiff's body, and plastered the walls with *Playboy* centerfolds.

Pervasive graffiti and pornography can give rise to an inference of knowledge on the part of the employer. In *Waltman v. International Paper Co.*, where there was graffiti on the walls of the powerhouse, the restroom and the elevator, the court held that the complainant had created a factual issue as to whether the employer had constructive knowledge of co-worker harassment.

When courts rule that the employer had no constructive knowledge, it is usually because the harassment was isolated rather than pervasive. In *Ukarish v. Magnesium Elektron,* however, the court held that the employer had no constructive knowledge because the plant atmosphere, though "distasteful," was simply a "fact of life." The reasoning in *Ukarish* seems to be that, because the prevailing environment in the plant always had been coarse, there was nothing to put the employer on notice that there was anything unwelcome about that atmosphere.

Similarly, the dissenting opinion in *Waltman* argues that the existence of sexual graffiti throughout the workplace is too "ordinary" to put the employer on constructive notice that the sexually charged environment was unwelcome. Thus, evidence of the culture of the workplace arguably may show that the employer lacked constructive knowledge of a hostile environment in that the activity was typical of the workplace.

c. The Complainant's Failure to Use the Employer's Grievance Procedure. In *Meritor*, where the complainant had failed to report any harassment through internal grievance procedures, the Supreme Court rejected the employer's view that the failure to complain insulated the employer from liability.

It will still be a good practical defense, however, if, where the employer has had a preventive procedure calculated to encourage victims of harassment to come forward, a hostile environment complainant has failed to report the sexual harassment to upper management (*Meritor Sav. Bank v. Vinson*). First, a general procedure that tells how to report harassment will undermine a complainant's claim that complaints made in some other manner were sufficient to impute knowledge to the employer. Second, that procedure will support an argument that the employer reasonably lacked notice of the sexual harassment and therefore had no opportunity to take prompt correction action. Third, the existence of the procedure enables the employer to challenge the complainant's credibility on the basis of a failure to invoke the procedure.

d. The Employer's Prompt Corrective Action. Once an employer is notified that sexual harassment has occurred, the employer may escape liability by taking prompt remedial action, but only if that action is reasonably calculated to end the harassment (*Sanchez v. City of Miami Beach*). The promptness and adequacy of the employer's response is evaluated on a case-by-case basis.

Once notified of harassment, the employer must investigate and take prompt remedial action reasonably calculated to end any harassment that is found. A test of whether the remedial action is adequate is whether the sexual harassment ends after remedial actions are taken (*Dornhecker v. Malibu Grand Prix Corp.; Brooms v. Regal Tube Co.*).

Both the promptness and the degree of remedial action that courts require of employers in a case of hostile environment harassment depend upon such factors as:

- the severity of the harassment,
- the degree of acquiescence in the harassment by supervisors,
- the promptness of the employer's responsive action,
- the effectiveness of any initial remedial steps,
- the credibility of the complainant's accusations, and
- the apparent sincerity of the employer's efforts to eradicate the harassment.

Depending on which of these factors is present, courts may reach different conclusions as to whether an employer's response is adequate. In *Dornhecker v. Malibu Grand Prix Corp.*, where the harassing conduct spanned only two days, the employer avoided liability with a promise to the complainant that she would not have to work with the harasser after their current business trip, which had a day and a half remaining. The court observed that society has seldom provided instantaneous redress for dishonorable conduct: "prompt" action is not necessarily "immediate" action. Conversely, the court in *Bennett v. Corroon & Black Corp.* upheld employer liability where a manager permitted "obscene" cartoons depicting the complainant to remain on the wall of the men's restroom for one day after he first saw them. The court concluded that the cartoons were so obviously offensive that the employer should have acted immediately rather than waiting for the complainant's reaction.

Employers do not necessarily excuse their failure to act because they do not know who was responsible for anonymous conduct. In *Waltman v. International Paper Co.*, unsigned notes and graffiti directed to employee Sue Waltman read: "Sue sucks everybody's dick," "Sue is a whore," "I am going to eat Sue's pussy," and "Sue has a nice pussy." The courts held that where harassment takes the form of graffiti throughout the workplace, the employer has an affirmative duty to address the problem even if the authorship is unknown. Waltman's employer apparently failed to find out who wrote the graffiti about her. The employer could not escape a trial on the issue of whether its response—washing the graffiti off the walls of the plant—was sufficient under the circumstances.

The employer's obligation to take prompt correction action, including appropriate discipline of offenders, is discussed in detail in Chapter 16.

B. Harassment by Co-Workers

Sexual harassment in the workplace is perpetrated by co-workers as well as by supervisors. Co-worker harassment is always hostile environment harassment. Quid pro quo analysis does not apply because co-worker harassment, by definition, does not involve the abuse of power delegated by the employer.

Some early decisions rejected claims of co-worker harassment on the ground that co-workers cannot affect conditions of employment. Courts now recognize that even without formal workplace authority, an employee can make his co-worker's environment so hostile, offensive, or intimidating as to alter the terms and conditions of her work (*Henson v. City of Dundee*). Co-worker harassment has included pulling a ladder out from under the victim and shoving a steel pipe into her ribs (*Egger v. Plumbers Local 276*), sticking a tongue into the victim's ear while she carried a vial of hot liquid (*Waltman v. International Paper Co.*), and warning a female resident in a surgery training program of a "reign of terror" against women and advising of the need to "keep a relationship" with a senior male resident (*Lipsett v. University of P.R.*).

Hostile environment harassment by co-workers can occur even where the harassers are subordinates of the complainant (*Erebia v. Chrysler Plastic Prods. Corp.*). One court, however, has held that where the complainant is capable of stopping the unwelcome conduct by means of supervisory power, a hostile environment claim will fail (*Perkins v. General Motors Corp.*).

The employer is liable for co-worker harassment, if at all, only under the negligence theory discussed in subsection VI.A.4. above. Thus, the inquiry as to employer liability for co-worker harassment focuses on whether the employer had actual or constructive knowledge of the harassment and, if so, whether the employer acted appropriately to control the harassment (*Katz v. Dole*; see also Appendix 1, EEOC Guidelines §1604.11(d)).

Co-workers themselves generally are not individually liable under Title VII. Their liability would arise under common-law theories (see Chapter 11), state employment discrimination statutes (see Chapter 7), or possibly criminal statutes (see Chapter 12).

C. Harassment by Nonemployees

The EEOC Guidelines provide that employers are liable for workplace sexual harassment perpetrated by nonemployees (such as independent contractors, customers, consultants, and vendors) "where the employer (or its agents or supervisory employees) knows or should have known of the conduct, and fails to take immediate and appropriate corrective action." Employer liability depends upon "the extent of the employer's control and any other legal responsibility which the employer may have with respect to the conduct of such nonemployees" (see Appendix 1, EEOC Guidelines §1604.11(e)).

Only a few reported decisions address sexual harassment by nonemployees. These decisions, which endorse the EEOC Guidelines, indicate that employers will be held liable for harassment by nonemployees when: (1) the employer imposes a job requirement, such as a dress code, that foreseeably subjects the employee to sexual harassment, or (2) the employer knows or should have known of the sexual harassment by nonemployees and fails to take prompt corrective action within its control.

1. Job Requirements That Foreseeably Provoke Sexual Harassment. Generally, dress codes that impose different standards for the sexes (*e.g.*, dresses for women, business suits for men) are not unlawfully discriminatory unless they reflect demeaning sexual stereotypes (*Carroll v. Talman Fed. Sav. & Loan Ass'n*).

A dress code for women may be unlawfully discriminatory if it foreseeably encourages sexual harassment. In *EEOC v. Sage Realty Corp.*, a female lobby attendant in a large Manhattan office building was required to wear a red, white, and blue uniform to commemorate the 1976 Bicentennial. The uniform, with slits down the front and up the sides, exposed the complainant's thighs, midriff, and buttocks as she performed her job. This situation prompted various nonemployees to whistle "Yankee Doodle" and "The Stars and Stripes Forever," and to offer the complainant to "run it up the flagpole anytime you want to." The complainant was discharged when she then refused to wear the uniform. The court found the employer liable under Title VII, reasoning that maintaining the uniform requirement, knowing that it would subject the complainant to sexual harassment, constituted sex discrimination.

In *EEOC v. Newtown Inn Associates*, the employer was found liable for retaliating against hotel cocktail waitresses who complained of a marketing scheme that required them to project an air of sexual availability to customers. The waitresses were directed to flirt with customers, to dance with customers in a "sexually provocative and degrading fashion," and to dress in revealing, thematic attire for events such as Bikini Night, P.J. Night, and Whips and Chains Night. In a similar EEOC decision, a receptionist was required to wear a sexually revealing costume that elicited verbal abuse from male visitors. Her costume consisted of a halter-bra top and a midi-skirt with a slit in front that ran up her thighs. The EEOC determined that the costume requirement unreasonably interfered with her work and created a hostile working environment (EEOC Dec. 81-17).

2. Failure to Take Prompt Corrective Action. Employer liability for harassment by nonemployees may arise if the employer fails to exercise reasonable control to prevent it. Where employers can control the conduct of nonemployees, the analysis strongly resembles that used for determining employer liability for co-worker harassment.

a. Independent Contractors. In a case brought under the New York State Human Rights Law, an employer had retained a polygraph examiner to administer lie detector tests. While administering the tests, the examiner allegedly touched the breasts of female applicants and asked them non-job-related questions of a sexual nature. The employer incurred liability for this conduct by continuing to use the polygraph examiner after it had notice of his improper conduct (*People v. Hamilton*).

b. Customers. The EEOC determined that a restaurant employer violated Title VII because the restaurant owner knowingly failed to intervene when a male customer made unwelcome sexual advances to a waitress. The employer had unusual ability to take corrective action because the harasser was a frequent customer and friend of the employer (EEOC Dec. 84-3).

c. Consultants. In *Dornhecker v. Malibu Grand Prix Corp.*, a consultant who had been retained by the complainant's employer dropped his pants, grabbed her hips, and touched her breasts. The court assumed that the employer had a legal responsibility to take prompt and decisive action to protect its employee from the consultant.

d. Vendors. Although there appear to be no reported decisions on the subject, sexual harassment by vendors of the complainant's employer is a problem that has drawn sustained attention. The California FEP agency has issued an internal memorandum detailing sample complaints by which an employee, sexually harassed by a visiting salesperson, may complain of her employer's failure to prevent or correct the vendor's harassment.

3. Liability of the Nonemployee Harasser. A sexual harassment claim against a nonemployee is possible under several theories of liability: common-law claims (see Chapter 11); state FEP statutes (see Chapter 7); federal employment or civil rights law (see Chapter 8); and criminal law (see Chapter 12). For liability of unions, see Chapter 13.

VII. THE EMPLOYER'S REBUTTAL

A. Disputing Elements of the Complainant's Case

The employer may defend a hostile environment charge by disputing one or more of the elements of the complainant's case: that the sexually harassing incidents occurred, that they were sex-based, that the incidents were unwelcome, that the incidents were sufficiently severe or pervasive to alter the conditions of the complainant's employment, and that the employer has legal responsibility for the conduct.

B. Articulating a Nondiscriminatory Reason

If the situation involves sexual advances, overt gender-baiting, or a sexually charged workplace, the harassment is facially sex-based discrimination and no nondiscriminatory reason likely can explain the defendant's actions.

If the complained-of conduct is not sexual, such as in a case of nonsexual hazing, the employer may argue that the conduct was based on factors other than sex. The employer may attempt to show, for example, that the conduct complained of was motivated by the complainant's personality, was directed indiscriminately against men and women, or that men and women were equally offended by the conduct.

Many cases contain too much sex-specific conduct to make the "personality clash" defense possible to sustain. In *Zabkowicz v. West Bend Co.*, the complainant's co-workers exposed themselves, verbally abused her, and made obscene gestures. When the complainant was pregnant and under a 25-pound lifting restriction, a co-worker grabbed his crotch and remarked, "Carol, I bet you'd have trouble handling this 25 pounder." The court found that the harassing conduct was on the basis of sex notwithstanding the employer's "personality clash" defense. Similarly, in *Morris v. American National Can Corp.*, an employer was unsuccessful in arguing that the complainant had "antagonized" the co-workers who threw objects at her, sabotaged her work, made her the target of openly displayed sexual graffiti, and adorned her work station with replicas and pictures of penises and obscene pictures and notes.

C. Rebutting Employer Responsibility

The employer also may argue that it cannot be held legally responsible for the harassment because it neither knew nor should have known of the alleged misconduct or because, upon learning of the misconduct, the employer took prompt and effective remedial action. (Employer responsibility is discussed in greater detail in section VI. above.)

VIII. THE PLAINTIFF'S ULTIMATE PROOF OF CAUSATION

A. Proof of Pretext

If the sex-based nature of the conduct is still at issue, the complainant must prove that the harassment was because of sex. Proof of a sexual advance is direct and sufficient proof of discrimination because of sex except where a bisexual harasser makes sexual advances regardless of gender.

Where the employer argues that harassment did not occur because of the complainant's sex, the complainant will offer circumstantial evidence to show that the unwelcome conduct was because of her sex.

B. Proof of Unreasonable Interference With Work

Where the complainant is alleging damages from an adverse employment action, and where the employer can prove that the immediate cause of an adverse employment decision was a nondiscriminatory business reason such as poor work performance or excessive absenteeism, complainants have still been able to prevail by proving that the performance or attendance problems were themselves the result of a hostile environment.

1. *Interference With Job Performance.* In *Weiss v. United States,* where a Jewish plaintiff was debilitated by repeated slurs such as "Jew faggot" and "Christ-killer," the employer could not rely on the plaintiff's decreased performance as a basis for discharge because the decreased performance itself resulted from the discriminatory behavior. While this case involved religious harassment, the same principle would apply to sexual harassment.

2. *Interference With Attendance.* In *DeGrace v. Rumsfeld,* a civilian firefighter received three threatening notes and found

some of his equipment damaged after complaining to his supervisor of racial slurs by his co-workers. The plaintiff alleged that the threats caused him to fear reporting to work, and he was eventually discharged for excessive absenteeism. The court concluded that because the absenteeism resulted from racial harassment, it could not be said that the discharge was free of racial discrimination even if the ultimate decisionmaker acted on legitimate reasons.

In an analogous sexual harassment case, the complainant challenging a disciplinary action may attempt to prove that the excessive absenteeism or poor work performance cited as the basis for the discipline was itself the result of sexual harassment.

4

CLAIMS BY THIRD PARTIES

I. OVERVIEW

The law clearly protects direct targets of sexual harassment. It is less clear whether the law also protects a person who is injured by gender-based conduct in the workplace that is directed at someone else or that is not directed at anyone in particular. This difficult issue arises in two basic contexts:

(1) A heterosexual employer hires, promotes, or otherwise favors his female lover, L, while passing over two better-qualified candidates—female X and male Y. Does either X or Y have a viable sex discrimination claim? Does it matter for this purpose whether the sexual advances to L were unwelcome?

(2) Female X or male Y objects to the employer's tolerance of sexual horseplay, explicit sexual language, and the public display of pornographic pictures and graffiti, none of which is specifically directed at X or Y. Does either X or Y have a viable hostile environment claim? Does it matter for this purpose whether others in the workplace find the conduct unwelcome?

The EEOC addressed most of these issues in its January 1990 Policy Guidance on Employer Liability for Sexual Favoritism (reproduced in Appendix 2). The Policy Guidance on Sexual

Favoritism addresses three situations: favoritism based upon quid pro quo harassment, isolated instances of favoritism toward a lover, and environmental harassment caused by widespread favoritism. This chapter addresses third-party claims in these three situations and also in a fourth situation: widespread sexual conduct not involving sexual favoritism.

II. THIRD-PARTY CLAIMS BASED ON UNDERLYING QUID PRO QUO HARASSMENT

A. Theories of the Third-Party Claim

A classic case of quid pro quo sexual harassment is the woman who loses a promotion because she has rebuffed her supervisor's advances. The third-party case arises where a woman, under duress, *accepts* her supervisor's unwelcome sexual advances and thereby wins a promotion for which another employee was better qualified. Under these circumstances, does the disappointed competitor of the woman have a viable sex discrimination claim? The EEOC endorses a third-party claim under these circumstances: "Where employment opportunities or benefits are granted because of an individual's submission to the employer's sexual advances or requests for sexual favors, the employer may be liable for unlawful sex discrimination against other persons who were qualified for but denied that employment opportunity or benefit." (Appendix 1, EEOC Guidelines §1604.11(g)).

The Policy Guidance on Sexual Favoritism, addressing this claim in more detail, describes two alternative theories in support of such a claim: (1) a disappointed female could claim that she was denied job benefits as an "implicit quid pro quo" that had become a general condition of employment; or (2) a disappointed female *or* male could advance a derivative claim on the basis of the unlawful sex-based coercion of the favored employee (Appendix 2, Policy Guidance on Sexual Favoritism §B.). These theories are discussed below.

1. Submission as a General Condition of Employment. If an employer tolerates a practice of granting job benefits in exchange for sexual favors, the EEOC says that employees of the same sex who lost those benefits because they did not confer sexual favors may recover on a theory that they were subjected to an implicit quid pro quo.

This theory of recovery is available only to members of the same sex as the favored employee. In *Toscano v. Nimmo*, the complainant was denied a promotion that was awarded to a female competitor who granted sexual favors to the male decisionmaker, a self-described "life-long 'womanizer' " who had propositioned many female workers. The court awarded judgment to the complainant on the theory that granting sexual favors was an implicit condition for receiving the job.

The theory based on *Toscano* provides that an employer discriminates on the basis of gender when it implicitly requires that members of one sex (*e.g.*, females) submit to sexual advances to receive job benefits. Cases of this kind will be relatively rare.

2. Derivative Claims. A theory of implicit quid pro quo is not available if a supervisor limits his sexual advances to a single subordinate. Liability to a third party may nonetheless result if the advances are unwelcome, are submitted to, and the supervisor confers rewards as part of a sexual quid pro quo. In this scenario, the EEOC considers that both female and male co-workers who are better qualified for the benefit in question may challenge the employment decision, for all such co-workers are injured as a result of the discrimination against the individual who was coerced (see Appendix 2, Policy Guidance on Sexual Favoritism §B.). This "derivative" theory of recovery is supported by cases holding that any person injured by an unlawful employment practice, regardless of whether that person was the target of the practice, may sue under Title VII (*Clayton v. White Hall School Dist.; Allen v. American Home Foods*).

B. Sex of the Third-Party Complainant

Under the EEOC's theory of submission to sexual favors as a general condition of employment, only a disadvantaged female competitor could claim that women, but not men, are generally required to submit to the sexual advances of a heterosexual male supervisor in order to enjoy the job benefit in question. Under the EEOC's theory of derivative liability, however, a discrimination action could be available to any better-qualified competitor, male or female.

III. THIRD-PARTY SEX DISCRIMINATION CLAIMS BASED ON UNDERLYING CONSENSUAL SEXUAL FAVORITISM

When a disadvantaged competitor challenges an employment decision based on a *consensual* sexual relationship, the EEOC and most courts have rejected claims of sex discrimination, whether or not the favored employee and the disadvantaged competitor are of different sexes (Appendix 2, Policy Guidance on Sexual Favoritism §A.; *Erickson v. Marsh & McLennan Co.*). The EEOC and most courts have likened the "isolated instance" of consensual sexual favoritism to nepotism: the practice may be unfair, but it is not sex discrimination, for in each case members of both sexes are equally disadvantaged for reasons other than their genders (*Platner v. Cash & Thomas*).

A minority position was adopted by the court in *King v. Palmer*, which permitted a female nurse to pursue a claim that she was unlawfully denied a promotion because her supervisor promoted another female nurse on the basis of his intimate relationship with her. The court assumed that Title VII's prohibition against sex discrimination is violated whenever sex is, without legitimate justification, a substantial factor in the employment decision. The court also held that, by presenting evidence that kisses, embraces, and other "amorous behavior" played a role in the promotion decision, the complainant had satisfied her burden of proof. She did not have to prove an "explicit sexual relationship."

The majority rule, stated in *DeCintio v. Westchester County Medical Center*, is that Title VII does not forbid isolated cases of consensual sexual favoritism. *DeCintio* involved seven male respiratory therapists who claimed they were denied promotion because of their gender. They alleged that the male decision-maker created a new job qualification—registration by the

National Board of Respiratory Therapists—in order to disqualify the males and enable him to hire a female applicant who happened to be his lover. The court held that sex discrimination does not include preferential treatment based on sexual liaisons or sexual attractions. The court emphasized that employment discrimination law forbids treating employees differently on the basis of gender; it is not unlawful to discriminate on the basis of a voluntary sexual relationship. Similarly, in *Miller v. Aluminum Co. of America,* the court dismissed a sex discrimination claim by a female employee who contended that she lost her job to a female co-worker because of the co-worker's consensual romantic relationship with the plant manager.

The EEOC, as indicated above, follows *DeCintio* rather than *King,* taking the position "that Title VII does not prohibit isolated instances of preferential treatment based upon consensual romantic relationships" (Appendix 2, Policy Guidance on Sexual Favoritism §A.).

IV. THIRD-PARTY HOSTILE ENVIRONMENT CLAIMS BASED ON UNDERLYING SEXUAL HARASSMENT

A. Theory of the Third-Party Claim

The typical hostile environment claim is by a female who has been the target of sexual harassment. The third-party issue is whether a hostile environment claim can be maintained by people in the workplace who were *not themselves* specific targets of the harassment. According to the EEOC, both men and women who object to an "atmosphere demeaning to women" can establish a violation if the conduct is sufficiently severe or pervasive to alter the conditions of *their* employment and create a hostile working environment for *them* (Appendix 2, Policy Guidance on Sexual Favoritism §C.).

Some authorities support the EEOC's theory of a third-party claim of hostile environment harassment based on sexual conduct directed at employees other than the complainant. In *Fisher v. San Pedro Peninsula Hospital,* the court recognized a nurse's sexual harassment claim against a doctor whose offensive remarks and touchings were directed at other nurses, but in the complainant's presence. Thus, even if the complainant was not the intended object of sexual harassment, she could state a claim because she saw the doctor hug and kiss other nurses, grab their breasts, make offensive sexual statements, and make lewd comments about the breasts of anesthetized female patients.

By contrast, in *Ross v. Double Diamond*, the court declined to consider harassment against others in the workplace in deciding a complainant's hostile environment claim. The court found that one of the complainant's co-workers had suffered a hostile work environment by virtue of several verbal and physical advances of a sexual and unwelcome nature. But the court refused to consider this evidence in hearing the complainant's own claim, even though the complainant knew about her co-worker's mistreatment and actively helped her to address it with their employer.

B. Sex of the Complainant

Courts and commentators have concluded that a sexually hostile environment in the form of widespread verbal and visual abuse tends inevitably to demean the status of women (*Drinkwater v. Union Carbide Corp.*). Women therefore have the clearest claim as third-party complainants in hostile environment cases. Nonetheless, the EEOC contends that when sexually offensive conduct occurs, "co-workers of any . . . sex can claim that this conduct, which communicates a bias against protected class members, creates a hostile environment for them" (Appendix 2, Policy Guidance on Sexual Favoritism §3.).

V. THIRD-PARTY HOSTILE ENVIRONMENT CLAIMS BASED ON UNDERLYING CONSENSUAL CONDUCT

A. Theory of the Third-Party Claim

Third-party hostile environment claims can challenge an atmosphere that *other* employees accept, and perhaps even enjoy, as a part of the culture of the workplace. Such a claim might involve any of three kinds of activity in the workplace:

(1) consensual sexual relationships between supervisors and employees, (2) sexual "horseplay" among male and female employees, and (3) displays of sexual graffiti or pornography. The consensual nature of the conduct is not a defense. As the EEOC has stated in the context of sexual favoritism, "the fact that it was exclusively voluntary and consensual would not have defeated a claim that it created a hostile work environment for other people in the workplace" (Appendix 2, Policy Guidance on Sexual Favoritism §C. n.13).

1. Consensual Sexual Relationships. In *Drinkwater v. Union Carbide Corp.*, the complainant alleged that an affair between her male supervisor and her female subordinate made the working environment sexually hostile. In discussing whether a consensual romantic relationship can create a hostile environment, the court first stated that this case differed from cases simply complaining about a consensual sexual relationship (see section III. above). The court found that the complainant here was claiming not simply a consensual relationship, but a hostile environment caused by that relationship. The court emphasized that in hostile environment claims, the environment, and not the relationship, is the basis of the claim, and that a sexual relationship may create a hostile environment if the complainant showed that "sexual discourse displaced standard business procedure" in a way that affected her job performance and evaluation. Such a claim would require more than proof of an unfair and unprofessional sexual relationship in the workplace; it would require a showing that the workplace was charged with "oppressive sexual accentuation."

2. Sexual "Horseplay." In the leading sexual "horseplay" case, *Broderick v. Ruder*, the complainant alleged that male managers and co-workers touched female employees, used sexual language, and told dirty jokes; that two managers had sexual relationships with female staff members who received promotions and cash awards; and that another manager was "noticeably attached" to a female subordinate whose career he promoted. The court found that this office atmosphere affected the complainant's job performance and deprived her of employment benefits and opportunities. Similarly, in *Priest v. Rotary*, the court found that a restaurant employer created a sexually hostile working environment by his consensual sexual horseplay with the complainant's co-workers, who received preferential job assignments.

3. Displays of Sexual Materials. Sexual materials can appear in the public areas of a workplace in the form of graffiti, cartoons, and sexually suggestive posters or pin-ups. To the extent that display of this material is tolerated, the display can be called consensual conduct. In one case, the trial court was directed to consider not only harassment directed at the complainant, but visual forms of harassment not specifically directed at her, such as graffiti on walls, in restrooms, in the elevator, "sexually explicit calendars" on walls and in lockers, and "used tampons" hanging from lockers (*Waltman v. Int'l Paper Co.*). Critics of this decision question whether a person who was not herself a direct target of the harassment, but who "feels" abused, can prove a hostile environment, particularly since (1) such displays may offend both male and female employees, (2) society's sexual mores are in a state of flux, and (3) the heightened sensitivities of isolated employees should not be sufficient to sustain a hostile environment claim.

Nonetheless, while no court has yet ruled that the display of pornography or sexual graffiti can itself constitute a hostile environment, courts have cited these displays as evidence supporting a hostile environment claim (*Robinson v. Jacksonville Shipyards*).

B. Sex of the Complainant

Male or female employees could challenge a hostile sexual environment not directed at them personally. Some offensive workplace conduct (*e.g.*, offensive talk about male homosexuality) arguably is equally offensive to both sexes (*Fair v. Guiding Eyes for the Blind*), while other conduct (*e.g.*, display of pictures of nude women in sexually submissive poses in a male-dominated workplace) may have an adverse impact on one sex (*Robinson v. Jacksonville Shipyards*).

5

Constructive Discharge

I. OVERVIEW

An employee who is discharged formally by an employer as a result of sexual harassment is entitled to legal remedies. The same remedies may be available to an employee who has been "constructively" discharged (*i.e.*, effectively forced to quit) by sexual harassment so severe that a reasonable person would quit rather than endure it.

Courts have identified the following elements that a complainant must prove to establish liability for constructive discharge:

(1) the complaint resigned or otherwise experienced some job detriment;

(2) the complainant was harassed because of the complainant's gender and the harassment caused the complainant to resign;

(3) the sexual harassment was so aggravated that a reasonable person in the same position would have felt compelled to resign; and

(4) the employer is responsible for the employee's action because (a) the employer intended to force the complainant's resignation, or (b) the employer or its agent knew of the harassment and failed to take corrective action before the complainant reasonably resigned.

The constructive discharge concept may also apply to job detriments other than the termination of employment. Thus, if the complainant, in order to avoid the harasser, took a demotion or an undesirable transfer or simply stayed at home on unpaid sick leave, there could be a case of constructive demotion or a case of "intermittent constructive discharge."

II. THE CAUSAL CONNECTION

The complainant must prove that the employment was terminated *because of* gender. Proof of this causal connection is two-pronged: (1) that the harassment was because of gender (see Chapter 3, section V.), and (2) that the harassment caused the complainant's resignation.

As to the second prong, the timing of the complainant's resignation often will show the causal connection. Closeness in time between the sexual harassment and the resignation will strongly support the causal connection. By the same token, long delays will tend to disprove any connection. Although constructive discharge may be found even where the resignation did not closely follow the last act of harassment, delays as short as four months, one month, and even eleven days have undermined a claim of constructive discharge (*Hirschfeld v. New Mexico Corrections Dep't*; *Benton v. Kroger Co.*; *Steele v. Offshore Shipbldg.*).

III. ESTABLISHING OBJECTIVELY INTOLERABLE WORKING CONDITIONS

A. Objective and Subjective Standards

To establish a constructive discharge, a complainant must prove not only that she felt forced to resign (a subjective test), but that the sexual harassment would have caused a reasonable person in the complainant's position to resign (an objective test) (*Bristow v. Daily Press*).

At least one court has held that this standard should consider a reasonable person of the same sex as the complainant, because men and women are vulnerable in different ways and offended by different behavior (*Yates v. Avco Corp.*).

B. Aggravating Factors

Courts generally hold that proof of constructive discharge requires proof of "aggravating factors" beyond the evidence required to establish mere employment discrimination. Thus, although a single incident of sexual harassment could be egregious enough to justify a resignation, generally the "aggravating circumstances" must consist of a series of sexually harassing incidents, such as unwanted touchings and repeated propositions.

Courts are most likely to sustain a claim of constructive discharge where the employer's corrective action is unduly mild or where remedial action is promised but not delivered. In one case, the harasser propositioned the complainant with a photograph depicting interracial acts of sodomy, showed her a racist pornographic picture involving bestiality, told her that was how she would end up, and then grabbed her arm and threatened to kill her when she tried to run away; she threw hot coffee on him, ran away screaming, and fell down a flight of stairs. The court found that the complainant's resignation was reasonable even though the employer had hired an attorney to investigate her complaint, had caused the harasser to apologize, had withheld the harasser's scheduled salary increase, and had threatened him with dismissal (*Brooms v. Regal Tube Co.*).

C. Proof of Sexual Harassment as Proof of Constructive Discharge

A complainant who proves a sexually hostile environment goes a long way toward showing the existence of aggravating factors, because by definition a hostile sexual environment involves severe or pervasive harassment. Thus, the same evidence used to show a hostile environment generally will be offered as proof of the aggravating circumstances compelling the complainant's resignation from employment. One court found that a reasonable person would resign from a work environment in which a supervisor made sexually offensive remarks to her, rubbed his hands on her back, and grabbed and kissed her against her will (*Paroline v. Unisys Corp.*).

IV. EMPLOYER RESPONSIBILITY

Courts differ as to the kind of employer intent a complainant must prove to establish a constructive discharge:

(1) All courts agree that an employee is constructively discharged where the employer communicates its intent to discharge the employee and the employee then quits before the employer's intent is ever formally expressed.

(2) All courts further agree that this intent may be inferred when an employer deliberately makes the working conditions intolerable, by sexual harassment or otherwise.

(3) Courts differ, however, as to whether a constructive discharge may also occur when the employer has no actual intent to force the complainant's resignation.

The controversy is thus whether an employer is liable for a constructive discharge only when the employer specifically intends to oust the complainant, or also when the employer did not intend the discharge but is responsible for the offensive conduct that causes the complainant to resign. Most courts take the latter position, holding that, even if the employer intended to retain the complainant, the complainant is constructively discharged whenever the work environment is so intolerable that a reasonable employee would have felt forced to resign, and the complainant in fact did feel forced to resign (the objective *and* subjective standard).

This controversy may be more theoretical than practical, for when the complainant is required to prove an employer's intent, that intent often is implied by the circumstances of the hostile environment (*Paroline v. Unisys Corp.*). Further, employer intent may be inferred from the employer's failure to take corrective action: where an employee's resignation because of sexual harassment was reasonable, it generally, if not invariably, was foreseeable to the employer (*Wheeler v. Southland Corp.; Yates v. Avco Corp.*).

Nonetheless, a finding of employer intent need not follow automatically from a finding that the employer failed to take fully effective remedial action. The employer can argue that its failure to act resulted from miscalculation or poor judgment rather than from a specific intent to cause the resignation. In this connection, the court will consider any evidence that the employer asked the complainant not to resign.

V. EMPLOYER REBUTTAL

A. Defeating the Underlying Case of Sexual Harassment

An effective defense to the underlying claim of sexual harassment also will defeat a claim of constructive discharge based on the same conduct.

Even where sexual harassment has occurred, complainants who have quit without resorting to adequate antiharassment procedures have been unable to prove constructive discharge. Thus no constructive discharge was established where:

- the complainant resigned the day after she first complained about the conduct of a consultant, even though the company president had already told her that she would not have to work with the harasser after another day and a half (*Dornhecker v. Malibu Grand Prix Corp.*); and

- the complainant easily could have escaped the supervision of the alleged harasser by working on another shift or at another mill near her home, yet chose not to do so (*Smith v. Acme Spinning Co.*).

B. Showing Other Reasons for the Employee's Action

In some cases the employer has defeated a constructive discharge claim by showing that factors other than sexual harassment motivated the complainant's resignation. One court concluded that no constructive discharge had occurred because the complainant, although sexually harassed, had resigned because her lover had been forced to resign from the police force on which they both worked (*Henson v. City of Dundee*). In another case, the court relied on the complainant's resignation letter, in which she said that she was resigning because of fears for herself and her daughter stemming from threats relating to an off-duty dispute that was unrelated to any sexual harassment at the workplace (*Huddleston v. Roger Dean Chevrolet*).

6

RETALIATION

I. OVERVIEW

Title VII and state FEP statutes prohibit retaliation against individuals who either *participate* in the statutory process or otherwise *oppose* discriminatory employment practices. Antiretaliation provisions thus prohibit discrimination on the basis of participation or opposition, just as basic employment discrimination provisions prohibit discrimination on the basis of race, color, sex, religion, and national origin.

Persons who may be protected from retaliation include employees, applicants, former employees, employees' relatives (*Wu v. Thomas*), employees who are merely potential witnesses (*EEOC v. Plumbers Local 189*), and persons who have opposed discrimination by employers other than their own (*Barela v. United Nuclear Corp.*).

Courts have identified the following elements that a complainant must prove to establish liability for retaliation:

(1) that the complainant engaged in statutorily protected participation or opposition;

(2) that an adverse employment action, such as a discharge, took place;

(3) that the adverse employment action was taken *because of* the protected activity (participation or opposition); and

83

(4) that the employer was responsible for the retaliatory conduct.

II. CLAIMS BASED ON PARTICIPATION

A. Activities Protected as Participation

1. Filing EEOC or FEP Charges. Activities protected as participation include nearly any activity related to communicating, or refusing to communicate, information to a civil rights enforcement agency. The clearest form of participation is filing an administrative charge of employment discrimination with the EEOC or a state FEP agency.

2. Other Forms of EEOC or FEP Participation. Employees have been protected from retaliation for participation where they have:

- communicated an intent to file a charge (*Gifford v. Atchison, Topeka & Santa Fe Ry. Co.*);
- testified on behalf of a co-worker who has filed a sexual harassment charge (*Ramos v. Roche Prods.*);
- refused to testify on behalf of the employer (*Smith v. Columbus Metro. Housing Auth.*); and
- filed charges against employers other than their own (*Barela v. United Nuclear Corp.*).

3. Internal Complaints. It appears that statements made in an internal complaint are *not* protected as participation. In *Vasconcelos v. Meese,* the complainant had drinks with another employee in a bar. The two then kissed and petted in a nearby parking lot. The complainant, claiming sexual harassment, lied during the internal employer investigation, stating that she had not invited the sexual advances. When the lie later emerged during the investigation of her EEOC charge, she was fired. The complainant then sued her former employer for retaliation. The court rejected the complainant's argument that the antiretaliation provisions of Title VII protects all statements, even lies, made in an internal investigation.

B. Legality of the Challenged Employment Practice

If a complainant files an EEOC charge alleging sexual harassment and is then fired because she filed the charge, she may prevail on her retaliation case without regard to the merits of the sexual harassment case. Thus, if a complainant suffers retaliation for her participation, she may prevail in a retaliation claim without proving that her underlying claim of discrimination is valid. Courts have not required that a complainant even have a good-faith belief in such a claim. In *Proulx v. CitiBank*, the court held that it was protected participation for a warehouseman to file a sexual harassment complaint with a state FEP agency, even though the claim was false and malicious.

III. CLAIMS BASED ON OPPOSITION

To be protected, the opposition must be to conduct that allegedly constitutes employment discrimination. Certain other forms of opposition, such as opposition to an employer's anti-union activities, are protected, if at all, only by other statutes, such as the National Labor Relations Act.

A. Activities Protected as Opposition

Activities protected as opposition range from the informal voicing of complaints to a supervisor to the formal invocation of an employer's internal grievance procedures (*Pettway v. American Cast Iron Pipe Co.; Rollins v. Florida Dep't of Law Enforcement*). Examples of opposition activity include:

- a communication between a waitress and an attorney about sexual harassment by customers (EEOC Dec. 84-3),
- a complaint by a loan officer to a bank vice president that she was sexually harassed by a co-worker (*Barrett v. Omaha Nat'l Bank*), and
- a report by a male employee that a supervisor sexually harassed female employees (*Fielder v. Southco*).

B. Legality of the Challenged Employment Practice

Authorities differ as to whether the opposed conduct must actually be a violation of employment discrimination law in order to be protected from retaliation. The EEOC and most courts protect opposition so long as the employee has a reasonable and good-faith belief that the practice opposed was unlawfully discriminatory; the employee need not show that the practice actually broke the law (*Drinkwater v. Union Carbide Corp.*). The minority view is that the protection for opposition activities applies only when the practice opposed actually did break the law (*Jordan v. Clark*).

The protection for opposition activity does *not* protect complainants who have absolutely no basis for believing that the conduct they oppose is unlawful. An employer may impose discipline on a complainant who is acting unreasonably or in bad faith in opposing conduct alleged to be sexual harassment (*Sand v. Johnson Co.*).

C. Activities So Disruptive That They Exceed Protection

Some opposition activity is so excessive as to lose the protection of the opposition clause. This question of the form of the protest typically arises only with respect to opposition activities; with respect to participation activities the use of statutory procedures is itself the form of the protest.

In determining whether the form of the opposition was excessive, courts balance the individual's right to oppose discrimination against the employer's right to operate its business. The antiretaliation provisions do not protect conduct that unnecessarily disrupts the workplace or that so interferes with the opposer's job performance that the opposer is rendered ineffective (*Hochstadt v. Worcester Found. for Experimental Biology; Jones v. Flagship Int'l*).

IV. THE ADVERSE EMPLOYMENT ACTION

A. Adverse Employment Actions That Constitute Retaliation

Not every job change made in reaction to a complaint of sexual harassment necessarily would be an adverse employment action. A temporary transfer to a job with the same pay and benefits may not be viewed as an adverse employment action (*Ferguson v. E.I. du Pont de Nemours & Co.*). Types of actionable job detriments found to be sufficient include:

- failure to hire (*Simmons v. Lyons*),
- failure to promote (*Broderick v. Ruder*),

- withholding pay increases (*Sowers v. Kemira, Inc.*),
- poor performance reviews (*Holland v. Jefferson Nat'l Life Ins. Co.*),
- spreading rumors of an affair between the complainant and the alleged harasser (*Toscano v. Nimmo*),
- abolishment of a position (*Barnes v. Costle*), and
- discharge (*Horn v. Duke Homes*).

B. Harassment as the Adverse Employment Action

Additional harassment of an employee who has protested sexual harassment can itself be unlawful retaliation if the harassment is motivated by the report and if the harassment is sufficiently severe or pervasive to alter the conditions of employment (*Cobb v. Anheuser-Busch*).

C. The Investigation as the Retaliatory Action

It is not retaliatory for an employer to conduct an otherwise lawful investigation. Nonetheless, certain investigations may be unlawful if they are conducted in a coercive or intimidating manner (*EEOC v. Plumbers Local 189*).

D. Defamation Lawsuits as the Retaliatory Action

Where charges of sexual harassment lead to a libel or slander suit by the employer or the alleged harasser, courts differ as to whether the suit is unlawful retaliation. Some courts reason that the complainant's statements to the investigating agent are absolutely privileged (*EEOC v. Virginia Caroline Veneer Corp.*). Other courts have suggested that an employer is entitled to vindicate its reputation by filing a defamation suit on the basis of a malicious complaint to the EEOC (*Pettway v. American Cast Iron Pipe Co.*). One court took a middle-ground approach, holding that some defamation suits will be unlawful retaliation, but not a defamation suit filed in good faith to rehabilitate the employer's reputation concerning defamatory remarks that were made *outside* of a pending EEOC proceeding (*EEOC v. Levi Strauss & Co.*).

V. ESTABLISHING THE CAUSAL CONNECTION

To succeed on a claim for retaliation, the complainant must show a causal connection between (1) the opposition or participation, and (2) the subsequent employment detriment, *i.e.,* that the second happened *because of* the first. The proof must show that a retaliatory motive played a part in the adverse treatment. This proof will consist of a showing that the employer had *actual or imputed knowledge* of the opposition or participation at the time of imposing the employment detriment and was motivated by that knowledge to retaliate (*Mandia v. Arco Chem. Co.*).

The proof that the employment detriment resulted from the protected activity can be inferred from several common types of circumstantial evidence:

- treating the employee differently from similarly situated nonprotesting employees (*Mosley v. General Motors Corp.*),
- deviating from the employer's own written procedures to take adverse action against the protesting employee (*EEOC v. Operating Eng'rs Locals 14 & 15*),
- beginning surveillance of the protesting employee (*Mead v. United States Fidelity & Guar. Co.*),
- the closeness in time between the employer's knowledge of the protected activity and the adverse action (*Minor v. Califano*), and
- attempting to conceal that the person who decided on the adverse action knew that the complainant had engaged in protected participation or opposition (*Minor v. Califano; Macey v. World Airways*).

VI. THE EMPLOYER'S REBUTTAL

The defenses commonly raised to retaliation claims are:
- that the employment practice opposed by the complainant could not reasonably have been believed to be unlawful under Title VII,
- that the form of the complainant's opposition was too extreme,

- that the employer was not retaliating because it was unaware of the protest or opposition, and
- that the discipline of the complainant was for legitimate business reasons rather than in retaliation for participation or opposition.

Discharges have been held not to be retaliatory where the evidence showed that they were based solely on such business reasons as the complainant's excessive absenteeism, the physical limitations of the complainant, and changing workloads at the employer's plant (*Tunis v. Corning Glass Works*). The employer's proof of nonretaliation may consist of a showing that similarly situated nonprotestors were disciplined just as harshly for the same infraction (*Kellin v. ACF Indus.*). In *Barrett v. Omaha National Bank*, the complainant, a banker, alleged that her employer began to review her loans as a result of her complaints of sexual harassment. The bank showed that loan reviews were not unusual and that the complainant had been selected for review before her reports of harassment, thus establishing a valid defense.

VII. ALTERNATE SOURCES OF PROTECTION AGAINST RETALIATION

Title VII is the main but not the only source of prohibitions against retaliation. Title VII will not apply where the employer is not covered by Title VII, where the Title VII filing period has elapsed, or where the damages sought are more than allowed under Title VII. Complainants may invoke alternative sources of relief under the Reconstruction Era Civil Rights Acts (Chapter 8), the National Labor Relations Act, state whistleblower statutes, state FEP statutes (Chapter 7), and various common-law theories (Chapter 11).

7

STATE FAIR EMPLOYMENT PRACTICES STATUTES

I. OVERVIEW

Fair employment practices (FEP) statutes have been enacted in almost every state, and differ from Title VII in various ways. One major difference is that many FEP agencies can decide employment discrimination claims in an administrative hearing, which can result in a judicially enforceable award of damages. The EEOC, by contrast, has limited power; it may seek to address violations of Title VII by means of informal conciliation and may itself sue in court to enforce a complainant's rights, but it has no power to decide cases on its own.

Because each state's statute and enforcement mechanism is different, readers should familiarize themselves with the requirements of the particular state with which they are concerned. A state-by-state discussion of FEP statutes, together with the text of each state's laws, can be found in the FEP Manual of BNA's *Labor Relations Reporter*.

II. SCOPE OF LIABILITY

A. Who Can Be Sued

Most FEP statutes apply to public and private employers, employment agencies, and labor organizations. Certain small

90

employers, religious organizations, and employers of domestic workers may be excluded from coverage. Unlike Title VII, many FEP statutes cover at least some employers with fewer than fifteen employees. California's FEP statute covers not only the traditional defendants, but any "person" (including a vendor or a customer) who engages in sexual harassment of an employee or a job applicant.

B. Employer Liability for Supervisor Harassment

Under FEP statutes, as under Title VII, employers are automatically liable for the actions of their supervisors in a quid pro quo case (see Chapter 2, section VI.). In cases of hostile environment harassment, the FEP statutes of some states, such as California and Illinois, differ from Title VII by holding employers automatically liable for sexual harassment by supervisors. Courts have interpreted the FEP statutes of other states, such as Michigan, Minnesota, and Washington, to follow the Title VII model for employee liability (see Chapter 3, section VI.).

C. Employer Liability for Co-Worker Harassment

FEP statutes follow Title VII in making an employer liable for sexual harassment by a nonmanagerial co-worker only when the employer or the employer's agents or supervisors either authorize the harassment or are negligent by, for example, failing to take prompt action to correct known sexual harassment.

III. EXHAUSTION OF ADMINISTRATIVE PROCEDURES

States vary with respect to whether employees must exhaust available FEP administrative procedures before commencing a court action under the FEP statute. In California, Illinois, Kansas, Maryland, Massachusetts, Montana, and Pennsylvania, employees must utilize administrative procedures before they can sue under the FEP statute. In other states, such as Minnesota, New York, and Oregon, employees may elect to proceed directly to court under the applicable FEP statute.

IV. EXCLUSIVITY OF FEP STATUTES

Acts that constitute sexual harassment may provide grounds for several common-law (nonstatutory) claims under state law (see Chapter 11). These include traditional claims such as battery and intentional infliction of emotional distress. A relatively new and particularly popular claim is "tortious wrongful discharge in violation of public policy," alleging that the complainant (1) was discharged after resisting sexual advances, (2) was discharged after protesting sexual harassment, or (3) resigned when sexual harassment made the work environment intolerable.

Courts have grappled with whether sexual harassment complainants may pursue these common-law claims independent of the FEP statute. Complainants generally argue that FEP statutes do not affect their common-law claims, but simply provide an additional remedy. Complainants want this result because they hope that if one claim fails another will succeed.

Employers typically argue that the FEP statute is the exclusive state-law remedy for sexual harassment, precluding any common-law action. Employers want FEP exclusivity because:

- a complainant already may have forfeited her FEP statutory remedy by, for example, failing to make a timely administrative claim;
- in states where the FEP statute provides limited relief, a sexual harassment complainant may not be able to seek the compensatory and punitive damages otherwise available in a common-law action; and
- a claim under the FEP statute may be harder to prove than common-law claims based on the same conduct, because the FEP action will require proof of all the specific elements of unlawful sexual harassment.

Courts generally hold that FEP statutes do not displace traditional common-law claims, such as claims for intentional and negligent infliction of emotional distress, assault, battery, negligence, intentional misrepresentation, invasion of privacy, and defamation (see Chapter 11 for a discussion of these claims). Courts differ more often on whether FEP statutes preclude a common-law public policy claim.

In Hawaii, Illinois, Maryland, Massachusetts, Montana, and Pennsylvania, courts have held that state FEP statutes provide the exclusive state-law remedies for employment discrimination. In Arizona and California, courts have held that FEP statutes provide simply a cumulative remedy that does not foreclose common-law claims for tortious discharge in violation of the public policy against sexual harassment. Title VII itself does not affect any state-law remedy.

V. REMEDIES

A. FEP Agency Proceedings

Courts have differed over whether state administrative agencies can award compensatory and punitive damages. In Alaska, California, Maryland, Pennsylvania, and Washington, courts have held that FEP agencies cannot award either compensatory or punitive relief, but are limited to issuing injunctions and awards of back pay.

By contrast, in Illinois, Iowa, Massachusetts, Minnesota, New Jersey, and Oregon, courts have held that FEP agencies may award compensatory damages or both compensatory and punitive damages.

B. Court Actions

Many FEP statutes, unlike Title VII, permit employees who sue in court to seek unlimited compensatory and punitive damages.

VI. SPECIAL OBLIGATIONS OF STATE CONTRACTORS

Nearly half of the states, and the District of Columbia, require certain state contractors to refrain from discrimination as a condition of their government contracts. These legal obligations are in addition to those imposed by state FEP statutes, Title VII, and federal executive orders. Few states investigate compliance with these contracts independent of other proceedings, so that sanctions are usually imposed only where there has been a finding of a violation under the state FEP statute.

Part II

Other Sources of Legal Protection

8

FEDERAL CONSTITUTIONAL, STATUTORY, AND CIVIL RIGHTS LAW

This chapter generally applies only to public employers. Other readers need not concern themselves with it unless they are federal contractors, in which case they need only read section VIII.

I. CLAIMS DIRECTLY UNDER THE UNITED STATES CONSTITUTION

Sexual harassment, when committed or condoned by a government official, may violate the constitutional right to equal protection (see section II.D.1. below). A direct constitutional claim of sexual harassment requires both governmental action and no alternative means of relief. A direct constitutional claim is very rare, because Title VII provides a means of relief for federal and state employees in the vast majority of cases, and because state and local government employees can also proceed under the Civil Rights Act of 1871 (42 U.S.C. §1983). Title VII has been explained in Part I; §1983 is discussed in section II. below.

Only government employees not covered by Title VII appear eligible to bring a direct constitutional claim. One such case was a congressman's employee who was not protected by Title VII (*Davis v. Passman*).

II. SECTION 1983

A. Introduction

Sexual harassment claims often have been brought under the Civil Rights Act of 1871 (42 U.S.C. §1983), which generally authorizes lawsuits by state and local government employees against their governmental employer for a violation of federal constitutional and statutory law. These are usually called "§1983 claims." The Act was passed to assist blacks during the Reconstruction Era after the Civil War, but now is used for many types of claims, some of which are discussed in section II.D. below. Section 1983 provides that "every person who, under color of state law, deprives another person of rights secured by federal law shall be liable." Thus, §1983 provides a mechanism for remedying violations of various federal laws or the Constitution. This differs from Title VII, which just provides a mechanism for addressing violations of Title VII itself.

Sexual harassment of an employee by a state governmental official may violate both Title VII and the Equal Protection Clause of the Fourteenth Amendment and, thus, create liability under both Title VII and §1983. The existence of a remedy under Title VII does not foreclose a §1983 claim; the two claims may proceed concurrently.

A §1983 claim has advantages for a sexual harassment complainant because, unlike a Title VII claim, it provides for unlimited compensatory damages and does not require the exhaustion of administrative remedies.

To prevail under a §1983 claim for sexual harassment in violation of a federal provision, the complainant must prove that the deprivation was by a "person" acting under "color" of state or local law, and that the harassment deprived the complainant of rights under the U.S. Constitution or a federal statute. These requirements are discussed below.

B. "Person" Liable Under §1983

Those who may be liable for damages as a "person" under §1983 include private parties, municipalities, counties, other political subdivisions of a state, and state officials who are sued *as individuals,* even if they were acting in an official capacity.

C. Action Under Color of State Law

Liability under §1983 exists only if the conduct in question was under color of state law. This "color" requirement is met when the defendant misuses power that is possessed only because the wrongdoer has authority under state law.

Generally, one acts under color of state law if one acts in an official capacity or while exercising responsibilities pursuant to state law. According to this standard, state government *supervisors* who perpetrate sexual harassment may be acting under color of state law, while rank-and-file government workers do not act under color of state law, because they do not exercise state-granted responsibilities.

Because of the "color of state law" requirement, employment-related sexual harassment claims under §1983 generally are limited to employees of state or local governments. Section 1983 actions are not available to federal employees or employees of private employers, except in those rare instances where a nonstate employer "is a willful participant in joint action with the state or its agents" (*Dennis v. Sparks*).

D. Deprivation of Federal Constitutional or Statutory Rights

The federal laws most frequently invoked by §1983 complaints are the Equal Protection Clause of the Fourteenth Amendment, the Due Process Clause of the Fourteenth Amendment, the First Amendment, and various federal statutes, discussed below.

1. The Equal Protection Clause. Most courts agree that sexual harassment by a state or municipal employer can violate the Constitution's Equal Protection Clause, which forbids certain arbitrary distinctions in government actions. The scope of protection afforded by the Equal Protection Clause in a sexual harassment case ordinarily should be the same as in a Title VII case. While the Supreme Court has not yet addressed this issue, it has held that the Equal Protection Clause prohibits purposeful gender discrimination that is not justified by an important governmental interest. Given the absence of any legitimate state interest in sexual harassment, the only real equal protection questions are whether sexual harassment constitutes *purposeful* discrimination on the basis of *gender.*

A denial of equal protection on the basis of gender requires proof that the sexual harassment constitutes intentional discrimination. This requirement is rarely a problem for a complainant to meet, in that a supervisor who makes unwelcome sexual advances toward an employee, or acts vindictively toward one who rejects those advances, is acting intentionally. Thus, if the unwanted attentions are by their very nature limited to one gender, the supervisor is intentionally treating an employee adversely on the basis of gender. The intent requirement of the Equal Protection Clause will create a problem, however, for a complainant who uses an adverse impact theory to challenge nondirected conduct, such as a work environment filled with sexual graffiti and visual displays (see Chapter 4, section V.). That theory is available to a complainant under Title VII, but not under the Equal Protection Clause.

2. The Due Process Clause. A sexual harassment complainant may also assert a §1983 claim on the basis of a Fourteenth Amendment right not to be deprived of property or liberty without due process of law.

a. Property Interests. A retaliatory dismissal for opposing sexual harassment may deprive a public employee of a property interest without due process of law, and so be unlawful. To make this claim, a complainant must prove a property *right* in *continued* employment. The property right is created from rules or understandings that are more than just a one-sided hope of continued employment. There must be a legitimate claim of *entitlement* to continued employment, absent valid grounds for dismissal. An example of this kind of entitlement would be a contract for a specific term of years.

b. Liberty Interests. The liberty interest may involve reputation, physical freedom, or privacy.

A loss of liberty interest based on a complainant's reputation may occur where the employer disseminates a false and defamatory impression about the employee in connection with the termination of employment.

If sexual harassment has involved physical restraint by a government official, that activity may be actionable under §1983 as a deprivation of physical freedom. In *Stoneking v. Bradford Area School District*, the complainant alleged that while she was a public school student she was sexually abused by the high-school band leader. The court held that the complainant was deprived of her liberty interest in being free from invasion of her personal security.

The liberty interest in privacy may involve "avoiding disclosure of personal matters" (*Whalen v. Roe*), and thus might involve a suit over the actions, not of the harasser, but of the employer trying to resolve the matter. A §1983 claim could thus arise by the complainant's being forced by her employer's investigator to reveal facts about her sexual history (*Eastwood v. Department of Corrections*).

3. The First Amendment. Retaliation against a public employee who has complained of sexual harassment can be the basis of a §1983 action. The constitutional bases of the action are the rights of free speech and of access to the courts (suing about sexual harassment). A First Amendment suit is available whenever the employee's speech is on a matter of "public concern" and the employee's interest in speaking out on public issues as a citizen outweighs the efficiency interests of the public employer. For example, a §1983 claim was upheld where the complainant alleged that a state university discharged the complainant in retaliation for filing a state court sexual harassment action against the employer and a supervisor (*Fuchilla v. Prockop*).

4. Asserted Statutory Bases. Not every federal statute necessarily is enforceable under §1983. Congress has foreclosed enforcement under §1983 of statutes that have their own enforcement provisions, such as Title VII, or that do not create

enforceable rights. The principal example of a federal discrimination statute that is enforceable under §1983 is Title IX of
the Education Amendments of 1972, which prohibits sex
discrimination in educational programs that receive federal
funding (see section IV.E. below).

E. Standards for Municipal and Individual Liability

Section 1983 liability for a municipality attaches only when
the injury is inflicted by a municipal official through the execu-
tion of a governmental policy or custom and by one who is a
"policymaker." A municipality is liable for harassment by non-
policymakers only if their harassment, or the failure to prevent
harassment, constitutes a well-settled practice that has been tolerated by the policymakers.

Individuals acting under color of law may be liable under
§1983 in their individual capacities for their own harassing
conduct. The officials responsible for supervising the harassers
may also be liable under §1983 if the supervising officials' action constitutes encouragement, condonation, acquiescence or
gross negligence amounting to deliberate indifference, or if the
officials have failed to act after receiving notice of the harassment.

III. SECTION 1985(3)

Part of the Civil Rights Act of 1871, 42 U.S.C. §1985(3),
authorizes damages suits arising from a *conspiracy* to deprive
complainants of equal protection of rights under the Constitution or federal law. Like §1983, §1985(3) does not create its own
substantive rights, but provides remedies for conspiracies to violate federal rights established in other laws. Section 1985(3) cannot be used to address violations of Title VII, which has its own
enforcement scheme.

Section 1985(3) covers conspiracies to discriminate against
those who have opposed sexual harassment. A §1985(3) claim
requires proof of:

(1) a conspiracy,

(2) a purpose of depriving someone of equal protection or privileges under the law,

(3) any act in furtherance of the conspiracy, and

(4) resulting injury.

At least one court has held that a §1985(3) complainant need not prove a class-based animus (*Volk v. Coler*). Courts differ as to whether agents of a single legal entity may "conspire" with one another for purposes of §1985(3).

IV. TITLE IX OF THE EDUCATION AMENDMENTS OF 1972

Title IX prohibits sex discrimination and, thus, sexual harassment, in any educational program or activity receiving federal funds. A university receiving federal funds may be sued for sexual harassment if officials of the institution knew or should have known of the harassment, unless the officials took appropriate steps to halt it. Title VII standards for proving discrimination apply. In 1992 the Supreme Court decided that Title IX entitles a victim of sexual harassment in education to money damages as well as injunctive relief and attorney's fees (*Franklin v. Gwinnett County Pub. Schools*).

V. FEDERAL EMPLOYERS' LIABILITY ACT

Courts differ on whether there is liability for sexual harassment under the Federal Employer's Liability Act (FELA), which holds certain employers, such as railroads, responsible for injuries caused by employer negligence. One court has held that a female railroad engineer who was forcibly kissed, hugged, and grabbed by co-workers had a valid FELA claim for sexual harassment on the basis of negligent failure to prevent it, and, further, that the claim was not preempted by Title VII (*Masiello v. Metro-North Commuter R.R.*). Another court, however, has upheld the dismissal of an FELA sexual harassment claim on the ground that there was no legislative history to suggest that the FELA, enacted in 1908, was intended to provide a remedy for racial or sexual harassment (*Griggs v. National R.R. Passenger Corp.*).

VI. FEDERAL EXECUTIVE ORDERS

Federal executive orders, enforced by the Office of Federal Contract Compliance Programs (OFCCP), prohibit discrimination in employment by certain federal contractors.

A. Obligations

Executive Order 11246 requires (1) nondiscrimination in employment and (2) affirmative action to use women and minorities in the contractor's work force. The OFCCP applies Title VII principles and specifically forbids sexual harassment (see BNA's *Affirmative Action Compliance Manual*). Further, the written affirmative action plan required of covered contractors and subcontractors must include assurances that supervisory personnel will prevent the harassment of employees who are placed through affirmative action efforts.

B. Enforcement

Executive Order 11246 is enforced through administrative proceedings, subject to judicial review. Sanctions for violations include debarment from contract activity, termination or cancellation of existing contracts, and withholding of progress payments. Courts have held that aggrieved individuals have no private right of action directly under the Order or as third-party beneficiaries of the Order; only the OFCCP can enforce the Order.

9

UNEMPLOYMENT COMPENSATION STATUTES

When sexual harassment results in the termination of the employment relationship—of either the complainant or the alleged harasser—it may become an issue in connection with claims for benefits under state unemployment compensation laws.

The laws governing unemployment compensation differ significantly from one state to another. Thus, readers dealing with claims for unemployment benefits should consult the laws of the involved state. Unemployment compensation claims are not decided by courts, but by special administrative agencies. Courts review agency decisions but usually play a limited role, deciding simply whether the agency has misinterpreted the law and whether the agency's findings of fact are supported by the evidence.

I. CLAIMS BY THOSE WHO RESIGN BECAUSE OF SEXUAL HARASSMENT

A. Sexual Harassment as Good Cause for Quitting

State unemployment compensation statutes generally provide that employees who quit their employment are disqualified

105

from receiving benefits, either completely or for a designated period of time, unless they have left their employment for "good cause." Several states provide by statute or judicial interpretation that the good-cause requirement is satisfied where a voluntary termination results from sexual harassment. In other states, the good-cause issue generally is decided by evaluating the harassing conduct to determine whether it would have forced a reasonably prudent person under similar circumstances to resign. Examples of cases on the good-cause issue include:

- Arkansas: A claimant had good cause to quit because her employer kissed her, grabbed her breasts, and patted her on the back and face. The harassment did not have to be "unbearable" to be good cause for quitting (*McEwen v. Everett*).

- New Jersey: A claimant had good cause to quit because her supervisor made sexual advances toward her, called her at home, asked her to cook breakfast for him, threatened her with physical harm, and made a racial comment about her in the presence of a co-worker (*Doering v. Board of Review*).

- Oregon: A claimant lacked good cause to quit where the plant manager displayed a postcard on his desk showing a woman with bare breasts, a poster on the office wall showed a bikini-clad woman whom male employees described as having "gorgeous tits," and a cartoon on the lunchroom wall entitled "The Perfect Woman" showed a woman's naked legs, hips, buttocks, breasts, and pubic area, with no arms, head, or upper torso (*McCain v. Employment Div.*).

B. The Complainant's Duty to Notify the Employer

In order to have good cause for quitting, a complainant usually must show that she made a reasonable effort to notify the employer of the harassing conduct so as to give the employer a chance to have the problem corrected. Thus, in some cases, claimants have been required to show that while employed they had used the employer's established procedure to report the sexual harassment. Other cases have held that a claimant need not register a formal complaint, but simply must make a reasonable effort to communicate the problem to the employer before quitting.

Where the alleged harasser is the claimant's supervisor, some cases have held that the claimant has a duty to report the matter to upper management, while other cases have held that the claimant has good cause to quit if the harassing supervisor is aware of the complaint and fails to take corrective action.

In some states, a claimant's obligation to attempt to resolve a sexual harassment complaint before resigning may be excused where there is reason to believe that the effort would be futile or dangerous (*Hussa v. Employment Sec. Dep't*).

C. Standard for Proving Sexual Harassment as the Cause for Quitting

An employer might argue that even if sexual harassment occurred, the claimant quit for other reasons. Several cases have held that a claimant had good cause to quit, even if sexual harassment was not the sole reason for quitting, so long as the harassment was a contributing factor.

D. The Burden of Proof

In most states, claimants have the burden of proving good cause for quitting. One notable exception is California, where courts require the employer to prove that the claimant quit employment without good cause.

II. CLAIMS FOR UNEMPLOYMENT COMPENSATION BENEFITS BY ALLEGED HARASSERS

Unemployment benefits also may be sought by those who have been discharged for alleged sexual harassment. The issue in these cases is whether benefits should be awarded, because state unemployment compensation statutes disqualify claimants who have engaged in conduct rising to a specified level of fault. The standards for disqualification vary from state to state, ranging from "just cause" to "misconduct." Under any of these standards, claimants who are discharged for sexual harassment risk a denial of unemployment benefits.

Where the employer challenges the claimant's right to receive unemployment benefits, the first question is whether the harassing conduct actually occurred. The burden for proving that harassment did occur typically is placed on the employer.

A second question is whether the harassment justifies a denial of unemployment compensation. In answering this question, agencies and courts measure the harassing conduct against various standards, including:

- the specific standard for disqualification under the unemployment compensation statute: in states that require proof of "misconduct," evidence of poor performance or poor judgment will not necessarily justify a denial of unemployment benefits;
- definitions of sexual harassment provided by state unemployment compensation statutes, Title VII, or state fair employment practice statutes;
- the terms of the employer's rules or policies concerning sexual conduct; and
- general standards of expected workplace behavior.

III. THE EFFECT OF UNEMPLOYMENT DECISIONS ON SEPARATE LITIGATION

An unemployment compensation claim is decided in a special administrative proceeding, where the claimant seeks a particular form of benefit. A sexual harassment complainant may also sue for other benefits and damages in other kinds of legal proceedings. The possibility of multiple actions raises the question of whether a decision in an unemployment compensation proceeding on an issue of sexual harassment will prevent the parties from relitigating the same issue in a separate action.

Several state statutes provide that decisions made in unemployment compensation proceedings cannot be used in separate actions. In other states, however, the result of an unemployment compensation decision may be used in a separate action, depending primarily on the similarity of issues in the separate action and whether the parties had a full and fair opportunity to litigate the issue of sexual harassment in the unemployment compensation proceeding.

IV. PRACTICAL CONSIDERATIONS

To avoid or minimize liability, the employer should establish and publish an appropriate sexual harassment policy, provide a meaningful reporting mechanism, and vigorously follow up on employee complaints. The employer will minimize liability by encouraging employees to report allegations of harassment promptly, through established procedures, to allow the employer an opportunity to correct any problems.

The employer should consciously decide whether and how to contest a claim for unemployment compensation regarding allegations of sexual harassment. As noted in section III. above, in some states, the result of an unemployment compensation proceeding may bind a party in a separate action. Even where it does not, the unemployment compensation decision may discourage or encourage the settlement of related claims. Furthermore, evidence given and findings made in the unemployment compensation proceeding, particularly when the complainant's testimony provides a sworn transcript of her version of the facts, may bolster or undercut claims in a later court or administrative action.

In states where unemployment compensation decisions bind parties in other actions, parties that decide to litigate the unemployment compensation claim must present the best possible case before the administrative agency. An employer may decide not to oppose a claim at all for the following reasons:

(1) The risk of liability in later court litigation may increase if the administrative agency rules against the employer on the merits, whereas an uncontested claim will have no effect beyond the unemployment compensation proceedings.

(2) Even if successful, the employer's opposition may prompt an administrative complaint or a lawsuit that otherwise would not have been filed—either by forcing

the claimant to obtain an attorney in connection with the unemployment compensation claim, or by making the claimant feel compelled to vindicate herself in a legal proceeding.

In states where unemployment compensation decisions cannot be given binding effect, the proceeding may be used as a discovery tool for potential civil litigation. This tool can benefit employers particularly, because they can obtain information from the claimant without necessarily subjecting their own witnesses to the same process. Thus, if the employer believes that the risk of a lawsuit outweighs the cost of an unemployment compensation award, it can choose not to present witnesses and proceed only through cross-examination of the claimant. This strategy, while often unlikely to produce a favorable result in the unemployment compensation proceeding, can be a useful technique where court litigation is expected. Moreover, the claimant is much less likely to be represented by counsel than in a court action, and as a result may be more likely to make damaging admissions that could be used in a subsequent proceeding.

Unemployment compensation cases usually are tried soon after the events in question. The hearing thus occurs when the recollections of witnesses will be fresh, but the parties also should consider the risk that witnesses may be locked into their testimony early on in the litigation process.

If a party intends to elicit testimony for potential use in a later proceeding, it is critical to have some method for preserving the record of the unemployment compensation hearing. Agencies in some states routinely tape-record unemployment compensation hearings; in other states it may be necessary to request in advance that a recording or transcription be made, or for a party to provide a court reporter if the agency does not provide one.

10

WORKERS' COMPENSATION STATUTES

I. OVERVIEW

Employees who are sexually harassed in the workplace may have a remedy under a state workers' compensation statute. All states have enacted some type of workers' compensation system. Federal civilian employees may be entitled to compensation under the Federal Employees' Compensation Act.

An employee who suffers a work-related disabling injury due to sexual harassment typically is entitled to four basic kinds of benefits:

(1) all past and future medical treatment necessary to cure the complainant from the effects of the injury;

(2) temporary disability payments, calculated as a percentage of lost earnings, during the time that a medical provider certifies that the complainant is unable to engage in any gainful employment;

(3) permanent disability payments, representing lost earning capacity and based on the residual disabilities caused by the injury that restrict the complainant from fully engaging in the labor market; and

111

(4) vocational rehabilitation to help the injured worker reenter the labor force.

Some states provide added benefits for employees who are injured by an employer's willful conduct.

II. INJURIES COVERED UNDER WORKERS' COMPENSATION

All jurisdictions cover specific physical injuries caused by industrial accidents. The evolution of knowledge about the work environment has expanded the covered injuries to those now commonly referred to as continuous or repetitive trauma. These are the injuries that result from the daily "micro-traumas" of repetitive work activities. As medical knowledge has grown, coverage has expanded to include injury from exposure to various noxious elements and emotional stress in the workplace.

Sexual harassment may cause a covered injury, either through a specific incident of a severe nature or on a continuous trauma basis (*i.e.*, by daily repetitive harassment). Sexual harassment generally is considered a psychiatric claim.

Situations in which sexual harassment has resulted in workers' compensation claims include a supervisor or co-worker:

- requesting sexual favors of an employee (*Fields v. Cummins Employees Fed. Credit Union*);
- commenting on the employee's sexual anatomy (*Busby v. Truswal Sys. Corp.*);
- making lewd comments to the employee (*Brooms v. Regal Tube Co.*);
- threatening the employee (*Cremen v. Harrah's Marina Hotel Casino*);
- touching and grabbing the employee (*O'Connell v. Chasdi*); and
- raping the employee (*Carr v. U.S. West Direct Co.*).

The principal issues raised by a claim for workers' compensation benefits are (A) whether the employee suffered an injury as defined by the particular state statute, and (B) whether the injury arose out of and occurred in the course of employment.

A. Nature of the Injury

1. Disabling or Requiring Medical Treatment. Workers' compensation statutes generally provide that an injury is not compensable unless it causes a disability or the need for medical attention, including psychiatric or psychological care. This requirement will preclude a claim for workers' compensation benefits where sexual harassment has neither disabled the employee nor caused the employee to require medical care. Emotional distress suffered by an employee as a result of sexual harassment may not entitle the employee to workers' compensation if the injury is not disabling (*Murdock v. Michigan Health Maintenance Org.*).

2. Physical Versus Mental or Psychological Injury. The most common injury suffered by sexual harassment complainants is mental and emotional stress, which may have physical manifestations (*Brooms v. Regal Tube Co.*—depression and physical illness; *Ford v. Revlon, Inc.*—high blood pressure, nervous tic, chest pains, rapid breathing). Some states limit workers' compensation to "physical" injuries and thus deny benefits to employees who, although suffering emotional stress, have not been injured physically by the sexual harassment. Other states seems to observe no distinction between physical and nonphysical injuries and also provide workers' compensation benefits for purely mental or psychological injuries. States that allow recovery for purely psychological injuries, however, still require that the injury be disabling or require medical treatment; workers' compensation does not provide a remedy for pain and suffering as such.

B. Connection With Employment

Any injury must be sufficiently connected to work to be compensable. The typical statutory formula is that the employee's injury must (1) "arise out of" employment, and (2) "occur in the course" of employment. Whether sexual harassment injuries meet these criteria may depend on which of the different tests a particular state follows.

1. Injuries Arising out of Employment. The requirement that the injury arise out of employment addresses the causal connection between the injury and the employee's work. States follow differing tests for resolving whether the requisite causal connection exists.

a. The "But For" Standard. Some courts have taken a very expansive view of this requirement, holding that an injury arises out of employment whenever there is any connection to the employee's job. That is, the injury arises out of employment if "but for" the employment, the injury would not have occurred; the injury is viewed as arising out of employment if the employment put the employee in the position to be injured. Thus, assaults by co-workers have been compensable, even if the subject of the dispute was unrelated to work, so long as the work of the participants brought them together and created the conditions for the clash. In a New Jersey case, *Cremen v. Harrah's Marina Hotel Casino,* a casino cocktail server was asked to report to her supervisor's office at the end of the day. When she did so, the supervisor locked the office door and sexually assaulted her. Employing the "positional risk" analysis, the reviewing court observed that because the workplace brought the employee and her supervisor together, the employment physically facilitated the occurrence. Thus, the sexual assault arose out of her employment, rendering the injuries compensable under the workers' compensation statute.

b. The "Normally Expected Risk" Standard. Some courts have held that an injury arises out of employment only if the injury is the result of a risk that would normally be expected in the workplace. These courts are reluctant to find that the risk of sexual harassment is one that an employee should expect when entering the workplace. Thus, these courts tend to hold that sexual harassment injuries do not arise out of employment. These cases arise largely in the context of whether the employee's common-law claim is barred by the exclusive remedy provisions of the workers' compensation statute (see section III. below). Taking a narrow view of the "arising out of employment" requirement therefore permits a complainant to pursue civil remedies but is not logically consistent with a philosophy of extending workers' compensation coverage to all work-related injuries.

In *Bennett v. Furr's Cafeterias,* a workplace risk analysis was used to permit the complainant to maintain claims of assault, battery, and outrageous conduct under Colorado law. The complainant, a management trainee, alleged that her supervisor sexually assaulted her during business trips. The employer moved to have the case thrown out of court on the ground that workers' compensation provided the exclusive remedy. Denying the motion, the court reasoned that the workers' compensation act would bar the complainant's common-law claims only if her injuries had been caused by employment-related risks. The court concluded that the alleged acts and the emotional trauma did not result from risks inherent to the position of management trainee. Similarly, in *Hart v. National Mortgage & Land Co.,* where a male supervisor grabbed the complainant's testicles, pinched his buttocks, mounted him, and showed him a dildo, a California court held that the workers' compensation act was no bar to an emotional distress claim because this behavior was not a normal risk of employment.

2. Injuries Occurring in the Course of Employment. The additional requirement that an injury occur in the course of employment refers to the time and place of the incident causing the injury. To satisfy this requirement, the incident causing the injury must occur while the employee is at the workplace, or a place where the employee reasonably is expected to be, and performing services for the employer. This requirement should present no problem to an employee who is sexually harassed at work. If the employee is harassed by a supervisor or co-worker in a social setting outside of the workplace, however, the injury may not be held to have occurred "in the course of" the victim's employment.

C. Requirement That the Injury Be Accidental

Many states limit workers' compensation coverage to injuries that are "accidental." Varying standards for determining what is considered "accidental" are discussed below.

1. The Employee's Perspective. A test used in some states is whether the injury was accidental from the perspective of the injured employee. Under this test, injuries from sexual harassment in employment would be covered by workers' compensation on the basis that they are not normally expected or foreseen.

2. *The Harasser's Perspective.* The alternative test is whether the injury was accidental from the harasser's perspective. Under this test, injuries from sexual harassment, which is inherently intentional, would not be considered accidental, and thus workers' compensation would not be applicable (*Ford v. Revlon, Inc.*).

III. WORKERS' COMPENSATION EXCLUSIVITY

Workers' compensation statutes began as legislative compromises between the interests of employees and those of employers. The statutes are intended to give employees an efficient and effective remedy for workplace injuries without regard to whether the employer was at fault. Thus, injured employees receive defined benefits and avoid the traditional defenses to personal injury litigation, such as contributory negligence, assumption of risk, and the fellow-servant doctrine. The workers' compensation scheme is also intended to benefit employers because many previously available tort remedies, such as emotional distress damages, are precluded by the exclusive— and limited—remedy provisions of a workers' compensation statute.

Workers' compensation statutes thus represent a trade-off: the employee gets a no-fault system of compensation, and employers are relieved of tort liability arising from work-related injuries to their employees. Thus, if an injury is compensable under workers' compensation, the benefits recovered may be the exclusive state-law remedy for that injury. The scope of this exclusivity varies from state to state.

When acts of sexual harassment have provided a complainant with grounds for a common-law claim, the employer often will argue that the applicable state workers' compensation statute provides the exclusive remedy. Accordingly, most of the judicial decisions addressing workers' compensation coverage for sexual harassment injuries arise in the context of the employer attempting to invoke, and the employee attempting to avoid, the exclusivity provision of a workers' compensation statute.

In some states, the exclusive remedy defense bars only suits against the employer, while in other states the exclusivity bar also applies to suits against co-workers. A state-law exclusivity defense bars only state-law claims, not federal claims such as those under Title VII.

A. Application of Workers' Compensation Exclusivity

In a sexual harassment case, the employer's use of the defense of workers' compensation exclusivity is most often successful against common-law claims of employer negligence. The defense has also been applied to a sexual harassment complainant's claims of assault and battery and intentional infliction of emotional distress. Exclusivity is far less likely to bar common-law claims for dignitary harms, such as defamation or false imprisonment, or claims that are asserted under a state FEP statute.

B. Rationales for Not Applying Workers' Compensation Exclusivity

Although a finding of coverage for purposes of workers' compensation generally will lead to a finding of exclusivity, courts have interpreted workers' compensation statutes to create exceptions to exclusivity with respect to particular injuries and particular causes of action.

1. Sexual Harassment as Causing Only a Nondisabling Injury. Where the complainant has alleged only nonphysical, nondisabling harm, some courts have rejected the application of the exclusivity bar on the basis that the workers' compensation system is designed to address only physical disabilities. Thus, some courts have held that where complainants allege that sexual harassment caused severe emotional distress but not physical injuries resulting in disability compensable under workers' compensation, their claims would not be barred by the exclusivity doctrine in these states (*Hogan v. Forsyth Country Club*).

In California, however, workers' compensation exclusivity may bar a common-law claim even if the work-related injuries are not disabling (*Livitsanos v. Superior Court*).

2. Sexual Harassment as Causing a Special Form of Injury. Courts that follow a workplace-risk analysis (see section II.B.1.b. above) conclude that because a complainant's injuries caused by sexual harassment are not covered by workers' compensation, a separate state-law claim against the employer may proceed unimpeded by the exclusivity provisions.

A related rationale for permitting sexual harassment claims to proceed, notwithstanding workers' compensation exclusivity, is that employment discrimination and workers' compensation laws address distinct injuries and should be read to provide supplemental, rather than exclusive, remedies. Under this rationale, the exclusivity provisions do not bar discrimination and common-law tort claims based on sexual harassment, because these claims address injuries separate from those covered under worker's compensation (*Byrd v. Richardson-Greenshields Sec.*).

3. Sexual Harassment as an Intentional Act. In many states, a factor determining whether the workers' compensation act provides an exclusive remedy is whether the harassment was "intentional" instead of "accidental." This factor may arise in one of two contexts.

First, in those states requiring that a compensable injury be "accidental," this factor bears on whether the workers' compensation act applies at all (see section II.C. above).

Second, in those states providing for an "intentional acts" exception to exclusivity, this factor may determine whether a tort claim will be permitted to proceed, notwithstanding workers' compensation coverage. Some courts have not applied the exception to torts committed by a co-worker or have limited the intentional torts exception to instances where the perpetrator intended the specific injury (as opposed to intending the conduct causing the injury).

11

THE COMMON LAW

The acts that constitute sexual harassment may not only amount to employment discrimination that is unlawful under statute, but may also be the basis for a tort or contract claim under the common law (the nonstatutory, judge-made law). The most frequent common-law claims asserted by sexual harassment complainants or their spouses are discussed below.

I. INFLICTION OF EMOTIONAL DISTRESS

A. Intentional Infliction of Emotional Distress

Intentional infliction of emotional distress is perhaps the common-law theory of recovery most frequently asserted in sexual harassment actions. Courts have identified four elements that a complainant must prove to establish liability for this tort: (1) extreme and outrageous conduct; (2) an intent to cause, or reckless disregard of the probability of causing, emotional distress; (3) severe emotional distress suffered by the complainant; and (4) proof that the conduct complained of caused the complainant's severe emotional distress.

Liability in sexual harassment cases almost always hinges on whether the conduct was sufficiently "outrageous." Outrageous conduct typically is found where the harasser has engaged in violent conduct, sexual exposure, or offensive touching of intimate areas of the complainant's body (*Gilardi v. Schroeder; Priest v. Rotary; Bushell v. Dean*). Courts also have upheld claims of intentional infliction of emotional distress when the harasser's conduct has included nonconsensual touching, kissing, fondling, or caressing the complainant's body, or exposing of the alleged harasser's body.

Absent this sort of activity, some courts have allowed claims only where the harasser has engaged in some kind of retaliatory, job-threatening conduct. These courts have dismissed claims that are based solely on verbal harassment or unwanted touching of a nonvulgar nature (*Class v. New Jersey Life Ins. Co.; Hooten v. Pennsylvania College of Optometry; Andrews v. City of Philadelphia*). Other courts have held, however, that sexual advances, verbal abuse, and sexual solicitations are themselves sufficient to establish outrageous conduct (*Bailey v. Unocal Corp.; Coleman v. American Broadcasting Co.; Young v. Stensrude*).

The workplace context makes the outrageous element easier to prove in sexual harassment cases, because the nature of the employment relationship may give the harasser extraordinary power to damage the complainant's interests. The standard for determining whether the conduct is "outrageous" for tort purposes, and the standard for determining whether conduct is "severe" or "pervasive" for Title VII purposes, generally seem to be about the same.

Both employers and unions may be directly liable for outrageous conduct for failing to respond appropriately to complaints of sexual harassment (*Ford v. Revlon, Inc.; Woods v. Graphic Communications*).

B. Negligent Infliction of Emotional Distress

Breach of a duty of care that results in emotional distress can result in legal liability, especially if there is physical injury. In the employment context, a sexual harassment complainant generally cannot recover for negligent (as opposed to intentional) infliction of emotional distress unless a physical injury also was suffered (*Rogers v. Loews L'Enfant Plaza Hotel; Miller v. Aluminum Co. of Am.*). This theory of liability is rarely relied upon, because sexual harassment is almost always intentional as to the individual perpetrator. In addition, courts usually analyze an employer's negligence in preventing sexual harassment as a matter of statutory discrimination law or as the separate tort of negligent retention or supervision, discussed in section XI. below.

II. ASSAULT AND BATTERY

The torts of assault and battery provide a common-law remedy for persons threatened with and subjected to offensive physical contact in the workplace. Although assault and battery are separate torts, they usually are asserted as companion causes of action in sexual harassment cases.

To prove assault, a complainant must show that (1) the actor intended to cause harmful or offensive physical contact, and (2) the complainant was put in apprehension of that conduct. Actual physical contact is not required—that is classified as battery. Verbal harassment alone does not constitute an assault unless the circumstances somehow warrant an expectation of imminent physical contact.

To prove battery, a complainant must show a harmful or offensive physical contact with a person resulting from an act intended to cause the complainant or a third person to suffer the contact. A battery results whenever the offensive contact extends to any part of the complainant's body or to practically anything attached to it. The complainant also must suffer mental or physical harm to justify any award of damages.

Damages have been awarded for assault and battery claims based on a harasser's unwelcome touching and other sexual advances. The touching need not be of private parts to warrant liability.

Civil assault and battery actions are particularly appropriate whenever an employee has been sexually molested by an employer, supervisor, or co-worker (*Valdez v. Church's Fried Chicken; Gilardi v. Schroeder*). Although the individual harasser is the obvious defendant, the employer also may be sued under a theory of negligence or *respondeat superior* (see sections XI. and XII. below).

III. FALSE IMPRISONMENT

The tort of false imprisonment involves an intentional act of confining another person "within boundaries fixed by the actor." Sexual advances sometimes involve aggressive physical conduct that can constitute false imprisonment. In one case, the court found two separate incidents of false imprisonment when a restaurant owner picked up a cocktail waitress and carried her across the room, then later physically trapped her while he fondled her body (*Priest v. Rotary*).

IV. INVASION OF PRIVACY

Several different torts fall under the general heading of invasion of privacy. The right to privacy has been deemed waived where a complainant has yielded to a supervisor's sexual advances (*Cummings v. Walsh Constr. Co.*), or has openly discussed a private matter in the work environment (*Moffett v. Gene B. Glick Co.*).

A. Intrusion Upon Seclusion

The tort of intrusion involves an intentional interference with the seclusion of one's person or private concerns. Courts have found the following situations to be intrusions:

- The complainant's immediate supervisor repeatedly called her at home and at work when he was off duty and made lewd comments to her about her personal and sex life, despite her requests that he stop (*Rogers v. Loews L'Enfant Plaza Hotel*).
- Female employees were subjected to unwanted touching of their thighs, breasts, and buttocks (*Pease v. Alford Photo Indus.*).
- The employer asked a female employee about her sexual relationship with her husband, told her that providing sexual services to him in his office was part of her job, and then covered his office window with paper to obscure the view of others (*Phillips v. Smalley Maintenance Servs.*).

- A co-worker placed a high-pressure air hose between the complainant's legs (*Waltman v. International Paper Co.*).

B. False Light Publicity

A second form of invasion of privacy is publicity that places the complainant in a false light before the public. One false light publicity action was based on statements made by the defendant at a news conference, in violation of the confidentiality provisions of the parties' settlement agreement, that described the complainant's lawsuit as unfounded and meritless (*Tomson v. Stephan*). Falsely implying that a complainant is promiscuous would be another example of possible false light publicity.

C. Public Disclosure of Private Facts

To establish public disclosure of private facts, a complainant must prove (1) the public disclosure of a private fact, (2) publicity that would be highly offensive and objectionable to a person of ordinary sensibilities, (3) no legitimate public interest in having the information made available, and (4) injury to the complainant as a result of the publicity. When an employee sued her employer for publicly disclosing their sexual relationship, the court dismissed her claim because she had discussed the relationship with others (*Cummings v. Walsh Constr. Co.*).

V. DEFAMATION

To prove defamation, a complainant must establish:
(1) a false statement concerning another that tends to harm the subject's reputation;
(2) an unprivileged disclosure, or "publication," to a third party;
(3) some fault amounting to at least negligence on the part of the person providing the information; and
(4) harm caused by the publication.

Written defamation is called libel, while oral defamation is called slander.

Courts have found defamation where a federal judge told others that his secretary was romantically interested in him (*Garcia v. Williams*), and where an employer who dismissed a female employee for rebuffing his sexual advances made statements implicating her in unlawful activity (*Chamberlin v. 101 Realty*). By contrast, an employer's publicized statement that an employee's sexual harassment claims were meritless were considered to be an opinion protected by the First Amendment (*Coleman v. American Broadcasting Co.*)

For a discussion of defamation claims by the alleged harasser, see Chapter 16, section VI.A.1.

VI. MISREPRESENTATION AND PROMISSORY ESTOPPEL

The torts of fraudulent and negligent misrepresentation can occur when one misrepresents facts or intentions for the purpose of inducing another to act or to refrain from acting, where justifiable reliance on the misrepresentation causes economic loss. One or both of these torts might be available to a sexual harassment complainant who has been persuaded to remain on the job by the employer's false assurances that the harassment will not recur (*Fawcett v. IDS Fin. Servs.*).

The same facts also could support a claim under a contract theory, as opposed to the tort theories discussed above, for what is called "promissory estoppel." This involves an agreement between employer and employee (*i.e.*, the employer agrees that there will be no more harassment if the employee agrees to continue working), where the employer's misrepresentations induced the complainant to act or refrain from acting in a specific way (*Kinnally v. Bell of Pa.*).

VII. BREACH OF PUBLIC POLICY

A. Basis of Cause of Action

Courts in most states recognize that "public policy" may limit an employer's right to discharge even an at-will employee. Courts typically have recognized a public policy claim where an employee has been discharged in a manner or for a reason contrary to public policy. The courts generally find the public policy implicit in state statutes and constitutions. Complainants alleging that they were fired for rejecting sexual advances, or in retaliation for opposing sexual harassment, have successfully based tort claims for wrongful discharge on the public policy contained in:

- the state FEP statute (*Dias v. Sky Chefs*; *Chamberlin v. 101 Realty*; *Holien v. Sears, Roebuck & Co.*);
- the state constitution (*Drinkwalter v. Shipton Supply Co.*; *Rojo v. Kliger*);
- statutes prohibiting prostitution (*Harrison v. Edison Bros. Apparel Stores*; *Lucas v. Brown & Root, Inc.*);
- statutes prohibiting indecent exposure (*Wagenseller v. Scottsdale Memorial Hosp.*); and
- general policies against retaliation for performing an act that the public would encourage or for refusing to perform an act that the public would condemn (*Handley v. Phillips*; *Clemens v. Gerber Scientific*).

B. Effect of Employment Discrimination Statutes

When an employee brings a claim for discharge in violation of the public policy against sexual harassment, courts have asked two basic questions. First, some courts have questioned the need to recognize a "public policy" tort action for sexual harassment, reasoning that a common-law action should be available only where there would otherwise be no remedy. By this reasoning, the fact that Title VII and the state FEP statute already provide remedies would undermine the justification for judicial recognition of a public policy tort. Second, courts in several states have held that the state FEP statute was intended to provide the *exclusive* state-law remedy for acts of employment discrimination (see Chapter 7).

VIII. BREACH OF IMPLIED CONTRACT OR COVENANT

A. Breach of Implied Contract

Under the general common-law rule, employment contracts for an indefinite term are presumed to be terminable at the will of either the employee or the employer. A complainant may rebut this presumption by proving that the parties expressly or impliedly agreed to limit or eliminate this right to terminate at will. The proof may include employment manuals, oral agreements, or written personnel policies (*Tuttle v. ANR Freight Sys.; Foley v. Interactive Data Corp.; Woolley v. Hoffman-LaRoche, Inc.; Toussaint v. Blue Cross & Blue Shield; Wolk v. Saks Fifth Ave.*).

Under these principles, a complainant might argue that the employer's failure to correct sexual harassment as impliedly promised in employer policies amounts to a breach of contract (see the Sample Antiharassment Policy in Appendix 4).

B. Breach of Implied Covenant of Good Faith and Fair Dealing

Courts in a few states have found an implied covenant of good faith and fair dealing that requires the employer to refrain from intentionally injuring an employee's right to receive the contractual benefits of the employment relationship. In those states some courts have concluded that sexual harassment can constitute a breach of the covenant (*Drinkwalter v. Shipton Supply Co.; Lucas v. Brown & Root, Inc.*).

IX. CONTRACTUAL INTERFERENCE

Some employees sexually harassed by co-workers have sued on a contractual interference theory. To prevail under this theory, the complainant must show that the harasser intentionally and improperly interfered with the complainant's performance of her employment contract. In sexual harassment cases, courts have found contractual interference where a supervisor caused a female employee's discharge after she rejected his advances (*Favors v. Alco Mfg. Co.*), and where a male co-worker's threats, insults, and intimidation forced a female employee to abandon her job (*Lewis v. Oregon Beauty Supply Co.*). The complainant must prove an unlawful motive and the existence of an enforceable employment contract (*Fisher v. San Pedro Peninsula Hosp.*). Normally the claim is brought against the individual harasser rather than the employer with whom the contract existed.

X. LOSS OF CONSORTIUM
BY THE COMPLAINANT'S SPOUSE

A suit for loss of consortium seeks compensation for the loss of the sexual attentions, society, and affection resulting from an injury to one's marital partner. The claim is not brought by itself; it is derivative of some other common-law claim. Loss-of-consortium claims have been asserted by men whose wives have suffered physical and emotional injuries arising from sexual harassment in the workplace. These claims may accompany the complainant's own actions for assault and battery, intentional infliction of emotional distress, and violation of a state FEP statutes (*Handley v. Phillips; Bowersox v. P.H. Glatfelter Co.; Spoon v. American Agriculturalist; Eide v. Kelsey-Hayes Co.*).

A loss-of-consortium claim does not require that the harassed spouse suffer a physically disabling injury. Manifestations of the effects of sexual harassment, such as depression, headaches, nausea, and severe emotional distress, can themselves cause loss of society and companionship, thereby warranting a remedy for loss of consortium (*Bowersox v. P.H. Glatfelter Co.*).

XI. NEGLIGENT RETENTION OR SUPERVISION

Complainants sometimes assert negligent retention or supervision claims against their employers in an attempt to hold them liable for acts of sexual harassment by other employees. A negligent retention or supervision claim requires proof that an employer knew or should have known of the alleged harasser's propensity to engage in sexual harassment and failed to address the conduct.

Claims against the employer for negligent retention or supervision usually accompany claims against the individual alleged harasser. It is no defense that the complainant assumed the risk of harassment by continuing to work with the harasser (*Perkins v. Spivey*).

Use of this theory of liability is limited because (1) the common-law duty to maintain a safe workplace concerns only physical injuries, and thus some jurisdictions do not permit suits for negligent supervision or retention absent some bodily injury (*Spencer v. General Elec. Co.; Perkins v. Spivey*); and (2) a negligent supervision or retention claim often will be barred by the exclusivity provisions of state workers' compensation statutes (see Chapter 10, section III.).

XII. *RESPONDEAT SUPERIOR*

For most of the sexually harassing conduct discussed in this chapter, the employer itself may be directly liable to a sexual harassment complainant on the basis of its own conduct (generally failure to investigate or stop the harassment). An alternative basis of indirect liability is provided by the common-law doctrine of *respondeat superior*.

Under *respondeat superior*, an employer may be *vicariously* liable for torts committed by one of its employees when the employee's act is committed within the scope of employment and in furtherance of the employer's business.

In the employment context, sexual harassment by a manager or supervisor rarely will be authorized by the employer or be in furtherance of the employer's business (*Dockter v. Rudolf Wolff Futures; Davis v. Utah Power & Light Co.*). Nonetheless, employers have been held liable under *respondeat superior* where:

- a manager discharged a complainant in retaliation for complaining about sexual harassment (*Dias v. Sky Chefs*),
- management reasonably could have anticipated that intentional misconduct of the sort in question could occur (*Spoon v. American Agriculturalist*), and
- the harasser acted with apparent authority of the employer (*Davis v. Utah Power & Light Co.*).

Such indirect liability also may attach, on the same principles, to nonemployer organizations such as unions.

XIII. DEFENSES

Two frequently asserted defenses to common-law claims are workers' compensation preemption (see Chapter 10, section

III.) and preemption by state FEP statutes (see Chapter 7, section IV.).

XIV. LIABILITY FOR PUNITIVE DAMAGES

Punitive damages in common-law tort actions are available upon proof that the defendant acted willfully or with malice (see Chapter 21, section II.C.3.).

12

CRIMINAL LAW

I. OVERVIEW

Acts of sexual harassment may violate criminal statutes. A corporate employer as well as an individual harasser may be criminally liable. Criminal prosecutions have unique consequences: they can lead to incarceration, fines, restitution, and can seriously damage a person's reputation. Criminal prosecutions can also tarnish the employer's image and establish civil liability that will not be covered by insurance, as insurance generally does not cover claims resulting from intentional conduct (see Chapter 19).

II. CRIMES COMMITTED BY SEXUAL HARASSERS

A. Rape and Sodomy

Several of the reported sexual harassment cases have involved rape. Most statutes define rape in terms of sexual intercourse accomplished with a person, against the victim's will, by means of force, violence, or fear of immediate and unlawful bodily injury.

Sodomy generally is defined to include sexual contact between the penis and the anus, the mouth and the penis, or the mouth and vulva. Whether this offense is a felony or a misdemeanor depends on the particular jurisdiction and whether the activity is consensual.

B. Sexual Assault and Battery

Many state statutes criminalize conduct known as sexual battery. The California statute makes it a misdemeanor to touch an intimate part of another for the purpose of sexual arousal, gratification, or abuse, if done against the will of the person touched. Touching is defined as physical contact that is direct or through the clothing of the victim or of the person committing the offense. Intimate parts are the sexual organ, anus, groin, or buttocks of any person, and the breasts of a female. This conduct, which frequently occurs in connection with sexual harassment, rises to the level of a felony if the victim is restrained by the perpetrator or an accomplice at the time of the touching.

A perpetrator who specifically intends to accomplish forcible nonconsensual sexual contact, but who does not actually complete the act, has committed a sexual assault. If the perpetrator is fought off while intending to commit rape, he has committed the crimes of attempted rape and, most probably, battery and sexual assault. The attempt to commit the most serious uncompleted act almost always will be included among the offenses charged. Attempt statutes provide that an individual perpetrates an attempt when, with intent to commit a specific offense, an individual does any act that constitutes a substantial step toward the commission of that offense.

C. Obscene Telephone Calls

Many states forbid making telephone calls with the intent to harass or abuse the recipient of the call. In addition, federal law makes it illegal to:

- use a telephone to make any comment that is obscene, lewd, lascivious, filthy, or indecent;
- make a telephone call, regardless of whether conversation ensues, without disclosing one's identity and with

intent to annoy, abuse, threaten, or harass any person at the called number; or

- make or cause another's telephone to ring repeatedly or continually with intent to harass any person at the called number.

D. Solicitation and Lewd Conduct

Some quid pro quo harassment—conditioning job benefits on providing sexual favors—may fall within the reach of statutes prohibiting the solicitation of prostitution. The typical prostitution statute prohibits a request that another person engage in lewd or sexual acts between individuals for money or other consideration.

Most jurisdictions also criminally punish any lewd or dissolute conduct, such as exposing oneself in a public place or in a location open to public view. The everyday workplace, of course, could constitute both a public place and a location where an individual's sexual behavior might be in the public view.

E. False Imprisonment

False imprisonment is the unlawful restraint of the personal liberty of another. The restraint need not involve violence or even physical contact; it may be accomplished by mere words accompanied by a show of force or authority to which the victim submits. The *crime* of false imprisonment differs from the *civil wrong* of false imprisonment (see Chapter 11, section III.), which involves a lawsuit by the complainant for damages, not a criminal complaint lodged by public prosecutors.

F. RICO

The Racketeer Influenced and Corrupt Organizations Act (RICO), or one of its state-law counterparts, can be the basis of both criminal and civil actions. Aimed at organized crime, RICO prohibits the use of a "pattern of racketeering activity" to establish, operate, or invest in an "enterprise." The prohibited conduct includes threats involving murder, extortion, obscene matter, and other subjects, but with exceptions immaterial here, does not usually include sexual activity.

There is no reported case of applying criminal RICO provisions to sexual harassment, but such an application is possible. One civil case upheld a sexual harassment complaint under RICO by a female carpenter against her union, where she alleged that union officials used sexual harassment to extort contributions from female members to support the union's political fund and to force her to withdraw a sexual harassment complaint against a co-worker (*Hunt v. Weatherbee*). The complainant was thus permitted to pursue an action under the civil provisions of RICO, which provide for attorney's fees and treble damages.

III. CRIMES COMMITTED BY EMPLOYERS

A. Aiding, Abetting, and Conspiracy

Criminal statutes make all persons who knowingly and intentionally involve themselves in the commission of a crime chargeable under criminal law as principals. If upper-level managers of a corporation effected a plan of sexual harassment to induce the resignation of an employee, for example, the managers and the employer could be prosecuted if the actual harasser committed criminal violations with the knowledge and approval of the employer.

Where an agreement exists to commit the offense or to assist in its commission, a participant may also be charged with the separate crime of conspiracy. A conspiracy violation requires that two or more individuals agree to commit a statutory offense, and that at least one of the conspirators knowingly and willfully performs some overt act to effect the object of the conspiracy. Most courts state that for conspiracy purposes a corporate employer is not liable for conspiring with its own employees.

B. Compounding, Concealing, and Obstructing

An employer and its personnel may incur criminal liability by engaging in conduct that conceals a crime. This conduct, known as compounding, commonly involves taking a bribe, or giving one, to conceal criminal activity. If a company, having knowledge of a crime, either takes or gives money in exchange for concealing the crime or withholding evidence of it, the employer may subject itself, as well as the individuals involved, to criminal prosecution for that behavior. A related crime—attempting to obstruct justice—results when one uses money or threats to induce a witness not to give testimony. Another related crime—subornation of perjury—results when one induces a potential witness to give false testimony.

C. Accessories After-the-Fact

An accessory after-the-fact is one who, knowing a crime has been committed, helps the violator to escape justice. The various accessory statutes provide that one may not harbor, conceal, or aid a principal who has committed criminal conduct with the intent that the principal avoid or escape arrest, trial, conviction, or punishment. Thus, an employer that protects an employee who has committed a sexual harassment-related crime by, for example, transferring him to another jurisdiction to help him evade prosecution, could be liable as an accessory after-the-fact.

IV. CRIMES COMMITTED BY COMPLAINANTS

A person who claims to have been victimized by sexual harassment at work may be tempted to threaten criminal action to obtain a cash settlement from the employer. This temptation may lead to criminal conduct on the part of the employer *and* the complainant. Therefore, as explained below, civil settlement negotiations in situations that involve a concurrent criminal prosecution should be handled only in consultation with counsel familiar with the criminal judicial process.

A. Extortion

The traditional crime of extortion involves obtaining property from another through the wrongful use of force or fear, or under color of official right. Extortion statutes may present traps for even well-meaning complainants who contemplate or participate in civil lawsuits. A traditional extortion statute may apply to any demand for money that is coupled with a threat to pursue criminal prosecution. Thus, a complainant lawfully may demand civil damages where crimes involving acts of sexual harassment have been committed, but may not lawfully threaten to press criminal charges if her demands for money are not satisfied.

B. False Reporting

In most jurisdictions, any person who knowingly makes a false report to a law enforcement official that a sexual or other crime has been committed is guilty of a misdemeanor. A false-reporting violation could become the basis for a subsequent civil suit by the employer or harasser alleging malicious prosecution.

C. Concealing Criminal Activity

Where a defendant offers to compensate the complainant if criminal charges are dropped, the offer itself may constitute a crime; accepting the offer may also constitute a crime by the complainant. Because criminal activity is prosecuted by governmental entities, a complainant retains no legal authority to decide, on her own, how a pending case should be resolved. Refusal by a sexual harassment complainant to proceed with an already-initiated criminal prosecution in exchange for a cash settlement by the defendant could result in the complainant becoming a defendant in a separate criminal prosecution.

D. Surreptitious Tape-Recording

Some jurisdictions make it a crime to tape-record a confidential communication without the consent of all parties. In these jurisdictions, sexual harassment complainants who wish to document unwelcome sexual advances or other verbal evidence of sexual harassment should rely on nonelectronic means. The same advice applies, obviously, to companies conducting surveillance as part of their investigation of complaints.

V. CONSIDERATIONS FOR THE EMPLOYER

Because early impressions by an investigating law enforcement agency can be critical, it is important to take all appropriate steps to influence that agency's favorable perception of the employer and its innocent personnel, and to fulfill the employer's obligations to protect both itself and the rights of all individual employees.

Employers should consult with counsel, once a sexual harassment complaint with criminal overtones is lodged, to determine how to handle information in the employer's possession and generally to guarantee appropriate conduct. Counsel then should contact all employees with pertinent knowledge to determine exactly what the individuals know and what they will say if questioned during the investigation, and to advise employees that they may be approached by law enforcement officers, without prior notice, outside of the workplace. Investigating officers may make surprise visits to prevent potential witnesses or defendants from consulting with others or preparing for interviews. This investigative technique often results in answers from employees based on insufficient knowledge, unreliable hearsay, or mere personal impressions that may be inaccurate. Investigating officers seldom advise their subjects not to speculate, and often encourage them to impress their listeners with the scope of their knowledge. In the event of civil litigation against the employer, these statements carry a potential for untold problems. If interviewees already have discussed the matter with counsel, however, they can be alerted to the possible pitfalls of the interview while maintaining their obligation to be truthful.

The safest course for both the employer and any employees contacted for an interview in a criminal investigation is for the employer to notify the potential witnesses, in writing, that an investigation may be conducted and that it is the employer's position that employees are to cooperate to the fullest extent. This document will evidence proper conduct by the employer and management personnel toward potential witnesses. Potential witnesses should also be informed, in writing, that counsel for the employer would like to be notified by the employee of any forthcoming interviews and would like to attend. The employee should further be advised of the right to retain private counsel and that, in any event, the employer's counsel is available to answer questions and is monitoring the investigation.

Finally, the employee should be informed in the letter that police investigators will not draw adverse inferences from being told that, although the employee has no objection to speaking with them, he or she requests a delay in order to speak with counsel, inasmuch as the matter potentially relates to legal positions of the employer.

If the employer has information that implicates an employee in wrongdoing, and the employer's counsel also represents that employee, there exists a conflict of interest. The employee should be directed, without delay, to an outside attorney from a list that can be furnished by the employer. It remains in the employer's best interests, for purposes of civil liability and public relations, to distance itself from those it has reason to believe have engaged in criminal sexual behavior that could in any way implicate the employer. For a discussion of whether the employer should pay for outside counsel, and of counsel's duty to the alleged harasser no matter who is paying, see Chapter 18, section V.

Positive early contact with the investigating agency can result in the employer being able to avoid search warrants directed at the premises. Searches can be disruptive, affect company morale, and result in adverse or embarrassing publicity. Prosecutors generally use search warrants where there is some reason to doubt the integrity of evidence procured through a direct request or subpoena.

Whenever use of a search warrant can be anticipated, all relevant employer documents or other company materials should be marked and stored separately from other business records. Law enforcement personnel who pay a surprise visit to the premises can then be directed to the desired records without disturbing employer operations and rummaging through unrelated files.

13

COLLECTIVE BARGAINING AGREEMENTS, UNION OBLIGATIONS, AND ARBITRATION

I. PROHIBITIONS AGAINST SEXUAL HARASSMENT IN THE LAW OF THE SHOP

A. Overview

In the organized work force, employers, relying on shop rules and the employer's interest in maintaining common decency, traditionally have disciplined employees for harassing conduct regardless of whether the basis of the harassment was sexual. Arbitrators have upheld such discipline of union-represented employees as consistent with the "just cause" for discipline that an employer typically must establish under a collective bargaining agreement. Since passage of Title VII, arbitrators have incorporated the developments of Title VII sexual harassment law into the arbitral concepts of just cause and acceptable workplace conduct.

B. Shop Rules

Employers have taken steps to curtail employee harassment, sexual or otherwise, by developing rules that govern conduct in the workplace. Employees who violate these rules are subject to discipline up to and including discharge. While these rules do not always specify sexual harassment, they cover most conduct that constitutes sexual harassment. For example, in *Powermatic/Houdaille*, an arbitrator upheld the suspension of a grievant for violation of a shop rule prohibiting immoral conduct where the grievant approached a female employee, placed his finger through the fly of his pants, and said, "Hey, big mama, look what I have for you."

C. Unwritten Law of the Shop

One line of arbitral authority holds that because sexual harassment is inherently impermissible, an employer may subject offenders to discipline, including discharge, without relying on any specific shop rule. In a discharge case involving a grievant who had forcibly grabbed a female co-worker's buttocks and kissed her, the arbitrator stated: "The Grievant cannot complain of receiving no express warnings [against engaging in such behavior]; such male versus female aggressions on the job predate the very first collective bargaining contract and such a prohibition remains part of the unwritten law of the shop" (*Dover Corp.*).

II. COLLECTIVELY BARGAINED PROCEDURAL LIMITS TO DISCIPLINE FOR SEXUAL HARASSMENT

Employers subject to a collective bargaining agreement requiring just cause for discharge must provide employees with procedural due process before imposing discipline. The procedure generally includes notice to the employee as to what conduct is prohibited, an adequate factual basis to conclude that prohibited conduct has occurred, and an opportunity for the employee or the union to present the employee's side of the story.

III. THE RELATIONSHIP BETWEEN TITLE VII AND ARBITRAL AUTHORITY

Rather than enforcing external law, arbitrators enforce the intent of the parties under the collective bargaining agreement. Where there is no conflict between external law and the terms of the collective bargaining agreement, an arbitrator is free to examine external law in interpreting a collective bargaining agreement. When evaluating discipline and discharge cases, arbitrators frequently rely on the EEOC 1980 Guidelines on Sexual Harassment (reproduced in Appendix 1).

In *Alexander v. Gardner-Denver*, the Supreme Court invited arbitrators to consider Title VII when dealing with discrimination issues. Arbitrators incorporate Title VII principles into collective bargaining agreements either because specific anti-discrimination provisions appear in collective bargaining agreements, or because discriminatory employment action is interpreted to be just cause for discipline.

IV. CONDUCT FOUND BY ARBITRATORS TO BE SEXUAL HARASSMENT

A. Vulgar, Hostile Work Environment

1. Verbal and Visual Harassment. Arbitrators routinely support management decisions to discipline employees for sexual harassment in the form of vulgar conduct such as:

- sexual or crude language directed at a co-worker (*Phillip Morris*),
- obscene sexual gestures (*Can-Tex Indus.*),
- exposing one's self to a female co-worker (*Porter Equip. Co.*),
- intentionally entering a women's restroom with a female co-worker present (*Island Creek Coal Co.*),
- spreading false stories about the sexual activities of a co-worker (*Social Security Admin.*), and
- other conduct creating a hostile environment (*Anaconda Copper Co.*).

2. Physical Contact. Arbitrators generally uphold severe discipline when the sexual misconduct involves offensive physical contact. One arbitrator upheld a discharge where the grievant grabbed the arm of a nurse's aide and kissed her on the cheek while she was preparing a patient's bath and hugged her against her will on three occasions, even though the grievant had worked for the employer for 24 years and had an unblemished work record (*Care Inns*).

3. General Considerations. In deciding whether discharge is the proper penalty, arbitrators will consider all circumstances of the grievant's misconduct, the effect of the misconduct on the complainant, whether the grievant was notified that sexual harassment was prohibited, the work record of the grievant, and the length of the grievant's service. Often in cases of long service and single violations, arbitrators are inclined to convert discharges into suspensions without pay. Thus, where a grievant pinched a female co-worker on the breast while making kissing sounds, the arbitrator reduced the discharge penalty to a seven-month suspension without pay in light of the grievant's 28 years of employment, good work record, and no prior disciplinary problems, and the fact that the complainant failed to report the incident to management (*Dayton Power & Light*).

One arbitrator has ruled that a single statement about sex, "I suppose you don't even like sexual intercourse," did not constitute sexual harassment or violate the shop rule prohibiting obscene or abusive language (*Washington Scientific Indus.*). An arbitrator also refused to find sexual harassment when an employee passed an obscene, sexually explicit note to a co-worker. The recipient of the note was not offended and simply tore up the note and threw it in the wastebasket. The arbitrator observed that, under the EEOC Guidelines, conduct is considered to be sexual harassment only if it is unwelcome (*Bakery and Confectionary Union*).

B. Nonvulgar but Unwelcome Sexual Advances

Arbitrators have upheld discipline for making unwelcome amorous advances toward other employees when the advances are persistent and annoying, even if the conduct is not crude or physical. In these cases arbitrators must distinguish harmless ineffectual romantic conduct from obsessive and compulsive behavior that reflect serious psychological problems. Prior warnings are usually necessary to support a discharge for this kind of conduct.

C. Harassment of Customers, Clients, and Other Nonemployees

Under the law of the shop, employees not only must refrain from sexually harassing their co-workers, but also must refrain from harassing customers, clients, and other nonemployees with whom they deal in their employment. Arbitrators have upheld discipline for:

- making offensive comments to a passing citizen (*City of Rochester*),
- making sexual advances toward the teenage daughter of a customer (*Pepco*),
- making sexually oriented jokes and comments to clients (*County of Ramsey*),
- touching the breast of a sales representative of another company (*Fisher Foods*),
- making sexual propositions to the employer's customers (*Nabisco Food Co.*), and
- sexually assaulting a customer (*Communications Workers v. Southeastern Elec. Co-op*).

V. GRIEVANCES FILED BY COMPLAINANTS

Arbitral decisions concerning sexual harassment typically result from grievances filed on behalf of men who have been disciplined for sexual harassment. Grievances may also be filed on behalf of women who are grieving the employer's failure to prevent or correct harassment or are grieving an adverse employment decision related to harassment.

A. Grievances Challenging Working Conditions

In *County of Oakland*, to comply with state requirements for special inmates, a county sheriff fitted behavior modification unit prison cells with glass doors and windows to permit constant observation of inmates. Female booking clerks within view of the cells filed a grievance because of their exposure to nudity and obscene gestures by the male inmates. In denying the charge of sexual harassment, the arbitrator emphasized that the booking clerk job is open to both genders.

B. Grievances Challenging Adverse Employment Decisions

Female employees may grieve adverse employment decisions on the ground that they resulted from sexual harassment. In *EZ Communications,* the arbitrator sustained a grievance over a radio station's denial of severance pay to a female newscaster who had walked off the job after a long series of on-air jokes about her sexual proclivities. The grievant's job was to read the news during a morning radio show featuring two male disc jockeys. Over a period of two years, the disc jockeys broadcast comments, intended in jest, that the grievant suffered from sexually transmitted diseases and regularly performed promiscuous oral sex with large numbers of casual acquaintances, including members of the Pittsburgh Penguins hockey team and the United States Marine Corps. Despite her complaints, the sexual remarks continued, with the final straw being a joke to the effect that a tattoo on her forehead read, "Let go of my ears, I'm doing the best I can." Hearing the joke just before she was to read the news, the grievant was too distressed to go on the air and left the station. This resulted in her discharge for flagrant neglect of duty and the denial of her claim for severance pay, which was due under the collective bargaining agreement if she was terminated on a "noncause" basis.

The arbitrator held that the grievant was relieved of an employee's general duty to "obey now, grieve later" because going on the air would have humiliated her. The arbitrator acknowledged that the nature of the grievant's entertainment job required her to participate in "banter and interplay with the other on-air talent," and that the First Amendment protects even jokes that are "lewd, offensive, sophomoric, in bad taste," but concluded that the disc jockeys' sexual comments created a hostile working environment.

Grievances by sexual harassment complainants often will be denied when the employer has imposed discipline on the alleged harasser. In one such case, an employee grieved a dismissal during her probationary period, claiming that her failure to learn her job duties was because she was so upset by the sexual harassment during her training period. The arbitrator denied the grievance because the grievant reported only the last of a series of incidents to the employer, which then acted promptly to address the conduct (*Amoco Texas Refinery Co.*). In another case, a female employee claimed that she had been discharged for refusing to "party" with her supervisor. The arbitrator denied the grievance because the evidence of the foreman's sexual advances was uncorroborated and unpersuasive in light of strong evidence of the grievant's poor job performance (*Paccar, Inc.*).

VI. UNION OBLIGATIONS

A. Duty of Fair Representation Under the NLRA

Unions, like employers, have a duty to treat sexual harassment complaints seriously. Under the duty of fair representation, established under the National Labor Relations Act (NLRA), a union must not abandon a grievance for any reason that is arbitrary, discriminatory, or in bad faith. While this duty does not require prosecution of every meritorious grievance, a union may not arbitrarily ignore a grievance or process it in a perfunctory fashion.

A union that fails to protect female employees from harassment while protecting male employees from comparable mistreatment could be violating its duty of fair representation by discriminating on the basis of gender. A union also might breach its duty if it simply fails to combat sexual harassment generally: this failure could be attacked both as arbitrary and as having an unjustified discriminatory impact on women employees, who are affected disproportionately by sexual harassment.

A union also may breach its duty of fair representation by its own discriminatory operation of a hiring hall. In *Seritis v. Hotel & Restaurant Employees*, the union, which referred members to jobs from its hiring hall, violated its duty to two teenage waitresses when a union officer conditioned their job referrals on their submission to sexual advances. The women lost access to jobs after rejecting union offers to be a "live-in sexual playmate" for two men, provide sexual services at parties, work as a topless waitress on a bus, work as a prostitute at a convention, live with a lesbian, and have sex with a dog in a Nevada stage show. The waitresses secured a judgment of $200,000 against the union for intentional infliction of emotional distress and breach of the duty of fair representation.

B. Duty Under Title VII

Unions may be liable for sex discrimination under Title VII if (1) the union intentionally fails to file a grievance concerning workplace harassment, (2) the union fails to impose discipline on union members who engage in harassment, (3) union agents engage in harassment, or (4) the union acquiesces in harassment.

VII. FAILURE TO ARBITRATE UNDER A COLLECTIVE BARGAINING AGREEMENT

A. Arbitration as the Exclusive Remedy

A union-represented employee who challenges employer discipline is limited to arbitration as the exclusive forum for resolving employment-related disputes that depend in any way upon an interpretation of the collective bargaining agreement.

B. Independent Right to Pursue Certain Claims

While the principle of arbitral exclusivity provides the employer with a defense to many common-law claims, a collective bargaining agreement cannot be used to preclude or even defer the claims of a sexual harassment complainant who brings a Title VII, state FEP, or state public policy claim, because these claims typically can be adjudicated without reference to the collective bargaining agreement. Thus, a union-represented employee may seek arbitration of a sexual harassment claim, and, notwithstanding the arbitrator's ruling, still pursue judicial remedies under Title VII. Alternatively, the grievant may bypass the grievance and arbitration procedure and rely solely on Title VII. The Supreme Court made these rulings in 1974 in *Alexander v. Gardner-Denver Co.*

VIII. SIGNIFICANCE OF THE ARBITRATION DECISION

A. Judicial Review of Arbitration Awards

The standards for judicial review of arbitration awards are extremely narrow. Courts are not free to substitute their interpretation of the labor agreement for that of an arbitrator. So long as the award draws its essence from the agreement between the parties, the court has no authority to review the merits of the award (*Paperworkers v. Misco*).

A narrow exception to this rule applies if the arbitration award is contrary to public policy (*W.R. Grace & Co. v. Rubber Workers*). One court set aside an arbitrator's decision to reinstate a habitual sexual harasser. The court reasoned that permitting reinstatement violated the public policy against sexual harassment as set forth in Title VII (*Newsday v. Long Island Typographical Union*).

B. Effect of Arbitration Decisions on Litigation

Where the parties proceed first to arbitration and then to litigation under Title VII, the Supreme Court in *Gardner-Denver* suggested that an arbitral award should be admitted as evidence for such weight "as the court deems appropriate." The Supreme Court instructed trial courts to assign weight to arbitral decisions on a case-by-case basis in accordance with the following factors:

(1) whether the decision applied to collectively bargained provisions in substantial conformance with Title VII,
(2) the degree of procedural fairness in the arbitral forum,
(3) the adequacy of the record with respect to the discrimination issue, and
(4) the special competence of the particular arbitrator.

Courts addressing the issue after *Gardner-Denver* generally have given "considerable" or "great" weight to the arbitrator's findings, but have not found them to be conclusive.

Part III

Preventive, Investigative, and Corrective Action

$L\!A\!S\!T$

DEVELOPING PREVENTIVE POLICIES

I. ELEMENTS OF AN EFFECTIVE SEXUAL HARASSMENT PROGRAM

A. Overview

The EEOC Guidelines state that employers must take all steps necessary to prevent sexual harassment (Appendix 1, EEOC Guidelines §1604.11(f)). To do this, employers should:

- express strong disapproval of harassment,
- develop methods to sensitize all concerned employees as to what constitutes sexual harassment,
- tell employees about their right to complain about sexual harassment through the company procedure,
- assure employees that complaints will be taken seriously and will be promptly and thoroughly investigated,
- assure employees that there will be no retaliation for lodging a complaint,
- develop appropriate sanctions, and
- take prompt corrective action when incidents occur.

Strong preventive and remedial action by an employer not only helps defend a claim of unlawful harassment and minimize the employer's liability, but also may prevent harassment in the first place. The more that employees are aware of their rights and are confident that disciplinary action will be taken against transgressors, the less likely it is that sexual harassment will occur.

B. Develop a Written Policy

Employers should develop a written policy that addresses sexual harassment, separate from and in addition to its general antidiscrimination policy (*Meritor Sav. Bank v. Vinson*). Because employees and supervisors may be confused about exactly what sexual harassment is, the policy should define it, with examples, so that employees do not mistakenly see offensive sexual conduct as simply misguided romantic overtures, harmless teasing, or practical joking (see the Sample Antiharassment Policy in Appendix 4).

C. Implement an Effective Complaint Procedure

Sexual harassment programs should identify an internal grievance procedure by which employees can report their complaints to management and have them investigated. Complainants who believe they will be treated fairly are more likely to pursue complaints internally and less likely to contact outside agencies or private attorneys. Resolving complaints internally is far less expensive than responding to a government investigation or defending a lawsuit. A policy that encourages early reporting and investigation of problems will place the employer in a better position to remedy the harm to the complainant. The prompt resolution of complaints not only will limit the scope of potential damages, but will also reduce the wider costs of sexual harassment that result from lowered morale, reduced productivity, increased absenteeism, and higher turnover rates.

1. Designating Where Employees Should File Their Complaints. The complaint procedure should specify the departments, positions, or individuals to receive sexual harassment complaints. The persons identified should be trained to follow an effective investigative procedure and should be authorized by top management to make any necessary inquiries. Whenever practical, to help ensure that sexual harassment complaints are treated like other allegations of misconduct, the designated recipient of complaints should be the same department or person ordinarily charged with investigating personnel-related matters. See Chapter 15, section II. for a discussion of selecting the investigator.

The complaint procedure should allow complainants to file complaints with at least one easily accessible person who is outside of their chain of command. It is unwise to give the complainant's immediate supervisor the exclusive responsibility for receiving reports and correcting harassment, because such a procedure would likely discourage reporting and diminish an employee's faith in the internal system—especially if the supervisor is the alleged harasser. Similar problems may befall a policy that requires complainants to go directly to upper management; lower-echelon women harassed by male supervisors could be less apt to report alleged harassment to the male president of a company if they felt awkward and intimidated.

2. Assuring Against Retaliation. Complainants should be assured that the employer forbids retaliation. Failure to protect complainants will subject the employer to claims of retaliation and discourage other employees from using the complaint procedure (see Chapter 6).

D. Communicate the Policy to All Employees

To make employees aware of the antiharassment policy and of its importance, the written policy should be distributed to each employee, either independently or with other employee materials, such as the employee handbook. Many employers collect written acknowledgments from employees as proof that the employer's policies have been disseminated, read, and understood.

E. Sensitize Concerned Persons

The written policy should be supplemented by personal meetings and written material. Training and education programs are also highly advisable to sensitize employees to sexual harassment concerns. It is generally advisable to conduct separate programs for supervisors and for nonsupervisory employees. Supervisors need to be reminded of their responsibilities and their duty to protect the company, and themselves, from legal liability; nonsupervisory employees need to be advised that they have the right and the responsibility to report unwelcome conduct as soon as it occurs.

These programs should inform participants, in detailed terms, of the kinds of conduct that may be viewed as sexual harassment, including:

- lewd or profane speech;
- sexually oriented verbal kidding, teasing, or jokes;
- subtle pressure for sexual activities;
- physical contact such as patting, pinching, or brushing against another's body; and
- the display of sexually suggestive objects, pictures, statements, or graffiti.

Training programs may be enhanced through the use of discussion groups involving male and female workers. Role-playing and dramatizations of sexual harassment situations are often more effective than simple lectures in sensitizing co-workers and supervisors to the nature of sexual harassment.*

The training also should impress upon supervisors and employees the economic consequences of sexual harassment—adverse effects on productivity, corporate reputation, and job turnover, and a supervisor's personal liability—in addition to the costs of investigation and litigation.

F. Investigate Thoroughly

Employees complaining of sexual harassment should be asked to write or help formulate a written claim. The interviewer should ensure that all of the facts are fairly and fully set forth in the complaint and that it includes any relevant detail

---

*Films on this subject are available for rental or purchase from BNA Communications, 9439 Key West Ave., Rockville, MD 20850, (301) 948-0540, and from other organizations.

or perception of the complainant. Written claims help the employer perform a thorough investigation. If litigation follows, it also may help to have a record of what was, and what was not, alleged in the original claim (see Chapters 15 and 17).

G. Take Prompt Corrective Action

The sexual harassment procedure should call for prompt and effective corrective action whenever a violation of company policy is found. This may require the employer to follow up to ensure that the remedial action is effective. If a finding of a violation warrants disciplinary action, the employer should advise the complainant that remedial action has been taken and that the complainant should report any further harassment immediately.

The procedure should further provide that, if after a full investigation sexual harassment is not found or no conclusion can be drawn, all parties will be notified of that fact and will be counseled that any future allegations of sexual harassment or retaliation should be promptly reported.

H. Assess Commitment to an Effective Program

The program should provide for regular monitoring to ensure that the program is understood by all employees and that it is being implemented by supervisors. The key to an effective sexual harassment policy is supervisor commitment. Making enforcement of an antiharassment program part of the supervisor's job performance evaluation is an effective method of ensuring this commitment. Performance factors that may be evaluated include:

(1) demonstrated commitment to the employer's equal opportunity and antiharassment objectives;
(2) avoiding the harassment of others;
(3) actions taken to prevent the harassment of employees by supervisors, co-workers, and nonemployees; and
(4) actions taken in response to complaints of sexual harassment.

Employee surveys and workplace audits can measure the workplace environment and create a more positive atmosphere. Employers can learn what employees believe is sexually harassing conduct, to what extent they understand the sexual harassment policies and procedures, and whether employees are aware of any sexual harassment within the company. This process will enable the employer to evaluate its policy's effectiveness and to modify training as needed. Such material, however, may be "discoverable" in litigation, where evidence that an employer learned of sexual harassment and failed to take corrective action would be very damaging.

II. REVIEWING RELATED POLICIES

A. Policies Involving Workplace Social Relationships

The law does not forbid all sexual relationships in the workplace or prohibit all types of sexual favoritism. Yet a consensual relationship between a supervisor and a subordinate can be a legitimate employer concern. These relationships can not only undermine efficiency and group morale but can lead to claims of favoritism by disadvantaged co-workers (see Chapter 4), and to claims of sexual harassment should there be discipline after the relationship ends (see Chapter 2, section III.).

To reduce the risk of these claims, some employers have imposed blanket prohibitions on relationships between supervisors and subordinates. Courts have upheld discipline resulting from the enforcement of these nonfraternization rules. To justify its nonfraternization policy, an employer can emphasize its intent to enforce its sexual harassment policy through this policy. An effective nonfraternization policy may also have the added benefit of encouraging earlier reporting of potentially harassing situations by subordinate employees receiving unwelcome invitations.

Nonfraternization rules, however, create problems of their own. The nature of an employer's work, or its corporate culture, may make such a policy untenable, as may legal or moral concerns about interfering with employees' nonworkplace conduct.

Moreover, if an employer prohibits such relationships, they may still exist covertly, and the clandestine nature of the relationship will mean that the employer lacks witnesses to the voluntary nature of the relationship.

Employers may wish to consider at least requiring that, when supervisors and subordinate employees do become romantically involved, they notify upper management and request a transfer of one of the parties so as to sever the supervisorial relationship. Under such a policy, an employer should not uniformly require the transfer of the lower-level or lower-paid employee. Typically these employees are women, and therefore the transfer policy itself could be challenged as unlawful sex discrimination. Employers may wish to permit the employees themselves to choose which of them will transfer.

B. "No-Spouse" Rules

An antinepotism policy prohibits the employment of relatives. A variation of the antinepotism policy, the "no-spouse" policy, may be adopted to combat co-worker complaints of unfair favoritism based on the sexual relationships between spouses. As long as the policy against hiring or continuing the employment of employees' spouses applies equally to male and female employees and does not have an adverse effect on women, it is lawful under federal law. Under no-spouse policies, employers may entirely ban the employment of married couples or may require that married couples work in different departments or otherwise have no supervisory relationship with each other. Employers should research the governing state law before implementing antinepotism policies, however, as many state statutes prohibit discrimination on the basis of marital status, and some of these laws are interpreted to ban or limit antinepotism rules.

C. Dress Codes

Concerns about sexual harassment also may influence an employer's dress code policy. Dress standards generally are not prohibited under Title VII. Employers can implement different dress standards for each sex, requiring men, but not women, to wear ties, and prohibiting women from wearing pantsuits in the executive office (*Fountain v. Safeway Stores; Lanigan v. Bartlett & Co.*). Employers may *not* impose dress codes that would cause an employee to be subjected to sexual harassment on the job, or that reflect offensive or demeaning sex stereotypes (see Chapter 3, section VI.C.1.).

15

CONDUCTING THE INTERNAL INVESTIGATION

I. THE EMPLOYER'S DUTY TO INVESTIGATE

An employer must investigate sexual harassment complaints to determine their merits and to fashion appropriate remedies. At the same time, an employer must be careful in responding to a harassment claim, because the response itself may lead to a claim by the alleged harasser (see Chapters 11; 13; and 16, section VI.).

The internal investigation is a crucial component of any effective antiharassment policy. An adequate investigation serves several important purposes. It can:

- identify instances of harassment,
- guide appropriate employment decisions regarding the harassment,
- protect the employer from liability for sexual harassment claims that the employer should have known about,
- identify a false charge of sexual harassment and protect the employer from liability for erroneous discipline,
- avoid or minimize employer liability,

- reduce the amount of any damages that may be obtained by the complainant,
- protect possible future victims of sexual harassment, and
- prevent any order of injunctive relief (see Chapter 21).

The duty to investigate arises as soon as evidence of sexual harassment becomes known to the employer. The duty exists regardless of whether a complaint arises formally, and even if the complainant has requested that the employer *not* investigate. An employer should never shirk its duty to investigate simply because an employee has said, "Don't worry about it." Even if no actual complaint is made, a court may find that an employer should have known about a sexually hostile environment, and therefore had a duty to investigate, if harassment is pervasive.

An employer increases its risk of liability by:

- telling the complainant not to let the offensive conduct bother her (*Katz v. Dole*),
- advising the complainant that an investigation of the complaint would harm her (*Waltman v. International Paper Co.*), or
- telling the complainant that she should expect improper sexual behavior while working with a predominantly male work force (*Continental Can Co. v. Minnesota*).

Even if a claim of sexual harassment appears to be prompted by the complainant's desire to forestall an anticipated disciplinary action, the wisest course is to investigate the claim seriously. Despite many employers' belief that some minimally responsive action, such as instructing the alleged harasser to steer clear of the complainant, will satisfy any responsibility to correct reported harassment, such a response is not an acceptable substitute for an investigation. An employer cannot simply hope or assume that acts of sexual harassment will not be repeated after a general instruction to "keep away." To avoid later liability, the employer must investigate to determine whether acts that would create an atmosphere of hostility did, in fact, occur (*Watts v. New York City Police Dep't*).

II. SELECTING THE INVESTIGATOR

A. Importance of the Investigator

The employer's choice of a person or persons to investigate claims of sexual harassment can determine whether the employer is later found to have an adequate antiharassment policy, and whether it took prompt and adequate steps to end the sexual harassment. Choosing the wrong investigator can discourage harassment victims from reporting meritorious claims, and may cause the employer to make a decision based on erroneous or incomplete information gleaned from an inadequate investigation.

The investigator's role is a demanding one. The most effective investigator has a high level of personal integrity, enjoys the respect and backing of both employees and upper-level management, is adept in the art of interviewing witnesses, and possesses both intellectual and interpersonal skills. The investigator must not appear to be an advocate for either the complainant or the alleged harasser; neutrality and objectivity in investigating and finding facts will enhance the credibility and effectiveness of the investigation. To achieve the best results, the investigator must understand the issues under investigation, have time to devote to the investigation, and be willing and able to get immersed in the details. The most effective investigators are tough enough to ask the hard questions and sensitive enough to gain the confidence necessary to draw out honest answers. An investigator with these qualities will be a credible and effective witness should the employer need to describe the investigation in a legal proceeding.

B. Providing Alternate Persons to Contact

Normally, sexual harassment policies allow the complainant either to contact persons up the chain of command or to contact a designated official in the human resources department. By providing a choice to employees, an employer encourages the reporting of sexual harassment claims.

Where the complainant is embarrassed by the unwelcome incident and is uncomfortable in the complaint process, the employer should consider using a qualified investigator who is of the same sex as the complainant if this is feasible and seems helpful.

C. Considering an Outside Investigator

In some cases, employers should consider retaining an independent fact finder. This option dispels any suspicion that an in-house investigator favored a more valued or higher-ranked employee or reflected the personal bias of the company employee who conducted the investigation.

D. Investigation by an Attorney

Employers should always consider whether to conduct the investigation under the protection of the attorney-client privilege and the attorney work product doctrine. Where an investigation is conducted by an attorney, the attorney-client privilege may keep the results of the investigation private and prevent the disclosure of poorly written, inaccurate, or incomplete investigative reports. (For a discussion of privileges, see section V. below.) On the other hand, investigation by an attorney can be very risky, because the employer may later have to prove the adequacy of its investigation and may be unable to prove the extent of the attorney's investigation without also waiving the attorney-client privilege covering sensitive legal advice given in connection with the investigation. An attorney often is most effective in the background, advising the investigator on the course and scope of inquiries and the legal consequences of the actions under consideration.

III. CONDUCTING THE INVESTIGATION

A. General Considerations

The thoroughness of the employer's investigation will be considered by courts in determining whether an employer took prompt corrective action reasonably calculated to end harassment.

Although it may be impossible to determine the truth of every allegation of sexual harassment, every investigation aims to determine certain basic facts:

- who the alleged harassers were,
- when and where the incident took place,
- precisely what was said or done by the parties,
- whether the incident was isolated or part of a continuing practice,
- the reaction of the complainant,
- how the complainant was affected,
- whether anyone else witnessed the incident,
- whether the complainant has talked to anyone else about the incident,
- whether there is any documentation of the incident, and
- whether the complainant has knowledge of any other target of harassment.

The law provides no hard-and-fast rule as to what constitutes a proper investigation. The adequacy of an investigation will be judged on the facts and circumstances of each situation. While the investigator should not be tied to a set procedure where circumstances warrant a variation, an employer can increase the likelihood that the investigation will be adequate by adopting and using a standard procedure for investigating complaints.

B. Interviewing the Complainant

When initially interviewing a complainant, the investigator should determine the facts outlined above. The complainant's statements should be put in writing. A copy of the complainant's statements should be made available to the complainant upon request.

If the complainant fails to cooperate, by withholding names and details, for example, this failure should be noted, for it bears on the reasonableness of the employer's response. While the employer cannot use the complainant's reticence as an excuse to do nothing, the employer obviously cannot investigate leads that only the complainant could provide and that the complainant chooses to withhold.

1. Advisories. The complainant should be assured that the employer will limit disclosure of the information obtained during the investigation to those persons who have a legitimate need to know. The complainant should be advised, however, that sexual harassment investigations almost always require that the identity of the complainant be revealed to the alleged harasser, and that it may be necessary to discuss the information with the alleged harasser and others. At the same time, the complainant should be assured that no retaliatory actions against the complainant will be tolerated.

2. Inquiries About the Harassing Conduct. Obtaining detailed descriptions of the alleged acts of harassment, including their nature and frequency, is crucial. The nuances of conversation and the circumstances of any physical contact may determine the issue of unwelcomeness. The questioning must explore in detail such matters as who said what, where the alleged incident occurred, for how long, and whether the complainant made efforts to terminate the sexual conduct. The questions also should seek the identity of all witnesses to the conduct. It may help to question the complainant about the alleged harasser's conduct toward male as well as female employees. If the alleged harasser was abusive to males and females alike, it is relevant to whether the offensive conduct was because of the complainant's sex.

3. Inquiries About the Effect on the Complainant's Employment. To be actionable sexual harassment, the conduct must affect the complainant's job. The investigation must address the relationship between the alleged harasser and the complainant, the nature of any sexual advances made, and whether the complainant contends that employment decisions were based upon her response to the alleged harassment. The investigator also needs to obtain the complainant's view of the accuracy of any adverse performance evaluations or criticisms of the complainant's job performance.

4. Inquiries About the Complainant's Conduct. It may be useful to explore the complainant's behavior toward the alleged harasser, such as sending gifts or notes or other conduct reflecting affectionate or friendly feelings. The complainant may claim that although there was initial consent to the conduct, the conduct continued after consent was withdrawn. Questions might focus on the method and manner by which the complainant communicated that the conduct was no longer welcome, and whether the offensive conduct ceased upon that request.

C. Interviewing the Alleged Harasser

The alleged harasser should be interviewed promptly. He may be surprisingly forthright, particularly if he thinks the behavior was trivial or misinterpreted. The investigator should advise the alleged harasser of the purpose of the investigation at the outset.

1. Advisories. The alleged harasser should be advised that:

- no conclusion has been reached regarding the investigation;
- the same rules of confidentiality that apply to the complainant apply to the alleged harasser;
- the employer requires truthful cooperation in the investigation, and forbids untruthful statements or attempts to interfere with the investigation; and
- retaliations against any complainant or witness are forbidden.

2. Inquiries About the Complainant's Allegations. The alleged harasser should be encouraged to disclose the times, places, and circumstances of each incident, as well as potential witnesses and documentation. If the alleged harasser asserts that the complainant had a motive to lie, the factual basis for this opinion should be fully explored. If the alleged harasser claims that the conduct was welcomed, all supporting facts should be obtained. The alleged harasser should be given harassment allegations in enough detail to be able to respond fully, and should be required to confirm or deny each specific charge.

D. Additional Interviews

In order to obtain a full picture of the claim, it is often necessary to interview potential third-party witnesses. Indeed, in some circumstances it is desirable to interview third-party witnesses before interviewing the alleged harasser. Unless the employer is confident that it knows what happened, all persons identified either by the complainant or by the alleged harasser as possibly having knowledge of the facts should be interviewed. Further, a party or witness may need to be reinterviewed to obtain a response to observations by another witness. It is generally useful to document all interviews with the complainant, the alleged harasser, and all significant witnesses.

All parties should have a full opportunity to rebut adverse statements. The investigator should consider sharing tentative determinations about the truth of a harassment claim with the alleged harasser in a final interview.

E. Reaching a Conclusion

In reaching a conclusion, the investigator needs to focus on whether the disclosed facts were based on firsthand knowledge. The investigator must also assess the parties' motives to lie or embellish, and assess the credibility of all persons interviewed. In one case, liability was found in an action brought by a person disciplined for sexual harassment where the decisionmaker failed to distinguish between information that was based on relatively reliable sources, such as firsthand knowledge and attributed hearsay, and information that was based on less reliable sources, such as gossip and rumor (*Kestenbaum v. Pennzoil Co.*).

IV. RECORDING THE INVESTIGATION

An important decision for the employer is whether to keep a written record of the investigation. Creating a complete and accurate record can illustrate that the employer took prompt and appropriate action. A record that is incomplete or inaccurate, however, may undermine the adequacy of the investigation and taint the employer's response to a sexual harassment claim.

On balance, it is generally wise to maintain a written record of all thorough investigations. If an employer finds that sexual harassment has occurred and takes responsive disciplinary action, the employer should record the investigation and witness statements in case the alleged harasser challenges the action taken. Similarly, if an employer finds insufficient evidence of harassment and thus no grounds for discipline, the employer's defense to any sexual harassment suit by the complainant will require full access to the statements of all witnesses to show that its decision was well-founded.

A record creates the additional issue of whether the investigative record will have to be made available to adverse parties in litigation. Employers may wish to consult legal counsel about these issues before undertaking any investigation.

The investigative materials typically are kept in a separate file, perhaps in the offices of the corporate or outside counsel, while copies of the investigation results are kept in the personnel files of the complainant and of the alleged harasser.

V. PROTECTING INVESTIGATION MATERIALS FROM DISCLOSURE

Investigations of sexual harassment complaints create communications and accumulate documents that may become "discoverable" by adverse parties in litigation. Legal privileges, discussed below, may protect the investigative materials from disclosure. Nonetheless, the employer may choose to disclose otherwise privileged information as proof that an extensive investigation was undertaken and therefore waive any privilege. It is important to remember that the privileges discussed below are general concepts, and their application is not necessarily clear-cut; the rules can be challenged by either side when they are applied to specific cases.

A. Attorney-Client Privilege

Communications between a corporate employer's employees and its legal counsel are protected by the attorney-client privilege if the communications are used to secure legal advice for the corporation (*Upjohn Co. v. United States*). In determining the extent to which internal sexual harassment investigations come under the attorney-client privilege, two issues cause the most problems. The first is whether the attorney-client privilege exists between the attorney and the employees he or she interviews. In order for the interview to be privileged, not only must the person requesting the information be an attorney, but the employee must be sufficiently high up in the company that he or she is, in effect, the "voice of the corporation" on the subject matter in question.

The second problem is that neither the attorney-client privilege nor the work product doctrine (discussed below) provides protection when the attorney is acting solely as a *business* advisor or investigator rather than as a *legal* advisor. The attorney-client privilege provides protection only when the attorney is in the process of providing *legal* advice.

B. Work Product Immunity

This doctrine gives *absolute* protection from disclosure of any documentation of the attorney's thoughts, conclusions, opinions, and legal theories prepared *in anticipation of litigation*. The work product doctrine gives a *qualified* protection to certain other materials, such as interpretive notes of witness interviews, so long as they have been prepared in anticipation of litigation.

Litigation may be anticipated before the filing of a lawsuit, and even before the filing of an administrative charge. On the other hand, if the investigation is conducted simply as an ordinary business practice or for business purposes—such as fostering employee relations, identifying potential personnel problems, or determining whether disciplinary action should be taken—work product protection may not apply.

Where a qualified work product privilege applies, documents need be disclosed only if the party seeking disclosure proves a substantial need for the documents and an inability to obtain the substantial equivalent by other means. Where the complainant can conduct an investigation parallel to that of the employer, no compelling need overcomes the work product privilege. Courts have found a compelling need, however, where witnesses interviewed by the complainant can no longer remember information given in earlier statements to the employer (*EEOC v. General Motors Corp.*).

VI. PROTECTION AGAINST A CLAIM OF DEFAMATION ARISING FROM THE INVESTIGATION

A. General Cautionary Instructions

An investigator should seek to protect the reputations of both the complainant and the alleged harasser in order to avoid potential liability for defamation on the part of the investigator, the witnesses, and the parties directly involved (see Chapter 11). The investigator should limit access to the investigative files to those persons with a clearly established "need to know." Each witness interviewed should be admonished not to discuss the matter with others, and should be informed of the risk of defamation if the incident were to be discussed outside the confines of the investigation.

Emphasizing the need for truthfulness and confidentiality should not result in intimidating the complainant or the supporting witnesses. Also, principals and witnesses should not be told that their statements will be kept "off the record." Complete confidentiality can never be assured, and a written record of the recollection of witnesses may be essential.

B. Defenses to a Defamation Claim

1. Truth. The truth of statements is an absolute defense against a claim of defamation in most states. In some states, however, truth is not an absolute defense where the statements are published for malicious reasons or for unjustifiable ends.

2. Qualified Privilege. A qualified privilege, a valid defense against a suit under certain conditions, generally exists where the information is given to persons who have a "need to know." Abuse of the privilege can occur where:

- the speaker acts with reckless disregard as to the falsity of the defamatory statements;

- the statements are published for reasons other than those intended to be protected, such as malice or ill will;
- there is excessive publication beyond those with a "need to know"; or
- the speaker does not reasonably believe that the statement is necessary to accomplish the purpose of the privilege.

To avoid arguments that it has abused a qualified privilege, the employer should not disclose information about an alleged instance of sexual harassment to anyone until the applicable law has been consulted.

a. During the Investigation. Allegations of sexual harassment inevitably must be shared to some extent during the investigation of the charge. Statements made during investigations may be protected by a qualified privilege. Although the law varies from state to state, the qualified privilege generally protects company investigators and witnesses who make statements, even if false, in good faith and for a proper purpose, to one with a legitimate interest in or duty to receive the information. Statements that are not made for good cause but are made maliciously or recklessly can result in the loss of the privilege.

b. After the Investigation. An employer sometimes may want to communicate that it has enforced its policy against sexual harassment in order to acquaint employees with the potential consequences of failure to abide by the policy. In many states, an employer may have a qualified privilege to report investigation results in a way that is calculated either to deter further harassment, to inform any complainants that their rights have been adequately addressed, or to emphasize a company policy to the entire work force (*Garziano v. E.I. du Pont de Nemours & Co.*). "Making an example" of a disciplined employee for an offense as potentially serious as sexual harassment is a temptation many employers wisely avoid.

3. Absolute Privilege. Alleged harassers have sued their co-workers for defamatory remarks made during their testimony at administrative hearings or in court. These statements, however, are usually absolutely privileged and thus will not result in liability. The purpose behind granting this privilege is to encourage witnesses in official proceedings to give information without fear of reprisal.

2ND

16

TAKING PROMPT CORRECTIVE ACTION

I. INTERIM CORRECTIVE ACTION

An employer may minimize the risk of liability by taking temporary measures to prevent serious harassment from recurring during the course of its investigation. Interim measures include temporary transfers and placing the alleged harasser on a nondisciplinary leave of absence (generally with pay). A failure to take interim action may result in employer liability, particularly if easily and immediately available action would have protected the complainant from continued and serious harassment.

II. RESPONDING TO THE INVESTIGATION

At the conclusion of the investigation, the results should be communicated to all involved parties, including the alleged harasser. The employer should be mindful of potential liability for defamation when disseminating information about *specific* sexual harassment allegations, and should not give information to anyone who has no "need to know" (see Chapter 15, section VI.).

III. WHERE THE EMPLOYER CANNOT DETERMINE WHETHER SEXUAL HARASSMENT HAS OCCURRED

Where factual accounts differ, the employer should not reflexively credit either the alleged harasser or the complainant, but should consider facts relevant to the disputants' credibility, such as their reputations, their motives to fabricate, and the observations of other employees.

If the employer cannot determine whether sexual harassment has occurred, it should advise the parties in a neutral manner that no conclusion was reached. A thorough investigation leading to no conclusion may preclude liability even if it later turns out that sexual harassment, in fact, occurred.

The complainant should be assured that the employer intends to protect the complainant and all employees against unlawful harassment and reprisal, and that any future instance of harassment should be promptly reported. The alleged harasser should be advised that although the truth of the claim has not been determined, all employees are expected to comply with the employer's policy against sexual harassment and retaliation. In addition, the employer may take the opportunity to review its sexual harassment policy and complaint procedures in light of the claim and investigation to ensure effectiveness and accessibility. The employer also may wish to communicate its policies again to its general work force or to the affected department or individuals to ensure that no misunderstanding flows from its failure to act in the individual case.

The employer also may consider the feasibility and "balance of hardships" of transfers or reassignments of work to prevent future contact between the complainant and the alleged harasser.

IV. WHERE THE EMPLOYER DETERMINES THAT FALSE REPORTING HAS OCCURRED

If the investigator determines that the report of the alleged harassment was a deliberate falsehood designed to damage the standing of another company employee, the employer must decide what, if any, disciplinary action should be taken against the complainant.

A. The Internal Investigation

Employers considering disciplinary action against complainants for false internal reports must distinguish between instances where the employee knowingly makes a false report and one in which there is an honest difference of interpretation of the incident that gave rise to the claim. An honest difference in perception should not warrant any disciplinary action. Under those circumstances, the complainant may be protected from any form of discipline by both federal and state statutes that prohibit retaliation for the filing of a claim, participating as a witness, or opposing a practice made unlawful by a state FEP statute (see Chapter 6).

Where the employer concludes that a sexual harassment claim was made in bad faith, however, the employer generally should apply the same level of disciplinary action against the complainant as it would for similar forms of dishonesty. The employer's record of similar disciplinary actions for other forms of dishonesty would be relevant in any claim of retaliation.

B. The Agency Investigation

An employer should refrain from any disciplinary action against a complainant for filing a charge with the EEOC or a state FEP agency. Statements made during agency investigations may be protected under federal and state law, even if they are deliberately false (see Chapter 6).

C. Defamation Actions Against the Complainant

Either the employer or the alleged harasser may want to bring a defamation action against a complainant who has made a false claim of sexual harassment. This option, while not necessarily unlawful, must be approached with caution, inasmuch as it may be prohibited by the antiretaliation provisions of federal and state laws. Defamation issues are discussed in Chapter

11, section V.; and retaliation issues covering defamation are discussed in Chapter 6, section IV.D.

V. WHERE THE EMPLOYER DETERMINES THAT SEXUAL HARASSMENT HAS OCCURRED

A. Ensuring That Discipline Is Adequate

If the employer determines that harassment has occurred, it must promptly sanction the alleged harasser, no matter how minor the infraction, and advise the complainant that action has been taken. It is important—both during the investigation and afterward—to ensure that the complainant does not take hasty action, such as quitting and filing a legal action. Possibilities include offering the complainant some time off with pay, offering to pay for counseling, and urging the complainant not to quit.

The employer must select disciplinary action appropriate under the circumstances, designed to ensure that the harassment will not recur. Several factors should guide that selection:

(1) the severity of the conduct;
(2) the pervasiveness of the conduct;
(3) the harasser's overall record of employment and employment history;
(4) the complainant's employment history;
(5) the notice that the harasser had of the employer's policy prohibiting sexual harassment;
(6) the discipline imposed for previous cases of sexual harassment and for violations of other company policies;
(7) the effectiveness of any initial remedial steps; and
(8) other company policies, such as any progressive discipline policy.

The discipline itself may range from an oral warning to discharge. In determining the appropriate sanction, it may be helpful to ask the complainant whether the employer can do anything more to assist in keeping the complainant's work environment free of harassment.

Employers who carefully document all steps taken in determining the correct level of discipline are best able to defend against either a discrimination or wrongful discharge suit (see section VI. below), or a grievance filed in opposition to the discipline (see Chapter 13). Documentation could include written acknowledgment of the company's policy from each employee involved, which could be placed in the employee's personnel file at the conclusion of the investigation.

The discipline imposed must be calculated to deter future harassment. Regardless of the extent to which discipline is imposed, the employer must follow through to ensure that the situation has been remedied and that the complainant has not been subjected to any type of retaliation. If the remedy imposed by the employer proves effective, then the employer is much less likely to be held liable for sexual harassment. If discipline is not initially effective, employers should impose harsher sanctions to ensure effectiveness.

B. Types of Disciplinary Action

Disciplinary actions can be imposed individually, sequentially (if a more moderate penalty is not effective, as in any instance of progressive discipline), or in combination. Thus, for example, an employer could impose an oral warning together with a transfer.

1. Oral and Written Warnings. Where the misconduct was minor, an oral warning may suffice. In *Barrett v. Omaha National Bank,* the employer avoided liability when it immediately investigated claims and, within four days of the report of unlawful harassment, reprimanded the alleged harassers, informed them that their conduct would not be tolerated, and told one of them that he would be fired for any further misconduct.

The employer should remind all involved employees about its policy prohibiting sexual harassment, tell them what activities constitute sexual harassment, and warn them that violation of the employer's policy may result in more severe disciplinary action, up to and including discharge. The employer should keep a record of the oral warning in the alleged harasser's personnel file, as well as in the investigative file. This notation should also specify who was present during the warning and what specifically was said to the alleged harasser. In general, a written reprimand is preferable to an oral one, for it creates in itself a record of the employer's action.

Simply admonishing employees to act more professionally, telling them to cease horseplay, or reminding them of company rules prohibiting harassment or abusive language will not necessarily insulate an employer from liability. The warnings should reprimand the alleged harasser and state that further harassment will result in further discipline.

If an employer knows that a warning has not deterred further harassment, it must increase the severity of the discipline. Progressive oral and written warnings will be insufficient where the harassing conduct is pervasive and repeated.

2. Transfers, Reassignments, and Restructuring the Workplace. Transfers, reassignments, and restructuring the work environment are other possible intermediate steps in the disciplinary process.

Of course, these measures should be handled in such a way that the complainant is not left worse off than before bringing the meritorious complaint. Transferring a vindicated complainant, instead of the harasser, to a less desirable position is thus inappropriate. A remedy that changes such a complainant's hours of work to less desirable hours or to a less desirable location is also unfair. In *College-Town v. Massachusetts Commission Against Discrimination,* the complainant was offered a transfer to another facility and then was dismissed when she failed to accept the transfer. The court found the dismissal to be retaliatory, faulting the employer for moving the complainant while failing to consider moving the supervisor.

3. Suspensions and Demotions. Suspensions and demotions are disciplinary options that may allow employers to deter future harassment, protect the dignity and security of the complainant, educate the work force, and "rehabilitate" an offending employee who is otherwise valuable.

Suspensions and demotions have consistently been upheld where the employer can prove that the disciplined employee actually harassed a co-worker. In *Spencer v. General Electric Co.*, a supervisor was demoted from a management position to a production position following an investigation of alleged sexual harassment, but his pay was not reduced and he received his next yearly raise without incident. Facts discovered thereafter revealed that he had lied when he denied having consensual relations with other female employees. He then was asked to resign. The reviewing court concluded that the employer had taken appropriate remedial steps.

Demotion may not be appropriate if it allows the harasser to continue working with the complainant. In *Department of Fair Employment and Housing v. Madera County*, the harasser initially was dismissed for his explicit sexual advances toward a female subordinate, but won reinstatement in a civil service commission appeal. Upon his return to the workplace, the harasser continued to bother the complainant. Although aware of the continued harassment, the employer, believing its hands tied by the order of reinstatement, did no more than issue a warning. The complainant eventually quit because of emotional distress and recovered substantial damages in her employment discrimination suit.

Madera County illustrates the need to use more severe discipline when intermediate sanctions fail to deter harassment. Consequently, employers, in considering disciplinary actions short of discharge, should consider not only the length of prior employment, the severity of the conduct that led to the complaint, and any prior disciplinary actions, but also the overall effectiveness of the disciplinary action in deterring repeated harassment.

4. Other Forms of Corrective Action. An employer can also delay planned promotions and salary increases, instruct the harasser to seek counseling or sensitivity training, tell the harasser to limit contact with employees to official company business, or terminate the harasser's access to certain company facilities.

5. Discharge. Many complaints of sexual harassment lead to the dismissal of the alleged harasser. In the unionized setting, dismissals on this basis have been met with mixed acceptance by labor arbitrators. In a number of decisions, arbitrators have converted "improper" discharges for sexual harassment into lengthy suspensions without pay, generally running from the original termination date to the date of the arbitrator's decision. Still, a substantial number of arbitrators have upheld dismissals for acts ranging from oral harassment to the exposing of genitalia (see Chapter 13).

Before dismissing an alleged harasser, an employer should attempt to ensure not only that the investigation was adequate, but that the discipline is not excessive and that the results are not too broadly disseminated.

VI. CHALLENGES TO DISCIPLINE

Discipline of the alleged harasser must take into account the potential legal claims that the disciplined employee may bring. Unemployment compensation claims are discussed in Chapter 9, section II.

A. Common-Law Claims by the Alleged Harasser

1. Defamation. A false complaint of sexual harassment may lead to a defamation suit by the alleged harasser. The alleged harasser also could base defamation claims on the statements of any witness who supplied exaggerated details concerning the events or the discipline imposed on the alleged harasser. However, at least one court has said that defamation claims cannot be based on intra-corporate communications among corporate officers (*Halsell v. Kimberly-Clark Corp.*). The defenses and privileges applicable to a defamation claim are discussed in Chapter 15, section VI.

2. Breach of Contract. To recover for a breach of contract, the harasser must show there was an employment contract that restricted the employer's right of discipline *and* that the discipline imposed was a breach of that contract.

Many states have permitted employees to challenge discharges on the theory that under the circumstances there was an implied contract, even if not stated in writing, that required "good cause" for discharge. In challenging good cause, the alleged harasser may emphasize mitigating circumstances, such as his prior work and disciplinary record, and any evidence that management may have condoned or contributed to the sexual harassment. Severe or repeated sexual harassment will often qualify as "good cause" for dismissal.

3. Breach of Implied Covenant. In cases alleging breach of the implied covenant of good faith and fair dealing, a key issue is the adequacy of the employer's investigation. In *Johnson v. International Minerals & Chemical Corp.*, three supervisors allegedly forcibly kissed an fondled the complainants, pinched their breasts, and made lewd remarks. After the complainants filed administrative charges, the employer settled their claims and then independently investigated the allegations and discharged the alleged harassers. In denying the alleged harassers' claim, the court held that the employer acted in good faith when it conducted a thorough investigation of the sexual harassment and sex discrimination charges against the supervisors before making a final decision to discharge them.

B. Discrimination Claims by the Alleged Harasser

To defend a discrimination claim by an alleged harasser, the employer must be able to substantiate the sexual harassment allegations and to demonstrate that employees who engaged in similar misconduct were subject to similar discipline. Employees have challenged their discipline for sexual harassment by alleging that it was a pretext for discrimination on the basis of a forbidden factor, such as race or gender. A black employee fired for sexually harassing white women was awarded damages for race discrimination where white men charged with more serious misconduct were not fired (*Marsh v. Digital Equip. Corp.*).

C. Claims by Government Employees

Government employees disciplined for sexual harassment may assert violations of "procedural due process"—*i.e.*, that they did not get a notice of the charges and a fair chance to tell their side of the story (see Chapter 8 for discussion of this legal theory). In *Huff v. County of Butler*, where an employee accused of sexual harassment was forced to resign without a hearing, the court said he had a valid suit for deprivation of liberty (here, the liberty to have a job) without due process, even though the employee had no property interest in his job because he was an at-will employee. In another case where an alleged harasser was discharged during a one-year employment contract, the court held that a midterm discharge without a prior hearing deprived the employee of both property and liberty interests without due process (*Vanelli v. Reynolds School Dist.*).

Federal employees subject to civil service protection may challenge discipline for sexual harassment through the Merit Systems Protection Board (MSPB).

17

THE AGENCY INVESTIGATION

Readers responding to administrative agency investigations should be generally familiar with how these investigations proceed. The description here applies primarily to Title VII investigations conducted by the EEOC, but applies generally to state FEP investigations as well.

I. PROCEDURAL PREREQUISITES TO A TITLE VII ACTION

A. Filing a Timely Administrative Charge

1. Untimely Charge. A prerequisite to suit under Title VII and many state FEP statutes is the exhaustion of administrative remedies. This process includes filing a timely administrative charge. In most states, the state FEP agency and the EEOC have agreed that a charge of discrimination filed with the EEOC is automatically simultaneously filed with the state FEP agency. Most agencies investigate only those charges that are filed directly with them.

A charge of discrimination under Title VII must be filed with the EEOC within 180 days of the alleged unlawful employment practice. In "deferral" states, in which the complainant must initially proceed with a state FEP agency, the time period for filing with the EEOC is extended to 300 days. In most deferral states, the state-EEOC agreement results in simultaneous filing.

These strict time limits for filing a charge may be relaxed or tolled under special circumstances, such as when the employee has been misled by the employer, or when there was a continuing violation.

Sexual harassment cases sometimes raise special issues concerning when the alleged unlawful employment practice occurred, and thus when the limitations period begins to run. The general principle is that the filing period starts when the discriminatory acts occur, not when the consequences of the acts become most painful (*Delaware State College v. Ricks*).

The complainant's perception of when the discrimination began is often important in determining timeliness, yet the date on which sexual harassment first occurred may be hard to identify. Welcome conduct at some point may become unwelcome, and trivial conduct may at some point become severe or pervasive. Moreover, incidents that collectively constitute a hostile environment are not routinely recorded in business records as are the promotions, discharges, or pay changes that are involved in more traditional Title VII cases.

In a quid pro quo case, the timeliness issue is complicated if the tangible job detriment does not closely follow the unwelcome sexual advances. In *Weide v. Mass Transit Administration*, a complainant filed a charge of sexual harassment within 300 days of a negative performance evaluation from a supervisor who allegedly had made an unwelcome sexual advance years earlier. Although the charge was filed more than 300 days after the sexual advance, the court found the charge to be timely because the filing was within 300 days of the negative evaluation, which allegedly was in retaliation for the complainant's rejection of the sexual advance.

Under the continuing violation theory, if the harassing conduct was part of a pattern of conduct that began outside of the charge-filing period (before 180 or 300 days of the filing) and continued into that period, the charge may include the entire history of harassment.

For an extensive discussion of timeliness, including the subject of amended charges, tolling of the limitation period, and continuing violations, see B. Lindemann Schlei & P. Grossman, *Employment Discrimination Law* (BNA Books), Chapter 28.

2. Filing an Adequate Charge. An administrative charge under federal law and in most states must state the facts constituting the alleged sexual harassment, identify the parties charged, and state when the alleged harassment occurred. A later court action generally cannot include facts or issues that do not relate to and grow out of the subject matter of the original charge. However, EEOC charges are construed liberally. The complainant need not specify details in the charge so long as the parties and the nature of the sexual harassment allegations are identified.

Generally, an individual must be named in the administrative charge to be named as a defendant in a later court lawsuit. Courts, however, have often permitted a complainant to sue a previously unnamed individual. For an extensive discussion of this issue, see B. Lindemann & D. Kadue, *Sexual Harassment in Employment Law* (BNA Books), Chapter 27.

3. Conciliation. The EEOC cannot sue unless it first finds reasonable cause to believe that Title VII has been violated and then exhausts reasonable efforts to resolve the violation through conciliation. Where conciliation fails, the EEOC must so notify the respondent in writing.

4. Right-to-Sue Letter. An individual complainant may sue once a right-to-sue letter is received, even if the EEOC has not found reasonable cause to believe that discrimination has occurred, and even if there has been no effort to conciliate.

B. Filing a Timely Complaint in Court

A Title VII lawsuit against a private employer is timely if filed within 90 days of the complainant's receipt of a right-to-sue letter. The 90-day period runs from the complainant's actual receipt of notice. This period, like the period for filing an EEOC charge, is subject to the doctrine of "equitable tolling."

The Supreme Court in *Baldwin County Welcome Center v. Brown* indicated that equitable tolling may occur where:

(1) the complainant has received inadequate notice of her rights;
(2) the complainant has been misled into believing that she had fulfilled all procedural requirements;
(3) the defendant, through affirmative misconduct, lulled the complainant into inaction; or
(4) the complainant's motion for appointment of counsel is still pending.

II. THE CHARGE-FILING PROCESS

To file a charge of discrimination, a complainant usually fills out a questionnaire, supplied by the agency, identifying the employer and the alleged harasser, describing the circumstances of the alleged sexual harassment, and identifying any witnesses and any other victims. The agency investigator will then meet with the complainant to discuss the allegations.

The investigator will examine the information to determine if the charge is timely (see section I. above).

The investigator will draft the formal charge from the information given by the complainant. The charge will contain the name and address of the parties, the date of the alleged harassment, and a short statement of the harassment alleged, including the harm suffered by the complainant. The charge must be in writing, under oath or affirmation. The procedure by which an agency investigator works with a complainant to file a charge is called the "intake process."

III. THE INVESTIGATION

A. The Respondent's Position Statement

The investigation begins with the service of the charge on the respondent (usually the employer, although unions, employment agencies, and apprenticeship training programs can also be respondents). Title VII requires that a respondent be given notice, within ten days, that a charge has been filed. Service of the charge will usually be accompanied by a request that the respondent provide a position statement setting forth its response to the allegations of the charge.

The position statement is vital to the respondent's defense of a sexual harassment charge. Determinations that the charge is meritorious are termed "reasonable cause" findings; determinations that the charge is without merit are termed "no-cause" findings. If thoughtfully prepared and persuasive, the position statement may form the basis for a no-cause finding, and the agency's role in the dispute will be finished. An inaccurate or incomplete position statement, however, can lead to a reasonable cause finding. If the agency finds reasonable cause to believe that sexual harassment has occurred, and efforts at conciliation fail, the position statement will be included in the materials submitted to the general counsel and commissioners when the decision of whether to litigate is made. If the agency decides not to litigate, the position statement will be available to the plaintiff's attorney both in determining whether to commence private litigation and in preparing for trial.

The position statement should contain a narrative statement of the facts, describe the respondent's sexual harassment policy, and should detail any steps taken under that policy to respond to the complainant's allegations. The position statement should clarify the relationship of the alleged harasser to the complainant—*i.e.*, whether the alleged harasser is a supervisor or coworker. The respondent should include in the position statement all relevant facts that help demonstrate that no unwelcome sexual advances occurred.

Major factual statements should be supported by documents, wherever possible. Where no documents exist, the employer may wish to consider providing declarations of the key witnesses attesting to the truth and accuracy of the position statement. Sexual harassment cases depend heavily upon credibility. The employer can increase its chances of prevailing if it can demonstrate that one or more of the complainant's assertions is contradicted by demonstrable facts.

B. Requests for Information

The investigator may send a written request for information (RFI) to the respondent. Examples of information typically sought in a sexual harassment RFI include:

- a copy of any existing policy on sexual harassment, including the procedure by which an employee may complain;
- a description of how employees are informed of the policy;
- a description of management training on how to handle sexual harassment;
- the personnel files of the charging party, the alleged harasser, and of other employees who have complained of sexual harassment;
- a description of any action taken in response to the charging party's complaint; and
- the name and sex of other employees working under the supervision of the alleged harasser.

In quid pro quo cases where the complainant alleges that there were employment-related consequences to resisting sexual advances, the investigator will request documentation of the relevant employment decisions.

C. Witness Interviews

Witness statements are critical to any employment discrimination investigation, but they are particularly important in cases of sexual harassment, due to the credibility issues so common to these charges. The complainant's statement will be taken at the start of the intake process. Witnesses identified by the complainant may be interviewed by the agency investigator as soon as they can be located. The respondent's witnesses typically are interviewed at the work site, with the employer's cooperation. While the respondent's attorney may attend the interview of management officials, the investigator generally will conduct interviews of nonmanagement employees only in private.

If the employer fails to respond to an RFI or refuses to allow the investigator to interview necessary witnesses, the agency may issue an administrative subpoena, which can be enforced in court.

D. Resolution of the Charge

When the investigator has obtained sufficient evidence to determine whether the charge has merit, he or she may conduct a "predetermination interview" with whichever party is not expected to prevail in the determination. During this interview, the investigator will review the evidence obtained, inform the party of the proposed determination, and invite the submission of additional evidence.

At the conclusion of the investigation, the agency will issue its determination. Title VII directs the EEOC to determine whether there is reasonable cause to believe that the charge is true. These determinations are sometimes admitted at trial.

If the EEOC renders a probable cause finding, Title VII requires that the agency attempt to resolve the matter informally by conciliation. A typical conciliation of a sexual harassment charge will require the employer to institute or reaffirm a sexual harassment policy, give relief to the complainant and any other victims, and discipline the harasser. If conciliation fails, the EEOC may file suit or issue a right-to-sue letter to the charging party. The charging party may file suit within 90 days of receipt of this notice.

IV. INVESTIGATORY ISSUES IN SEXUAL HARASSMENT CHARGES

The EEOC has provided the following guidance on investigative issues posed by sexual harassment charges (see Appendix 3, Policy Guidance on Sexual Harassment).

A. Unwelcome Nature of the Conduct

Investigators must determine unwelcomeness from the totality of the circumstances. When unwelcomeness is at issue, evidence of contemporaneous protest is particularly persuasive. Protest is not a necessary element of a claim, for victims reasonably may fear reprisal in some circumstances. If there was no protest, however, the investigator must try to find out why the victim did not complain at the time of the alleged harassment.

B. The Complainant's Relationship to the Alleged Harasser

Whether the employer is responsible for sexual harassment may depend on whether the alleged harasser was a supervisory employee, a co-worker, or a nonemployee. In quid pro quo cases, an employer is automatically liable for harassment by a supervisor. In hostile environment cases, the investigator must determine whether the employer knew or should have known of the alleged sexual harassment and whether it took prompt corrective action. The investigator will ask whether the complainant or others made contemporaneous reports of harassment, or if a management employee knew or should have known of the alleged conduct (see Chapter 3, section VI.).

C. Determination of Hostile Environment

In a hostile environment case, the EEOC uses the "reasonable person" standard to see if the harassment is severe or pervasive enough to violate Title VII. Under this standard, a hostile environment generally is created by a pattern of offensive conduct. While one incident usually will not suffice unless it is egregious, a single instance of unwelcome, intentional touching of a charging party's intimate body areas may itself create a hostile environment.

In evaluating allegations of verbal harassment, the EEOC investigator will determine the nature, frequency, context, and intended target of the remarks. The investigator will consider whether the alleged harasser singled out the complainant, whether the complainant participated in the exchange, the relationship between the complainant and the alleged harasser, and whether the remarks were hostile and derogatory (see Chapter 3, section IV.).

D. The Respondent's Internal Response to the Complaint

If the employer asserts that its internal response to an informal complaint remedied the situation, the investigator will determine whether the employer conducted a prompt and thorough investigation of the allegations and whether, if warranted, the employer took prompt and appropriate corrective action. The investigator will ask what steps were taken, when they were taken, and whether the steps fully remedied the conduct without adversely affecting the complainant's employment status.

If it finds that the harassment has been eliminated, the appropriate remedies were applied, and measures were taken to prevent future problems, the EEOC generally will close the case.

Part IV

Special Litigation Issues

18

THE DEFENSE LITIGATION STRATEGY

This chapter contains an overview of the tactical concerns of defense attorneys. The subjects covered are (1) new judicial interpretations enabling employers to negotiate for jury-free resolutions of employment disputes, (2) initial tactics in response to a sexual harassment lawsuit, (3) the deposition of the complainant, (4) the use of expert witnesses, (5) the defense of both the corporate employer and individual defendants, and (6) anticipating the complainant's strategy.

I. NEGOTIATING INDIVIDUAL AGREEMENTS TO ARBITRATE

Just as an employer and a union may bargain collectively to arbitrate employment disputes, an employer may reach such an agreement with individual, unorganized employees. Both parties may prefer arbitration over court litigation, because arbitration is quicker and cheaper. Employers especially may favor arbitration as an alternative to a jury trial.

The enforceability of agreements to arbitrate is not yet fully established. Employers seeking to enforce individual agreements to arbitrate have cited the Federal Arbitration Act (FAA), which requires enforcement of written agreements to arbitrate transactions involving interstate commerce, even as to most statutory claims. The Supreme Court in *Gilmer v. Interstate/Johnson Lane Corp.* ruled that an age discrimination claim can be subject to compulsory arbitration under the FAA, at least when arbitration is called for by an agreement separate from a formal employment agreement. Cases following *Gilmer* have enforced agreements to arbitrate sexual harassment claims asserted under Title VII and state FEP statutes.

There is still a question as to whether the FAA covers arbitration agreements that appear in employment contracts. The question arises because the FAA expressly excludes from coverage the "contracts of employment of seamen, railroad employees or any other class of workers engaged in foreign or interstate commerce." Some courts say that this exclusion applies only to transportation workers; others interpret the exclusion to cover virtually any employment contract. The Supreme Court has yet to decide the issue. In an attempt to finesse this issue, many employers have proposed free-standing arbitration agreements by which the employer and an employee agree to arbitrate all disputes regardless of whether they are employment related.

Many state statutes authorize the enforcement of arbitration agreements even if they are in employment agreements. Thus, even if the FAA does not apply, employers can seek to enforce arbitration agreements under state law. The agreements should bar a court lawsuit to assert a state-law claim even if they do not bar a federal claim.

II. CORRECTIVE ACTION AFTER LITIGATION

A. Unconditional Offer of Reinstatement

In a discharge or constructive (forced-quit) discharge case, the employer may be able to limit any economic damages by making the complainant an unconditional offer of reinstatement. The Supreme Court has held in a sex discrimination case that an unreasonable rejection of the employer's unconditional "good faith" offer of reinstatement, to a position "substantially equivalent" to the plaintiff's former position, ends the accrual of any back-pay liability (*Ford Motor Co. v. EEOC*).

An unconditional offer of reinstatement obviously could undercut the employer's case if the employer contends that the complainant was discharged for misconduct or poor work performance. In that case, the offer would indicate that the reasons for discharge were only excuses, because the employer would be offering to take back an employee it previously claimed was not fit to work for it. In a constructive discharge case, however, an unconditional offer of reinstatement can often be effective, for the employer's desire to reemploy the complainant can be perfectly consistent with the complainant's decision to quit.

To help ensure that the offer of reinstatement will be understood as unconditional, the employer should state expressly that accepting the offer will not waive the complainant's right to pursue legal claims. The employer also should make clear that the job being offered is comparable to the complainant's former job in terms of promotional opportunities, status, responsibilities, working conditions, and compensation.

An offer of reinstatement is best made early, even before a complaint is filed. A long delay between the termination of employment and the offer of reinstatement may lead to increased liability, make reinstatement less feasible, and make the employee's rejection of the offer seem more reasonable.

To determine whether the complainant's rejection of the offer is "reasonable," courts examine the surrounding circumstances, including the reasons for the rejection and the terms of the offer. Rejection may be considered reasonable if the complainant objects to returning to work with or for the alleged harasser. The employer can meet this objection by offering the complainant a substantially equivalent job at a different location. The employer can also remove objections by agreeing to expunge from the complainant's personnel file any information relating to the circumstances of the harassment charge and the complainant's termination of employment.

The unreasonable rejection of an offer of reinstatement may be the basis for (1) a summary judgment motion by the employer asking the court to rule without a trial to limit back-pay damages, or (2) negotiating a settlement favorable to the employer because the complainant has lost some "leverage," in that potential damages will be less. In constructive discharge cases, a good-faith unconditional offer of reinstatement that does not reexpose the complainant to a harassing environment also may buttress a defense argument that the employer did not previously know about the alleged conduct, and now has taken appropriate steps to remedy it. A rejection of the offer would bolster a defense contention that the complainant had left the job for reasons other than an intolerable work environment.

B. Offer of Judgment

An "offer of judgment," available under federal or state rules of civil procedure, is exactly what it says: a formal offer to let the complainant win a specified amount, anticipating what she could obtain if the case went to trial. If the complainant prevails at trial, but in an amount less than the offer, she then is not entitled to any costs or attorney's fees incurred after the offer, but must pay the employer's post-offer costs and may even be liable for the employer's post-offer attorney's fees. If, after an offer of judgment, the complainant prevails at trial in an amount more than the offer, the offer has no effect.

An offer of judgment should state expressly whether the amount offered includes all costs and fees. If the complainant accepts an offer of judgment that is silent on this point, the court may hold that the complainant is entitled to the amount of the offer *plus* costs and attorney's fees.

C. Letter Threatening Sanctions

Federal and comparable state rules provide for sanctions, including an award of the employer's attorney's fees, for filing a pleading that is not well-grounded in law or fact. If, after review of the complaint, it appears that the plaintiff's allegations are frivolous, defense counsel will consider sending a letter to opposing counsel explaining why the case lacks merit, attaching key documents, such as poor performance evaluations, and, when appropriate, giving notice of the defendant's intention to seek sanctions if the action is pursued.

III. DEPOSITION OF THE COMPLAINANT

In a sexual harassment case, the deposition of the complainant is the cornerstone of the defense strategy. The deposition serves several objectives, not all of which are always mutually consistent:

- preparing for trial;
- creating a record on which to base a pretrial motion;
- persuading the complainant that the case has no merit by confronting her with inconsistencies in testimony or other information not previously disclosed; and
- demonstrating to the complainant and the complainant's counsel that litigation is a major commitment of time, energy, and emotions.

In taking the complainant's deposition, the defendant should address all facts relevant to proving sexual harassment and any defenses that the employer may raise, such as lack of knowledge of the alleged harassment.

The following discussion of the topics frequently explored at a complainant's deposition may provide some insight for company representatives who are furnishing the defense attorney with information in preparation for the deposition.

A. Failure to Use the Employer's Grievance Procedure

Where the complainant failed to notify the employer immediately upon first experiencing what later was claimed to be harassing conduct, the examiner will inquire into the extent of the notice that the complainant had concerning the employer's sexual harassment complaint procedure, when and how, if at all, it was used, and why it was not used promptly. The complainant should be asked to acknowledge receipt of any literature describing the employer's procedures for filing an allegation of harassment, and to acknowledge the failure to follow them.

If the complainant did report harassment to the employer, the examiner should explore any explanation for any delay in the report. The complainant should be asked to describe exactly the complaint that was finally made. The examiner also should inquire as to the complainant's response, if any, when approached by management about the alleged problem. Nonchalance or indifference on the part of the complainant will undermine her case.

B. Intent

The alleged harasser's intent to harm the complainant may be relevant where the claims include intentional torts, such as intentional infliction of emotional distress, or where the exclusive remedy for a work-related injury may be under the state workers' compensation laws (see Chapters 10 and 11). Intent also may be relevant to the question of insurance coverage (see Chapter 19).

C. Emotional Distress

To explore any claim of emotional distress, the examiner should inquire into the complainant's emotional condition and any psychological treatment received prior to the alleged harassment, the current claimed symptoms, and their onset and severity. The complainant should be questioned about treatment by physicians and therapists, any medication being taken, and why it was prescribed. There may be an argument that the medication or the underlying condition being treated is an independent source of emotional stress.

"Causation" is an element of the complainant's proof. The defense may seek to show that other events or circumstances caused the complainant's emotional distress. Therefore, counsel can explore other possible causes of emotional distress, such as family and personal relationships, traumatic experiences, moving of residence, death of family members, job-related stress, other incidents of harassment, illness, and other causes of tension.

D. Mitigation

Sexual harassment complainants, like other plaintiffs, have a duty to mitigate damages. In actual or constructive discharge cases, complainants may be questioned about their efforts to find new employment and, if they have secured a new position, about their new salary, fringe benefits, and other conditions of employment. To limit the period of the defendant's potential back-pay liability, the defendant must establish when the complainant obtained other employment with comparable pay and working conditions, or stopped seeking employment.

IV. EXPERT WITNESSES

Both the complainant and the employer often use expert witnesses in sexual harassment litigation. An expert is qualified to help the trier of fact understand the evidence or find a fact because of the expert's knowledge, skill, experience, training, or education in the area in question, but the expert's opinion may be inadmissible if the question at issue is not so technical that it exceeds the jury's understanding. For example, a court reasonably may conclude that the issue of whether gender was the basis of differential treatment is not so technical that it requires the aid of an expert. For a further discussion of expert witnesses, see Chapter 20, section X.

A. The Complainant's Experts

Complainants have used experts such as psychotherapists, medical doctors, sociologists, social workers, and employment professionals.

B. The Defendant's Experts

If the complainant has a professional expert witness likely to function as an advocate, the defendant might wish to counteract the impact of that testimony with its own professional advocate. If the complainant's witness is a treating therapist, however, that sort of expert witness may be sufficiently candid to provide as much helpful information as could be obtained from an independent expert retained by the defendant. A defendant may effectively undermine the complainant's expert with additional facts unknown to the expert when the expert's opinion was formed. Ordinarily, an expert who has not seen a patient frequently over a lengthy period of time cannot testify definitively about the cause of the stress, but only as to the nature and extent of the problem.

If the evaluation of the case suggests that a defense expert is advisable or necessary, a request for a mental examination should be considered. Most courts will find that plaintiffs have placed their mental condition at issue when they seek to recover damages for mental distress (see Chapter 20, section V.).

V. THE JOINT DEFENSE OF THE EMPLOYER AND AN INDIVIDUAL DEFENDANT

Sexual harassment complainants often sue both the employer and the individual alleged harasser. In that event, the employer and the individual defendant must decide whether to present a joint defense. A joint defense, while promoting coordination and minimizing litigation costs, creates potential conflicts of interest and raises issues of attorney-client privilege and attorney work product (discussed in sections C. and D. below).

A. Joint Defense Strategy Issues

1. Relevant Considerations. Evaluating the desirability of a joint defense first requires a thorough investigation of the sexual harassment complaint (see Chapter 15). The employer then must decide whether it believes that the alleged harassment actually occurred. This decision will determine whether the theory of the defense will be "it didn't happen," or "we don't know what happened, but it's not our fault."

If the investigation reveals independent evidence in support of the claim, the employer's strategy generally will be that "it's not our fault," and the employer will not offer joint representation to the individual defendant. Any other position would suggest that the employer approves of the conduct, and also would increase the employer's potential liability. Although selecting this strategy may alienate the alleged harasser, the employer's objective should be to direct the complainant's focus where it belongs—on the individual alleged harasser.

If the investigation establishes that the claim is false, the defense strategy is again clear—"it didn't happen." In this case, the employer likely will decide to offer joint representation. A joint defense has cost advantages if the employer is obliged to pay the individual defendant's attorney's fees, and if the employer is likely to be found liable if the claim is sustained against the individual. A joint defense also permits the defendants to adopt one common approach toward the litigation. This strategy should also secure the cooperation of the alleged harasser and thus increase the probability of a correct result. Should the strategy prove factually erroneous, the chance of significant employer liability increases. That, however, is a risk that cannot be avoided. The employer can ameliorate this situation by cautioning the alleged harasser, after its investigation, that sexual harassment will not be tolerated and that if it is determined that sexual harassment did occur, proper and prompt disciplinary action will be taken.

More difficult questions arise when, as often happens, the alleged harasser denies the allegations and the only evidence is the complainant's allegation. The most cautious approach here is for each defendant to retain separate attorneys. This approach will ensure that each defendant will have an attorney who can act on behalf of the client without facing any conflict of interest. The alleged harasser then would be able to confide fully in his attorney without fear that disclosure would lead to discharge or other disciplinary actions. Independent attorneys also could tell a more personalized story to the judge or jury deciding the case.

If the individual defendant is a nonsupervisory employee, the question of joint representation is still more difficult. A joint defense should increase the level of the alleged harasser's cooperation because of the perceived unity of interest among the defendants. Because a co-worker harasser is less likely to be ruled an agent of the employer, however, the potential for employer liability, and thus the employer's incentive to provide an employer-paid defense, is decreased.

2. Investigative Procedures. An employer's strategy alternatives will dictate its investigative procedures. Unless evidence from other sources is unusually convincing and the employer can decide what to do before interviewing the alleged harasser, the employer's attorney should not commit to any position at the initial investigative interviews following the filing of a lawsuit. The attorney generally advises the alleged harasser that the attorney represents only the employer, and that while the employer may decide to offer legal representation in the future, after all of the facts are gathered, joint representation will not be offered if there is a serious question of the individual's liability.

3. Indemnification. The individual defendant's limited ability to pay damages usually will lead the complainant to try to hold the employer responsible for the individual defendant's acts. When an individual defendant is held personally liable for sexual harassment under a common-law tort theory, state law may require an employer to indemnify (pay back) the individual defendant if the individual's losses occurred as the direct consequence of the individual defendant's discharge of employment duties.

Where the individual defendant is the alleged harasser, indemnity under common-law theories of liability generally would not extend to acts of sexual harassment that are not known to the employer, because there is ordinarily no duty to indemnify for losses arising from an unauthorized or negligent act. Where the individual conduct was intentional and willful, one court has specifically ordered the employer *not* to indemnify the individual defendants for punitive damages (*Kyriazi v. Western Elec. Co.*). Moreover, in a case of intentional, unauthorized misconduct, the employer may be entitled to indemnity from the individual harasser in the event that the employer is held liable for the individual's misconduct.

B. Conflicts of Interest

An attorney who jointly represents an employer and an alleged harasser has two separate clients, each of whom deserves the attorney's independent representation, even though the employer may be paying the fees for both defendants. Under ethical rules, a lawyer may not represent two different clients unless the lawyer reasonably believes that their interests are not adverse and unless each client consents after a full disclosure of the implications of multiple representation. The attorney should inform the parties in writing, before undertaking representation, of the potential conflicts and the fact that future conflicts may require one or both parties to obtain a new attorney, which will cost both time and money. The initial disclosure should include all material facts and an explanation of their legal significance, including which party, if any, the attorney may continue to represent in the event of a conflict. After fully disclosing potential conflicts, the attorney should obtain each party's written consent to joint representation, demonstrating that the party assumes the risks associated with the attorney's withdrawal, be it voluntary or by disqualification.

An actual conflict of interest will arise for the attorney if it is discovered that the alleged harasser did engage in the wrongful conduct alleged. In those circumstances, the employer may decide to sever the joint defense to diminish its exposure to liability for the alleged harasser's conduct. The employer then may seek to show that the alleged harasser is entirely responsible for the alleged conduct, and that the conduct occurred without the knowledge or approval of the employer. If the alleged harasser expressly waives any objection to the possibility of adverse representation after consultation and explanation by the attorney, some courts have permitted the attorney to continue representing the employer in the same matters. Where the employer severs the joint defense, however, the employer's continued representation by the same attorney will leave the attorney with a dilemma concerning how to use any privileged information received from the alleged harasser during the joint representation.

C. The Attorney-Client Privilege

1. During Joint Representation. The attorney-client privilege may be maintained in a joint defense of an employer and an alleged harasser so long as the defendants share a "common interest."

2. After Joint Representation Has Ended. When the joint defense of the employer and alleged harasser ends, a question may arise as to the employer's right to use, in its own defense, what it learned during the joint defense. Whether a new attorney is retained for each of the parties, or whether the former joint attorney continues to represent one of the parties, the privileged nature of the earlier disclosures must, unless the former clients' consent is obtained, be retained throughout the litigation. Although the employer should be able to use any unprivileged evidence that has confirmed the complainant's allegations, privileged information obtained directly from the alleged harasser must remain confidential.

Before joint representation commences, employers generally attempt to obtain the individual defendant's specific voluntary consent to use information acquired during the joint representation in the event the joint representation is ended. Whether such a consent will be considered valid in later litigation is open to question.

D. The Work Product Doctrine

1. During Joint Representation. Two parties jointly represented by the same counsel may use their attorney's "work product" for their mutual benefit without threat of the complainant's attorney obtaining access to the material. The work product doctrine is not waived by mere disclosure to a third party. The doctrine is designed to promote the adversary system by safeguarding the fruits of an attorney's trial preparation from the discovery attempts of an opponent. Because co-defendants need not be represented by the same counsel to maintain a joint defense and to enjoy the protections of the work product doctrine, a separately represented alleged harasser and the alleged harasser's employer, to the extent they retain a community of interest in the litigation, may share work product materials without any waiver of work product protection.

2. After Joint Representation Has Ended. There is little authority concerning whether one co-defendant may withhold from the other the work product that was generated when both defendants had the same counsel. In *Rudow v. Cohen*, the individual co-defendant obtained the work product of the employer's counsel, which was created before the interests of the two defendants diverged. Documents prepared by the employer concerning the employer's dismissal of the harasser, however, were not discoverable because they did not relate to the subject matter of the joint representation or the common interest of the employer and harasser.

Employers should be alert to occasions when their interests diverge from those of the individual defendant, since work product created before that time may be obtained by the alleged harasser. Voluntary disclosure thereafter may constitute a waiver of the protection. Company personnel always should check with counsel before releasing *any* documents to an individual codefendant or his attorney. For a discussion of the attorney-client and work product privilege in the context of the employer's internal investigation, see Chapter 15, section V.

VI. THE COMPLAINANT'S LITIGATION STRATEGY

A. Investigation by the Plaintiff's Attorney

Complainants typically will seek a copy of their personnel files prior to any litigation. Some state laws grant employees access to at least some part of their personnel files upon written request. Even in the absence of a legal requirement, the employer may make the files available voluntarily in the hope of deflecting a lawsuit. The file may reveal the employer's version of the events, and is likely to contain evidence of the complainant's performance and disciplinary record, general policies and practices of the employer, and other potentially relevant documents such as time cards, logs, attendance records, medical history, and workers' compensation claims. A barren personnel file may indicate employer laxity in personnel matters.

B. Interviews With Other Witnesses

The complainant's attorneys will want to talk to corporate employees. The complainant's co-workers may be able to corroborate or controvert the claim and provide evidence of their own behavior, which may bear on the issue of "unwelcomeness."

Co-workers also may identify other employees who have been victimized by the same harasser, have observed similar behavior, or who have taken actions sufficient to put management on notice of the harassment.

Nonetheless, there are legal and ethical constraints on the complainant's attorney's freedom to interview employees of an adverse corporate party *ex parte* (without the opposing party's knowledge or consent). A violation of *ex parte* communication rules could lead to sanctions, disqualification of the attorney, or rulings precluding the use of admissions obtained through an improper employee interview. As a general rule, most decisions allow the complainant's counsel informal access only to those employee witnesses whose acts or statements cannot bind the employer.

C. Use of Publicity

Because sexual harassment allegations are a public relations nightmare for many employers, it should not be surprising to see a complainant's attorney invite settlement discussions, before an action is filed, by sending the employer a draft complaint detailing the charges. With many employers, receipt of an explicit draft complaint is sufficient to raise the specter of adverse publicity and to generate substantial interest in a quiet settlement before litigation commences.

The complainant's leverage in forcing a settlement by threatening publicity depends to a large degree on the standing of the employer in the community. Large employers who are sensitive to their public image obviously are more vulnerable to this tactic. The timing of any threat is also critical. Once charges have been made public, the employer may decide that it has little to lose by proceeding with a defense. Thus, a pre-filing threat is often more effective in achieving a settlement, because the employer is still in a position to bargain for confidentiality.

In some instances, the threat of publicity may in fact be counterproductive. Many defense attorneys and employers perceive publicity threats as a form of blackmail used by unscrupulous opponents to pressure an employer into settlement without regard to the validity of the accusations. Overt or heavy-handed threats to try the case in the press may destroy any chance of settlement. Publicity can also be damaging to the complainant in terms of emotional well-being and future career prospects.

19

INSURANCE COVERAGE

I. NOTIFYING THE CARRIER

As soon as the employer has notice of a sexual harassment claim, it should collect and review all pertinent insurance policies. In light of the significant costs associated with sexual harassment litigation, the need to investigate potential insurance coverage cannot be overstated.

If it appears that a policy may provide coverage, the insurance carrier (the insurer) should be notified promptly, before any deadline for filing a proof of loss expires. If the insurer denies coverage, the employer should review any contractual limits on the insured's time to sue the insurer on the policy and take the necessary steps to preserve the employer's right to recover under the policy.

II. DUTIES TO INDEMNIFY AND DEFEND

An employer faced with costly litigation should remember that an insurance policy typically creates two separate obligations for the insurer: a duty to defend claims and a duty to indemnify for liability for those claims. The duty to defend is broader than the duty to indemnify, meaning that an insurer

208

must defend against a lawsuit if the complaint alleges any facts that, if proven, would trigger liability covered under the policy, even though the insurer would not be obligated to pay a judgment if the facts ultimately bring the case within a policy exclusion. Even unpleaded theories of liability may trigger a duty to defend if facts known to the insurer suggest a potential liability, so long as the theory of liability is not too tenuous.

By assuming the defense of its insured, the insurer generally acquires the right to control the defense and select defense counsel. The insurer must, however, pay the reasonable fees of the insured's own selected attorney if there is an irreconcilable conflict of interest between insurer and insured. In some states such a conflict arises whenever the insurer reserves its rights as to coverage of liability (*i.e.*, the insurer agrees to cover *some* of the claims but not *all* of them). Moreover, some insurers may allow the employer's regular attorney to represent the employer.

III. POTENTIALLY APPLICABLE POLICIES

Various types of policies may provide coverage in a sexual harassment case. Comprehensive general liability insurance typically covers the insured employer's liability for any "occurrence," typically defined as an "accident," that the insured employer "neither expected nor intended" and causes "bodily injury" or property damage. The legal issues, which may be decided differently in different jurisdictions, are (1) whether the alleged acts of sexual harassment constituted an unexpected "occurrence," and (2) whether any psychological damage and emotional distress incident to sexual harassment constitute a "bodily injury" (see section IV. below).

Errors and omissions liability policies cover risks inherent in the practice of a particular profession and may be construed to cover some intentional torts.

Excess and umbrella liability policies provide coverage in areas that might not be included in basic coverage, or liabilities that exceed the insured's primary policy limits.

Directors' and officers' liability and general partners' liability policies cover the actions of a company's directors, officers, and certain managerial or executive employees while acting within the scope of their authority.

Comprehensive personal liability policies and homeowner's policies also may cover the actions of individual defendants without regard to whether the actions were within the scope of their authority.

Workers' compensation policies may cover some or all of the damages alleged by the complainant. These policies are not necessarily limited to claims brought under workers' compensation statutes.

IV. COVERAGE OF SEXUAL HARASSMENT CLAIMS

A. Issue of Intentional Conduct

Many liability insurance policies do not cover injuries that are intentionally caused by an insured party, either because the act in question is not considered an accidental "occurrence" or because it falls within a policy exclusion for intentional acts. Accordingly, sexual harassment claims are not likely to trigger insurance coverage to the extent they are litigated under a theory of intentional tort or under the disparate treatment theory of employment discrimination. For the same reason, insurance coverage likely will be denied in a pure quid pro quo case where the offending supervisor is the employer's agent and is authorized to take the challenged personnel action. Thus, when a complaint alleges that a company owner, manager, partner, or corporate officer committed an intentional tort as a managing agent of the insured corporate defendant, an insurer may have no duty to defend.

However, if an individual harasser is acting to further personal interests and not those of the insured corporation, as is typical in sexual harassment cases, then the intentional nature of the tort might not justify denying coverage, for in such a case the corporate insured's potential liability may be not for its own or its manager's own intentional conduct, but for negligence in supervision.

Insurance coverage is most likely in a hostile environment case, where an offender may be shown to have acted beyond supervisory authority. Coverage is also more likely if the alleged harasser is a nonmanagement employee, for then it is not likely that the employee's intentional tort will be imputed to the employer and thus be excluded from coverage under the employer's policy.

B. Issue of Bodily Injury

Coverage under the occurrence/bodily injury formula may be denied if the complainant alleges only emotional distress of a nonphysical nature, as some courts do not recognize such distress as a "bodily injury." Moreover, even where bodily injury is recognized to exist, coverage has been denied on the basis of a policy exclusion for "bodily injury to any employee of the insured arising out of and in the course of employment."

C. Other Coverage Issues

Some policies expressly provide additional coverage in the form of coverage for "personal injury" liability in connection with such claims as libel, slander, and false arrest, all of which have been claimed in sexual harassment cases (see Chapter 11).

The public policy of some states may prohibit the insurer from indemnifying the insured for willful acts of discrimination, even where the policy itself would appear to provide coverage. Thus, even if an insurer is funding the defense, the employer still may be liable for damages.

Some states forbid insurance coverage for punitive damages on public policy grounds. Other states permit insurance coverage for punitive damages, at least with respect to vicarious liability.

20

EVIDENCE AND DISCOVERY

I. OVERVIEW

"Discovery" is the fact-finding process that occurs in litigation before trial. Generally, a litigant may discover all information reasonably calculated to lead to admissible evidence. Thus, the law of evidence will determine a party's obligations to provide and ability to discover information from the other side.

Human resources personnel should be aware of what is the most important evidence in order to alert the company's attorney to anything that may be significant, and assist in contacting other employees for additional information.

A sexual harassment case involves many different categories of evidence. The primary evidence consists of the complainant's testimony and the alleged harasser's denial or explanation. Each side will also seek corroborating testimony from other witnesses.

Other evidence typically includes:

- the timing and nature of the complainant's report of unwelcome conduct,
- the complainant's behavior as noticed by co-workers and friends following the incident(s),
- the sexual atmosphere of the relevant workplace,
- expert testimony as to whether the complainant's behavior is consistent with sexual harassment,

- the complainant's and alleged harasser's prior conduct, and

- facts that bear on the complainant's and alleged harasser's credibility.

II. RULES OF EVIDENCE

A. Balancing Relevance Against Unfair Prejudice

Generally, a party may introduce any evidence relevant to any element of a sexual harassment claim or defense. The rules of evidence used in federal courts say that evidence is "relevant" if it makes the existence of any significant fact more probable or less probable than it otherwise would be.

The Supreme Court in *Meritor Savings Bank v. Vinson* interpreted Title VII to permit the broad admissibility of evidence of prior workplace activities in a sexual harassment case, unless its probative value is substantially outweighed by the danger of unfair prejudice, confusion of the issues, misleading the jury, or by considerations of undue delay, waste of time, or needless presentation of cumulative evidence. For evidence to be excluded, it must be more than merely prejudicial: it must create unfairness to a party that substantially outweighs its probative value. An example of unfairly prejudicial evidence might be evidence of the sexual promiscuity of the complainant in a quid pro quo case: although sexual promiscuity logically may bear on whether a sexual advance was welcome, sexual promiscuity also may prejudice the jury unfairly against the complainant and confuse the issues at stake.

B. Character Evidence

Evidence of a person's character—whether in the form of reputation, opinion, or evidence of past acts—generally is inadmissible to prove that the person acted in conformity with that character on a particular occasion. Character evidence usually is excluded because its probative value is outweighed by the risk that the finder of fact will rule against a party for "being a bad person," regardless of the facts in the present case.

Character evidence can enter the record, however, through one of the exceptions to the general rule against its admission. The most common exception is for evidence of prior acts to prove motive, opportunity, intent, preparation, plan, knowledge, identity, or the absence of mistake or accident.

III. PRIOR BEHAVIOR OF THE COMPLAINANT

A. Sexual History

The prior behavior of the complainant is relevant to whether the alleged conduct occurred at all and, if so, whether it was welcome. Defendants therefore have an interest in proving the sexual promiscuity of the complainant, on the theory that sexual promiscuity tends to show a receptiveness to the sexual activities in question. Still, complainants have generally succeeded in resisting inquiries into their sexual history because:

- modern amendments to federal and to many state rules of evidence have generally limited these inquiries,
- the complainant's prior sexual behavior may be excluded whenever it is unduly prejudicial,
- courts are concerned that unnecessary inquiries into the sex lives of sexual harassment complainants may discourage valid complaints, and
- the fact that complainants may welcome sexual advances from certain individuals has no bearing on the emotional trauma they may feel from sexual harassment (*Mitchell v. Hutchings*).

In *Priest v. Rotary*, the defendant tried to admit evidence that the complainant, a waitress in the defendant's bar, had a history of engaging in sex for economic gain and thus had a "motive" for soliciting men at the bar, which was the alleged reason for her discharge. The court ruled, however, that even if the evidence could be admitted under the "motive" exception to the rule against character evidence, the probative value of the evidence was outweighed by the danger of undue prejudice.

Where a complainant makes a state-law claim for intentional infliction of emotional distress, the defendant's awareness of the complainant's sexual activity with others may be considered relevant to whether the defendant intentionally inflicted distress. To the extent that the alleged harasser knew of the complainant's conduct toward co-workers, that evidence might show that the harasser believed his conduct would not be offensive.

The fact that the complainant had been fired from a previous job for propositioning a married man was held to be relevant to whether she was the sexual aggressor (*Gan v. Kepro Circuit Sys.*). Similarly, where the complainant alleged that her supervisor forced her to have intercourse while visiting her at home, the defendant was allowed to cross-examine her regarding her subsequent sexual relationships, including an allegation she made of date rape (*Kresko v. Rulli*).

B. Behavior With the Alleged Harasser

Although a complainant's sexual history is generally protected from inquiry, virtually any interaction between the complainant and the alleged harasser is fair game. Thus, courts have ruled that employers could introduce or discover evidence that the complainant:

- had an affair with the alleged harasser (*Bigoni v. Pay'N Pak Stores*; *Evans v. Mail Handlers*),
- visited the alleged harasser in nonemployment contexts and invited him for home-cooked meals (*Reichman v. Bureau of Affirmative Action*), and
- presented a "sexually explicit gift" to her alleged harasser (*Steele v. Offshore Shipbldg.*).

C. The Complainant's Workplace Conduct

In *Meritor Savings Bank v. Vinson*, the Supreme Court held that the workplace conduct of the complainant, such as sexually provocative speech and dress and "publicly expressed sexual fantasies," is "obviously relevant" to whether particular conduct was unwelcome. The Court concluded that although such evidence creates a risk of unfair prejudice and must be carefully weighed before it is admitted, it could not be excluded as a rule.

In *Gan v. Kepro Circuit Systems*, the court found admissible evidence that the complainant had frequently used crude and vulgar language in the workplace, had initiated sexually oriented conversations with male and female co-workers, had frequently asked male employees about their marital and extramarital sexual relationships, had volunteered intimate details about her own marital and premarital sexual relationships, and had volunteered information about her menstrual cycle. The court also admitted evidence that the complainant had called a co-worker "nigger" and pinched him on the buttocks before the co-worker, in retaliation, had grabbed the complainant's breasts. There was also evidence that when male employees compared the complainant to the female subjects of photographs in sexually oriented magazines, she had opined that she was much prettier.

In *Swentek v. USAir*, it was found relevant that the complainant, a flight attendant, placed a dildo in her supervisor's mailbox to "loosen her up," urinated in a cup and, pretending that it was a drink, passed it to another employee, and made a frank sexual invitation to a pilot as she grabbed his genitals. Although the court said that use of foul language and sexual innuendo in a consensual setting does not waive legal protections against unlawful harassment, these activities were admissible as evidence because the court said they tended to prove that the alleged harassment was in fact welcome. In *McLean v. Satellite Technology Services*, evidence was admitted that the complainant had lifted her dress to show her supervisor, who was the alleged harasser, that she was not wearing undergarments.

Courts generally have excluded evidence of the complainant's sexual behavior with third parties outside of the workplace as being too remote in time or place to the working environment.

IV. PSYCHOLOGICAL HISTORY AND MEDICAL EVIDENCE

For the same reasons that defendants cannot usually investigate a complainant's general sexual history, they may have difficulty attacking the credibility of the complainant's story with evidence that the complainant had been sexually assaulted as a child or has a history of imagining sexual assaults or overreacting to trivial actions. In one case where the complainant, in reporting a sexual assault by a co-worker, had mentioned sexual assaults suffered in childhood, the complainant successfully resisted discovery even though the defendant's forensic psychiatrist opined that the childhood incidents bore upon her current perceptions (*Knoettgen v. Superior Court*).

The complainant's physical symptoms following the alleged harassment will be admissible as bearing on whether the complainant found the alleged harassment unwelcome. The evidence might include unusual nervousness, crying, vomiting, sleeplessness, nightmares, headaches, or other common symptoms of stress-related disorders (*Priest v. Rotary*). Courts routinely permit inquiries, addressed to the complainant or others, into the complainant's psychological reaction to the alleged abuse as relevant to whether the conduct actually occurred and whether it was welcome. Thus, courts have admitted:

- testimony that the complainant was a vindictive person who threatened suits against co-workers over imagined wrongs, and who bragged that she was going to get the alleged harasser fired (*Swentek v. USAir*); and
- psychiatric testimony of chronic anxiety following the boss's demands for oral sex (*Phillips v. Smalley Maintenance Servs.*).

Where sexual harassment claims have placed the complainant's medical and psychological history at issue, the defendant may seek access to medical or psychological records of prior similar symptoms and stress-related disorders to discover other stressful events that could have caused the complainant's symptoms. In *Broderick v. Shad*, where the complainant alleged insomnia and nervousness because of harassment, the defendant was permitted to inquire into medical records reflecting any such conditions reported to the complainant's physician. Both discovery and a psychological examination have been allowed where the complainant claimed severe emotional problems arising from harassment (*Vinson v. Superior Court*).

The defendant may take a deposition of the complainant's treating psychologist, and may inquire into all information on which the psychologist relied in reaching an expert opinion concerning the complainant's emotional trauma and its causes (*Mitchell v. Hutchings*).

V. MENTAL EXAMINATION OF THE COMPLAINANT

When the complainant's mental condition is in controversy and there is good cause shown, a defendant may be entitled to compel the complainant to undergo a psychiatric and psychological evaluation. Each motion to compel a mental examination is decided on a case-by-case basis, under all of the relevant circumstances (*Schlagenhauf v. Holder*).

A. The "Mental Condition in Controversy" Requirement

A defendant moving for an order of examination obviously has a better argument that the complainant's "mental condition is in controversy" where the complainant claims emotional distress damages, but that is not necessarily dispositive with all courts (*Lowe v. Philadelphia Newspapers; Robinson v. Jacksonville Shipyards*).

B. Good Cause

"Good cause" for a mental examination requires a showing that the examination could bring out specific facts relevant to the cause of action and necessary to the defendant's case. In sexual harassment cases, defendants may argue that they have good cause because they need to:

- show that the complainant was "oversensitive" to sexual banter,
- show a psychological condition that caused the complainant to imagine that sexual advances were being made, or
- probe the complainant's allegations of severe emotional distress.

VI. THE COMPLAINANT'S REPORTS
OF SEXUAL HARASSMENT

A. Absence of Complaints

The absence of timely complaints to management regarding misconduct is relevant to whether harassing conduct ever occurred, whether it was welcome, and whether the employer knew or should have known about it. In *Evans v. Mail Handlers*, the court admitted evidence that the complainant failed to complain until a consensual affair soured, for the purpose of showing that the complained-of conduct was welcome at the time it occurred.

B. Complaints to Management

Complaints of sexual harassment to management are admissible to prove that the conduct was not welcome, and to prove that the employer had notice of the misconduct that it then failed to correct (*Bundy v. Jackson*). To the extent that any prior complaint conflicts with the complainant's testimony in deposition or at trial, the defendant may use the prior statement to impeach the complainant's testimony. In *Highlander v. KFC National Management Co.*, the fact that the complainant made light of an alleged pass at the time that it occurred was admitted to show that the comment actually was welcome.

If the complaint is excessively late or closely follows some disciplinary action against the complainant, the timing would be admissible to show that the complaint is unreliable or influenced by an improper motive. A complainant's failure to complain about sexual joking and touching of her shoulder until weeks after she was discharged was admitted to show that the conduct was not unwelcome (*Neeley v. American Fidelity Assurance*).

C. Informal Complaints

The defendant is entitled to discover whether the complainant made prior inconsistent statements. Accordingly, the defendant generally has broad latitude in discovery to inquire into the alleged incidents, what was said, and when it was said. These individuals, in turn, may be questioned regarding their conversations with the complainant and the reports made by the complainant as to the incident.

VII. THE ALLEGED HARASSER'S KNOWLEDGE OR BEHAVIOR

A complainant often will offer evidence of the knowledge or conduct of the alleged harasser, and evidence of harassment of other employees by other alleged harassers. Although this evidence will raise issues of privacy, undue prejudice, and the ban against the admission of character evidence, such evidence often is ruled admissible.

A. Evidence of the Harasser's Intent

The alleged harasser's knowledge of the complainant's severe financial straits can be used to prove motive, opportunity, and intent with respect to threatening job loss if sexual favors are not extended. In *Priest v. Rotary*, the harasser's knowledge of the complainant's economic dependence on her job was used to show the outrageousness of the harasser's actions for purposes of a claim of intentional infliction of emotional distress.

B. Evidence of Plan

Prior-acts evidence may be admitted to prove a plan of harassment. In *Phillips v. Smalley Maintenance Services*, a quid pro quo case, the complainant's boss told her that part of her job was to give him oral sex three times a week, and began to put paper over the window in his office door to prevent anyone from seeing inside. The complainant was then fired after she rejected this demand. The court admitted testimony by another female employee that she had been subjected to treatment "similar" to that alleged by the complainant, and testimony by another witness that he had seen other female employees leave the alleged harasser's office when there was paper over the office door window.

C. Evidence of Habit

At least one court has upheld the use of an alleged harasser's sexual history as "habit" evidence. In *Chomicki v. Wittekind*, where the jury found that the defendant landlord terminated the plaintiff's tenancy for spurning his sexual advances, the trial court admitted testimony of four other females that showed a "routine practice of demanding sexual favors." Other courts have held, however, that "characteristics of one's personal relationships" do not constitute habits (*Priest v. Rotary*; *Kresko v. Rulli*).

D. Evidence of Hostile Environment

Evidence that the alleged harasser sexually harassed other employees in addition to the complainant routinely is admitted in hostile environment cases to demonstrate that the incidents of harassment were pervasive rather than isolated (*Broderick v. Ruder*). In one case, two women other than the complainant were permitted to testify that a company officer had fondled them in his office while discussing business, just as the complainant testified he had done with her (*Rudow v. New York City Comm'n on Human Rights*).

Evidence of other harassment also may be introduced for the related purpose of showing the effect of the conduct on the complainant's working conditions. In *Robinson v. Jacksonville Shipyards*, the court admitted evidence concerning the harassment of the complainant's co-workers because, among other grounds, one's perception of a hostile environment may be influenced by the treatment of other members of one's protected class, even if that treatment is learned of second-hand. While a complainant generally cannot rely on incidents of sexual harassment of which she was unaware, a supervisor's "widespread reputation" as a "womanizer" might be admissible as helping to create a hostile environment (*Jones v. Lyng*). One court held, however, that evidence of a pattern of behavior by a supervisor toward other employees was irrelevant (*Kresko v. Rulli*).

E. Evidence of Other Kinds of Sex Discrimination

Evidence of the harassment of employees other than the complainant may also be admitted to show the employer's sexually discriminatory motive in making an employment decision. A history of vulgar and indecent language, directed toward women employees and tolerated by the employer, has been admitted to prove that sex played a role in decisions adverse to women complainants (*Morgan v. Hertz Corp.; Contardo v. Merrill Lynch*).

F. Evidence of Employer Notice

Evidence of harassment of other employees by the alleged harasser can also prove that the employer knew or should have known of the problem and is liable for failure to take reasonable steps to correct the harassment. In *Hunter v. Allis-Chalmers Corp.*, evidence of pervasive harassment by co-workers was admitted to support a finding that the employer was directly liable, either because the employer acted negligently in failing to stop the harassment or because the employer actually condoned the harassment.

Conversely, in order to justify not having imposed more severe disciplinary action, an employer may introduce evidence that the alleged harasser had never before harassed co-workers (*Barrett v. Omaha Nat'l Bank*).

VIII. THE EMPLOYER'S RESPONSE TO REPORTS OF HARASSMENT

An employer has every incentive to offer evidence of its response to the complainant's allegations, in order to show that it did not authorize the harassment and took prompt remedial action to correct it. The evidence may include facts concerning the employer's investigation of a sexual harassment complaint and the discipline that the employer imposed. The employer also might introduce evidence that the complaints were insufficient to warrant taking any disciplinary action. The fact that the complainant at the time made light of the alleged pass, and asked that management take no action, is admissible on the issue of whether the employer was justified in taking no action (*Highlander v. KFC Nat'l Mgmt. Co.*).

It is less clear whether a complainant can offer proof that the employer improved its antiharassment policy after the incidents in question to show that the employer's previous policy was inadequate. Most jurisdictions prohibit evidence of subsequent remedial measures designed to prove "negligence or culpable conduct." These jurisdictions do, however, permit evidence of remedial actions when offered to prove control over the subject matter or the feasibility of precautionary measures. The court in *Shrout v. Black Clawson Co.* admitted evidence that, after the alleged harassment, the employer changed its procedure for reporting incidents of harassment. This evidence showed that the employer's previous "open-door" policy was inadequate, so that the harassed employee reasonably could fail to use it to report harassment.

IX. PRIVILEGES INVOKED REGARDING INTERNAL INVESTIGATIONS

Employers who investigate sexual harassment complaints often will create documents that may be discoverable in subsequent litigation. Various privileges may justify nondisclosure of some aspects of the investigation, although, as a practical matter, the employer may choose to permit discovery because it will want to prove that an extensive investigation occurred. For a discussion of these issues, see Chapter 15, section V.; and Chapter 18, section V.

X. EXPERT TESTIMONY

Rule 702 of the Federal Rules of Evidence authorizes opinion testimony by an expert who is qualified by knowledge, skill, experience, training, or education to help the trier of fact understand the evidence or find a fact in issue. The admissibility of expert testimony is in the discretion of the trial judge, whose decision will not be overturned unless it is clearly erroneous or an abuse of discretion. Expert testimony has been admitted on several issues in sexual harassment litigation.

A. Whether Harassment Occurred

Expert testimony has been admitted as to whether the complainant reacted in a manner consistent with a person who has suffered sexual abuse. In *Robinson v. Jacksonville Shipyards,* a consultant opined that, using typical coping strategies, women may not complain about sexual harassment because of fear, embarrassment, and feelings of futility.

One court, however, has held that a complainant may not use expert psychological testimony that the alleged harasser fit the "profile" of a person who would have a tendency to harass, or testify as to general traits that are true about harassers. The court reasoned that this evidence should be excluded because its probative value was substantially outweighed by the prejudice to the defendant, and because it amounted to inadmissible character evidence (*Bushell v. Dean*).

B. Causation

Testimony by an expert mental health professional may be admissible as to whether the complainant has experienced emotional distress caused by sexual harassment. Expert psychiatrists have opined on whether the harassment caused medical depression, whether the complainant suffered from post-traumatic stress disorder (PTSD), and whether the complainant had a paranoid personality disorder evidenced by pervasive suspicion of all supervisors.

C. Damages

If continuing treatment is required for psychological effects such as PTSD, the expert may estimate the time and cost of therapy.

D. Personnel Procedures

Consultants have also given expert testimony on what steps are reasonably designed to prevent and remedy sexual harassment in the workplace. Similarly, where an employer has based its decision to discharge a complainant on performance evaluations, or seeks to use them at trial for other purposes, a human resources expert can address both the procedures in general and the ways in which they were applied to the complainant.

E. Sexual Attitudes and Stereotypes

Sociologists have been permitted to give expert testimony on the sexual connotations of the complained-of acts. In *Eide v. Kelsey-Hayes Co.*, a sociologist familiar with research and literature on sexual harassment was found qualified to testify about subtle forms of sexual harassment, which included the use of nicknames and sexually suggestive posters in the workplace. Psychologists have been permitted to testify on sexual stereotyping to the effect that permitting sexual joking and the display of pornographic material in the workplace is a form of discrimination against women and contributes to a sexually hostile environment (*Robinson v. Jacksonville Shipyards*).

In addition, EEOC investigators have been permitted to testify concerning EEOC findings in determinations admitted into evidence. Where suit is filed after a "no-cause" determination has been issued by the EEOC, the defendant may produce the EEOC investigator as an expert witness regarding the agency's findings.

XI. PRIVACY CONSIDERATIONS

The complainant's as well as the defendant's discovery may be limited by considerations of undue embarrassment or invasion of privacy. In *Boler v. Superior Court,* the court upheld an alleged harasser's refusal to answer deposition questions about female employees with whom he had had sexual relations. The questions were assertedly relevant to such issues as the employer's knowledge of a propensity to coerce sexual favors from subordinates, but the court held that the inquiries were unduly invasive of the privacy not only of the harasser, but of the women in question. The court indicated, however, that it would permit discovery of a list of the women who had worked for the employer during the relevant time frame.

Even this much discovery was too much for the court in *Cook v. Yellow Freight System,* where the complainant requested the names, addresses, and telephone numbers of each female office employee who had worked with the alleged harasser. The court, citing privacy considerations, denied the complainant's motion to compel discovery. Though recognizing that the information directly related to a claim that the alleged harasser had a history of harassing women in the workplace and that the employer had failed to respond appropriately, the court held that the privacy interests of the absent third parties—the women whose identities were sought—could be asserted by the defendant employer, and that those interests justified narrowing the discovery request. The court ordered that the complainant submit for court approval a letter to be sent to the women in question, that the defendant provide the complainant with mailing addresses to allow her to mail the letter, and that further discovery of the women and their files be subject to their individual consent and be used only for the lawsuit.

21

REMEDIES

I. INJUNCTIVE AND AFFIRMATIVE RELIEF

Title VII and state FEP statutes entitle a successful plaintiff in a sexual harassment case to a monetary award for any economic loss suffered. Thus, for example, a plaintiff who was discharged for resisting sexual harassment can be awarded back pay. Employment discrimination statutes also authorize certain nonmonetary injunctive relief, such as prohibiting the company from continuing to engage in harassing conduct, and affirmative relief, such as compelling the company to take certain steps to remedy the problem. Until the Civil Rights Act of 1991, injunctive relief was the only relief available under Title VII to victims of harassment who had not been fired or demoted.

A. When Injunctive or Affirmative Relief Is Available

A person subjected to sexual harassment is entitled to injunctive relief against future discrimination unless the employer proves that it is unlikely to repeat the harassing conduct (*EEOC v. Goodyear Aerospace Corp.*). Courts have granted this relief when the hostile work environment continues to exist or when an employer has taken corrective action only after being sued (*Sanchez v. City of Miami Beach; EEOC v. Hacienda Hotel*).

227

B. Types of Injunctive and Affirmative Relief

The type of relief awarded depends on the facts of each case. Common forms of injunctive relief include court orders that forbid a company to:

- encourage, create, or condone a sexually hostile environment;
- give negative references to prospective employers of the complainant;
- retaliate against the complainant; or
- refuse to discipline the sexual harasser (*Bundy v. Jackson; EEOC v. Fotios*).

Common forms of affirmative relief include commands in a court order that an employer:

- implement a company-wide sexual harassment policy,
- educate employees and supervisors about the nature of sexual harassment and the disciplinary steps that will be taken against harassers,
- develop grievance procedures,
- hire an equal employment opportunity expert to evaluate the company's sexual harassment policies,
- reinstate the complainant to the job,
- transfer the complainant to another division within the company,
- promote the complainant, and
- reimburse the complainant for medical and other expenses (*Robinson v. Jacksonville Shipyards; Meritor Sav. Bank v. Vinson; Broderick v. Ruder; EEOC v. FLC & Bros. Rebel*).

Courts sometimes monitor the employer's corrective actions by inspecting the company premises or by requiring the employer to report periodically the steps it has taken to prevent sexual harassment (*Arnold v. City of Seminole; EEOC v. Fotios*).

C. Preliminary Injunctions

Sexual harassment claims sometimes require expeditious judicial action. Under severe circumstances, a complainant may obtain preliminary injunctive relief to prevent irreparable harm (*Aronberg v. Walters; O'Connor v. Peru State College*). Mere job loss generally is not considered to be an irreparable harm because the complainant can be compensated monetarily for such a loss.

Section 706(f)(2) of Title VII authorizes the EEOC itself to request preliminary relief pending final disposition of a sexual harassment charge. The most common types of this preliminary relief are orders to prevent the employer from retaliating against or threatening to harm the complainant, and to prevent interference with the agency's investigation.

Some state antiharassment statutes, which prohibit telephone calls, touching and other threatening activities, provide for an antiharassment injunction (Cal. Code of Civ. Proc. §527.6).

II. MONETARY RELIEF

Several types of monetary relief are available to victims of sexual harassment. Courts generally award a prevailing plaintiff monetary relief that includes back pay from the time of any discharge to the time of reinstatement (*Albemarle Paper Co. v. Moody*)(see section A. below). Courts may also award "front pay," which compensates the complainant for anticipated future earnings loss caused by the sexual harassment (see section B. below). In addition, the Civil Rights Act of 1991 amended Title VII to provide that, in cases of intentional discrimination, the complainant may recover compensatory and punitive damages (see section C. below).

A. Back Pay

1. Computation. Back pay may be awarded to redress any economic injury that the complainant has suffered as a result of the sexual harassment (*Brooms v. Regal Tube Co.*). The calculation of back pay encompasses not only lost "straight-time" salary, but also overtime, shift differentials, commissions, bonuses, pay raises, tips, vacation, sick pay, pension, severance pay, profit-sharing and insurance (*Arnold v. City of Seminole; Huddleston v. Roger Dean Chevrolet; Priest v. Rotary; Yates v. Avco Corp.; Meyers v. ITT Diversified Credit Corp.; Ross v. Twenty-Four Collection*).

2. Deductions. Certain deductions must be made from the back-pay calculation. One deduction is for the amount of interim earnings. Accordingly, if the complainant's interim earnings exceed the amount of any possible back-pay award, back pay is denied. In addition, some courts have deducted taxes, public assistance, unemployment compensation, and social security benefits from the back-pay award (*EEOC v. Wyoming Retirement Sys.*), although other courts refuse to make those deductions (*Guthrie v. J.C. Penney Co.*).

3. Mitigation of Damages. The complainant who loses her job because of employment discrimination must attempt to minimize damages by using reasonable diligence to seek other employment substantially equivalent to her previous position. Failure to do so will defeat, to that extent, the complainant's claim for back pay. But a failure to get a new job may be excused if the sexual harassment has caused psychological problems that interfere with working (*Brooms v. Regal Tube Co.*; *EEOC v. Gurnee Inn Corp.*).

4. Interest. In Title VII cases, courts generally exercise their discretion to order an employer to pay prejudgment and postjudgment interest on the back-pay award (*Loeffler v. Frank*; *Pease v. Alford Photo Indus.*).

5. Period of Recovery for Back Pay. Back pay is recoverable for a period that begins no earlier than two years before the EEOC charge was filed. In actual or constructive discharge cases, back pay accrues from the date of discharge or resignation (*Horn v. Duke Homes*). Where the complainant was denied a promotion, the back-pay period begins when the promotion was denied (*Bundy v. Jackson*). Where the sexual harassment caused an unpaid leave of absence, the back-pay period commences on the date the leave began (*Zabkowicz v. West Bend Co.*).

The back-pay period typically ends when the court renders judgment (*Anderson v. Group Hosp.*). It can end sooner, however, if the complainant ceases to suffer adverse economic consequences, such as by securing a higher-paying job (*DiSalvo v. Chamber of Commerce*). The back-pay period also may end when the defendant offers the complainant unconditional reinstatement or transfer to another location, or when the complainant voluntarily withdraws from the job market (*Ford Motor Co. v. EEOC; Miller v. Marsh*).

B. Front Pay

If reinstatement is not ordered (where, for example, continuing hostility makes reinstatement unwise), sexual harassment victims also may be entitled to front pay. Front pay is the difference between what the complainant would have earned in the absence of discrimination and what she will earn on a new job. The court determines, in its discretion, the point at which front pay will be terminated (*Parker v. Siemens-Allis, Inc.; Sowers v. Kemira, Inc.*).

C. Compensatory and Punitive Damages

1. Title VII. Under the Civil Rights Act of 1991, punitive damages are available in Title VII suits whenever the employer engages in a discriminatory practice with malice or with reckless indifference to the legally protected rights of the employee. Further, compensatory damages may be awarded for future pecuniary losses, emotional pain, suffering, inconvenience, mental anguish, loss of enjoyment of life, and other nonpecuniary losses. The total amount of compensatory and punitive damages is subject to a cap that varies with the size of the employer:

Number of Employees	Cap on Total Award
15–100	$50,000
101–200	$100,000
201–500	$200,000
more than 500	$300,000

The 1991 Act provides that when compensatory or punitive damages are sought, any party in the lawsuit can demand a jury trial, and the court is forbidden to inform the jury of the cap on the damage award.

2. State Statutes. Many fair employment practices statutes permit complainants to recover compensatory damages in sexual harassment suits, and some also permit punitive damage awards. Some of these states, however, limit the amount of recoverable compensatory and punitive damages (*Wirig v. Kinney Shoe Corp.*).

3. Common-Law Torts. A victim of sexual harassment may file a variety of tort claims, all of which allow for awards of punitive and compensatory damages (see Chapter 11, section XIV.). In awarding damages for emotional distress, the trier of fact considers the duration and intensity of the harassment and the degree of emotional harm suffered by the complainant (*Shrout v. Black Clawson Co.*).

To obtain punitive damages in a tort suit, the complainant generally must show that the harasser acted willfully or with malice (*Dias v. Sky Chefs*). One court has ruled that conduct sufficient to create a sexually hostile environment also suffices to support punitive damages (*Fisher v. San Pedro Peninsula Hosp.*).

In some states, the employer is liable for punitive damages even if the harasser was merely an employee and not an officer, director, or managing agent of the company, and the company neither participated in nor ratified the conduct. In other states, however, the company is liable only if one of its officers, directors, or managing agents participated in or ratified the sexual harassment (*Shrout v. Black Clawson Co.; Hart v. National Mortgage & Land Co.*). Ratification may be inferred where the employer is informed of the sexual harassment but does not fully investigate and fails to repudiate the conduct by disciplining or terminating the harasser.

There should be no liability for punitive damages in a sexual harassment case based on mere negligence. However, failure to investigate and correct known sexual harassment may effectively ratify the harassing conduct, thereby entitling the complainant to punitive damages (*Fisher v. San Pedro Peninsula Hosp.; Shrout v. Black Clawson Co.; Rogers v. Loews L'Enfant Plaza Hotel*).

III. ATTORNEY'S FEES AND COSTS

Prevailing parties in sexual harassment suits brought pursuant to civil rights statutes, such as Title VII or state FEP statutes, may recover their reasonable attorney's fees and costs.

A. The Prevailing Plaintiff

1. Judicial Proceedings. In order to "prevail," the complainant must succeed on any significant issue in the litigation that achieved some of the benefit sought. The complainant need not prevail on each claim or even the main claim, but must force some material alteration in the parties' legal relationship (*Texas State Teachers Ass'n v. Garland Indep. School Dist.*). Courts are split on whether a party must obtain back pay, injunctive relief, or at least some voluntary action by the employer to be entitled to an award of attorney's fees (*Moran v. Pima County; Swanson v. Elmhurst Chrysler Plymouth*).

A complainant may be considered to have prevailed, even if all relief is obtained voluntarily, if the lawsuit prompted the employer to provide the relief (*Maher v. Gagne*). The complainant is also generally entitled to attorney's fees, unless she expressly waives them, if the parties settle the lawsuit and give the complainant relief, or if the complainant accepts the employer's offer of judgment (*Maher v. Gagne; David v. AM Int'l*).

2. Administrative Proceedings. Courts also may award attorney's fees for hours expended in an administrative proceeding that the complainant was required to exhaust or that were reasonably expended in preparation for the subsequent litigation (*New York Gas Light Club v. Carey; Webb v. County Bd. of Educ.*).

B. Computation of Fee Awards

In computing fee awards in sexual harassment cases, the court initially determines the "lodestar" amount, which is the number of hours reasonably expended multiplied by a reasonable hourly rate. The fee applicant has the burden of establishing the reasonableness of the number of hours expended and the hourly rate. Once the lodestar amount is determined, the court, in its discretion, may adjust it downward or upward, typically weighing such factors as (1) novelty and difficulty of the case, (2) skill required, (3) preclusion of other employment caused by the case, (4) contingent or fixed nature of the fee, and (5) awards in similar cases (*Johnson v. Georgia Highway Express*).

One factor that may justify a downward adjustment in the lodestar figure is a partial success. Where the complainant has succeeded on some but not all claims, and the successful and unsuccessful claims are unrelated, hours expended on the unsuccessful claims are excluded from the fee award (*McHenry v. Chadwick*).

A second circumstance under which the fee award is limited is when a prevailing party receives an award at trial that is less than a previously rejected offer of judgment. Under such circumstances, the prevailing complainant may not be entitled to recover her post-offer costs, which include attorney's fees, because as to the post-offer litigation she has not "prevailed" (*Marek v. Chesny*). For a discussion of offers of judgment, see Chapter 18, section II.B.

C. The Prevailing Defendant

A prevailing *defendant* in a sexual harassment case may obtain attorney's fees under Title VII only if the plaintiff's suit was "frivolous, unreasonable or without foundation." (*Christiansburg Garment Co. v. EEOC*). Two factors courts have considered in determining the amount of fees to be awarded a prevailing defendant are (1) the complainant's motivation in bringing the lawsuit, and (2) the relative ability of the parties to absorb the cost of litigation (*Hill v. BASF Wyandotte Corp.; Kota v. Abele Tractor & Equip. Co.*).

In *Jackson-Colley v. Army Corps of Engineers*, a Title VII action, the court found that the complainant had acted in bad faith by raising sexual harassment allegations that had not been raised in a prior administrative appeal of her performance-based discharge. Moreover, she had attributed sexual motivation to a supervisor's "gawking" and scratching of his groin, when in fact the supervisor had a vision problem and a medical condition that induced the scratching. Calling the complainant's allegations "grossly aggrandized" and "mean-spirited," the court imposed costs and attorney's fees on the complainant.

Courts also have awarded attorney's fees to prevailing defendants when the complainant has acted in bad faith during the course of the litigation and the complainant's counsel has engaged in misrepresentations and abuses of the litigation process (see *Perkins v. General Motors Corp.*, where the complainant continued to prosecute the claim after a judicial finding of no harassment and also made misleading statements to the court).

D. Costs

Prevailing parties in sexual harassment cases generally are entitled to have their costs paid by the other party. "Costs" include court reporter fees, docket fees, and photocopies of papers necessarily obtained for use in the case (28 U.S.C. §1920).

The Civil Rights Act of 1991 amended Title VII to provide that an award of reasonable attorney's fees may include an award of expert fees.

For purposes of awarding costs, the complainant is considered to be a "prevailing party" if she succeeds on any significant issue in the litigation that achieved some of the benefit she sought in the lawsuit (*Texas State Teachers Ass'n v. Garland Indep. School Dist.*). When the defendant prevails, courts routinely award costs. Still, courts have discretion to disallow costs that are unreasonable, unnecessary, or excessive, or when the complainant has limited financial means (*Zabkowicz v. West Bend Co.; Wrighten v. Metropolitan Hosp.*).

22

SETTLEMENT

I. OVERVIEW

The possibility of adverse publicity, dissemination of highly personal information, costs of litigation, loss of management time, and the risk of liability all lead employers to settle even cases that are not clearly meritorious. Complainants settle to obtain monetary and other benefits and to avoid the uncertainty and delay inherent in litigation. Thus, many sexual harassment cases are settled before trial, before the filing of a complaint, and even before administrative charges have been filed.

II. VALIDITY OF WAIVER OF SEXUAL HARASSMENT CLAIMS

A. Introduction

Virtually all settlements involve a written release or waiver of claims by the complainant, since this is typically the most important consideration for the employer. Releases of past claims are valid, providing the release is "voluntary and knowing."

The validity of a release may come into question if the complainant settles and then files suit. Factors that affect the validity of a release include:

(1) the complainant's education and business experience;
(2) whether the release is part of a written agreement that is understandable by the average person;
(3) whether the release specifically refers to the statutory rights or claims being waived;
(4) whether the release is given in return for consideration (money or benefits) that is in addition to what the complainant already would be entitled to receive;
(5) the amount of time given to the complainant to consider the settlement and release before signing it;
(6) the role the complainant had in deciding the terms of the settlement;
(7) the clarity of the settlement agreement; and
(8) whether the complainant was represented by counsel, encouraged to seek counsel, or given a fair opportunity to consult with counsel.

Waivers of an employee's future claims under Title VII are not valid (*Alexander v. Gardner-Denver Co.*).

B. Confidentiality

To avoid adverse publicity and to discourage unmeritorious claims by others, employers often bargain for confidentiality clauses. At the start of negotiations, the complainant should be counseled that the negotiations themselves should be kept confidential to prevent widespread discussion of the terms. A confidentiality clause should clearly define the scope of the obligation and specify any disclosure exceptions (such as to legal counsel, to tax advisors, to a spouse, in response to a court order, and, when necessary, to enforce the settlement). The provision should also oblige the complainant to instruct any individual who is permissibly informed about the settlement to maintain the confidentiality of the information.

In many instances, particularly if litigation has commenced, the parties should agree upon a statement (*e.g.,* "the matter has been resolved to my satisfaction") that they will use in response to inquiries after a settlement agreement has been reached. Care also must be used in crafting such statements to avoid defamation arising out of allegations of sexual harassment.

Allowance must be made for the employer's reasonable need to communicate within the company and to third parties, such as auditors and legal counsel. Broad promises of confidentiality on behalf of all employees should not be made if the employer cannot ensure compliance. An alternative is to promise to instruct designated individuals to hold the matter in confidence.

C. Acknowledgment Concerning Legal Advice and Voluntariness

The settlement agreement should recite that the complainant has consulted an attorney or was given sufficient time to do so, and that the complainant has read the agreement, understands it, and is signing it voluntarily.

D. Additional Provisions

Other common provisions include:

- a nonadmission of wrongdoing or liability,
- an integration clause stating that the writing constitutes the total agreement,
- a choice-of-law clause,
- an indemnity provision,
- a provision stating whether the settlement payment includes attorney's fees,
- an "after-acquired facts" clause stating that information discovered later will not affect the validity of the settlement, and
- a severance clause that eliminates any unlawful provision so that the rest of the agreement remains in effect.

A provision may also be included for the resolution of any future dispute over any breach of the agreement; attorney's fees in such event; and the right of the employer to respond with an "offensive action" to recover its legal expenses in the event a lawsuit is filed in breach of the complainant's covenant not to sue. Arbitration clauses are frequently being added to provide for resolving any disputes over alleged breaches of the settlement agreement.

III. TAX CONSEQUENCES

The "take-home" value of the settlement to the complainant will be substantially greater to the extent that taxes are not withheld on all or a portion of the settlement. Thus, whether a settlement payment is to be considered wages for withholding purposes is an important factor in settlement negotiations. The decision of whether to withhold and pay employment taxes on some or all of a settlement's proceeds can be very important. If a settlement amount from which no taxes are withheld is later found to constitute wage income, the necessary taxes, plus interest and penalties, will be due from both employer and complainant. The employer can be held liable for both the employer's and employee's portion. The advice of competent tax counsel can therefore be critical in structuring a settlement agreement and in understanding the risks of failing to withhold taxes on settlement payments. Some general concepts, however, can be stated here.

The Internal Revenue Code excludes from taxable income "damages received" on account of "personal injuries or sickness." Treasury regulations define "damages received" as "an amount received (other than workers' compensation) through prosecution of a legal suit or action *based on tort or tort type rights*, or through a settlement agreement entered into in lieu of such prosecution" (emphasis added). Under this regulation, whether settlement proceeds will be excluded from income depends upon the facts and the nature of the claim, not its effect or consequences.

In *United States v. Burke,* the Supreme Court has given some limited guidance as to the taxability of settlement proceeds in employment discrimination cases. The Court generally indicated that settlements of these cases might permissibly be free of tax and approved the test in the Treasury regulations—that the "personal injuries" exemption from taxation depends not on whether the harm alleged is health-related, but rather on whether the claim being settled is tort-like in nature. Under this test, the settlement proceeds in *Burke* were taxable, because the claims being settled arose under Title VII as it existed prior to the Civil

Rights Act of 1991. Title VII at that time did not permit compensatory or other tort-like remedies. The *Burke* Court did not have occasion to address the issue that is likely to arise now—the taxability of payments to settle claims arising under employment discrimination statutes that *do* permit tort-like remedies—but the Court's language indicates that such a settlement may be tax-free.

If some claims of a former employee are tort-like in nature and other claims are contractual in nature, one technique in settlement negotiations is to allocate part of a settlement payment to wages (subject to withholding) and part to nonwages (not subject to withholding). In *Metzger v. Commissioner*, the Tax Court upheld an allocation in a settlement agreement that treated half of the $75,000 settlement payment as a settlement of wage claims (taxable) and the other half as a settlement of all claims other than wages (not taxable). The settlement involved both employment discrimination claims and a claim for breach of contract. The Tax Court held that the violation of the taxpayer's constitutional and statutory right to be free from discrimination was a claim for redress of personal injuries. The extent to which this holding—that money paid in settlement of Title VII claims is excludable from income—will be followed by the Tax Court and the IRS is uncertain. In a private letter ruling, the IRS has stated that it has not acquiesced in a general way to the *Metzger* decision.

In sexual harassment cases, statutory employment discrimination claims frequently are accompanied by common-law tort claims and common-law contract claims. If consistent with the allegations in the case and the course of settlement negotiations, it is advisable to state expressly whether all or a portion of the settlement is allocable to the complainant's tort or tort-like personal injury claims and to include a recitation of the tort claims being released.

Part V

Appendices

EEOC 1980 GUIDELINES ON SEXUAL HARASSMENT

Sec. 1604.11. Sexual Harassment

(a) Harassment on the basis of sex is a violation of Sec. 703 of Title VII. * Unwelcome sexual advances, requests for sexual favors, and other verbal or physical conduct of a sexual nature constitute sexual harassment when (1) submission to such conduct is made either explicitly or implicitly a term or condition of an individual's employment, (2) submission to or rejection of such conduct by an individual is used as the basis for employment decisions affecting such individual, or (3) such conduct has the purpose or effect of unreasonably interfering with an individual's work performance or creating an intimidating, hostile, or offensive working environment.

(b) In determining whether alleged conduct constitutes sexual harassment, the Commission will look at the record as a whole and at the totality of the circumstances, such as the nature of the sexual advances and the context in which the alleged incidents occurred. The determination of the legality of a particular action will be made from the facts, on a case by case basis.

(c) Applying general Title VII principles, an employer, employment agency, joint apprenticeship committee or labor organization (hereinafter collectively referred to as "employer") is responsible for its acts and those of its agents and supervisory employees with respect to sexual harassment regardless of whether the specific acts complained of were authorized or even forbidden by the employer and regardless of whether the employer knew or should have known of their occurrence. The Commission will examine the circumstances of the partic-

---
*The principles involved here continue to apply to race, color, religion or national origin.

ular employment relationship and the job functions performed by the individual in determining whether an individual acts in either a supervisory or agency capacity.

(d) With respect to conduct between fellow employees, an employer is responsible for acts of sexual harassment in the workplace where the employer (or its agents or supervisory employees) knows or should have known of the conduct, unless it can show that it took immediate and appropriate corrective action.

(e) An employer may also be responsible for the acts of non-employees, with respect to sexual harassment of employees in the workplace, where the employer (or its agents or supervisory employees) knows or should have known of the conduct and fails to take immediate and appropriate corrective action. In reviewing these cases the Commission will consider the extent of the employer's control and any other legal responsibility which the employer may have with respect to the conduct of such non-employees.

(f) Prevention is the best tool for the elimination of sexual harassment. An employer should take all steps necessary to prevent sexual harassment from occurring, such as affirmatively raising the subject, expressing strong disapproval, developing appropriate sanctions, informing employees of their right to raise and how to raise the issue of harassment under Title VII, and developing methods to sensitize all concerned.

(g) Other related practices: Where employment opportunities or benefits are granted because of an individual's submission to the employer's sexual advances or requests for sexual favors, the employer may be held liable for unlawful sex discrimination against other persons who were qualified for but denied that employment opportunity or benefit.

Reprinted from *Fair Employment Practices, Labor Relations Reporter,* The Bureau of National Affairs, Inc., Washington, D.C.

EEOC POLICY GUIDANCE ON EMPLOYER LIABILITY FOR SEXUAL FAVORITISM

Following is the text of an EEOC policy guide issued January 12, 1990, providing guidance to the Commission's field staff on the extent to which an employer should be held liable for discriminating against qualified individuals based on the employer's favoritism toward another individual who submitted to sexual advances or requests.

EEOC POLICY GUIDE

Subject Matter

Background

The Commission and the courts have declared that sexual harassment violates Section 703 of Title VII. *Meritor Savings Bank v. Vinson,* 477 U.S. 57, 64, 40 EPD ¶31,159 [40 FEP Cases 1822] (1986); EEOC's Guidelines on Discrimination Because of Sex, 29 C.F.R. §§1604.11(a). EEOC's Guidelines define two kinds of sexual harassment: "quid pro quo," in which "submission to or rejection of [unwelcome sexual] conduct by an individual is used as the basis for employment decisions affecting such individual," and "hostile environment," in which unwelcome sexual conduct "unreasonably interfer[es] with an individual's job performance" or creates an "intimidating, hostile or offensive working environment." 29 C.F.R. §§1604.11(a)(2) and (3).

Subsection (g) of EEOC's Guidelines provides:

> where employment opportunities or benefits are granted because of an individual's submission to the employer's sexual advances or requests for sexual favor, the employer may be held liable for unlawful sex discrimination against other persons who were qualified for but were denied that employment opportunity or benefit.

As discussed below, sexual favoritism in the workplace which adversely affects the employment opportunities of third parties may take the form of implicit "quid pro quo" harassment and/or "hostile work environment" harassment.

Discussion

A. Isolated Instances of Favoritism Towards a "Paramour" Not Prohibited

Not all types of sexual favoritism violate Title VII.[1] It is the Commission's position that Title VII does not prohibit isolated instances of preferential treatment based upon consensual romantic relationships. An isolated instance of favoritism toward a "paramour" (or a spouse, or a friend) may be unfair, but it does not discriminate against women or men in violation of Title VII, since both are disadvantaged for reasons other than their genders.[2] A female charging party who is denied an employment benefit because of such sexual favoritism would not have been treated more favorably had she been a man nor, conversely, was she treated less favorably because she was a woman. *See Miller v. Aluminum Co. of America,* 679 F.Supp. 495, 47 EPD ¶38,112 [45 FEP Cases 1775] (W.D. Pa.), *aff'd mem.,* 856 F.2d 184 (3d Cir. 1988);[3]

---

[1] The material in §615 of the Compliance Manual on subsection (g) of the Guidelines (at pp. 615-10 and 11) is superseded by this Policy Guidance.

[2] *See Benzies v. Illinois Dept. of Mental Health,* 810 F.2d 146, 148, 39 EPD ¶35,870 [42 FEP Cases 1537] (7th Cir.), *cert. denied,* 107 S.Ct. 3231 [43 FEP Cases 1896] (1987) (denial of promotion to woman is not violation if motivated by personal or political favoritism or a grudge); *Bellissimo v. Westinghouse Electric Corp.,* 764 F.2d 175, 180, 37 EPD ¶35,315 [37 FEP Cases 1862] (3d Cir. 1985), *cert. denied,* 475 U.S. 1035, 39 EPD ¶35,875 [40 FEP Cases 192] (1986) (discharge of female employee violates Title VII only if it is done on a basis that would not result in the discharge of a male employee).

[3] The plaintiff in *Miller* alleged that her supervisor treated her less favorably than her co-worker because the supervisor knew that the co-worker was engaged in a romantic relationship with the plant manager. *Miller,* 679 F.Supp. at 500-01. The lower court held that in order to establish a Title VII

Reprinted from *Fair Employment Practices, Labor Relations Reporter,* The Bureau of National Affairs, Inc., Washington, D.C.

DeCintio v. Westchester County Medical Center 807 F.2d 304, 42 EPD ¶36,785 [42 FEP Cases 921] (2d Cir. 1986), cert. denied, 108 S.Ct. 89, 44 EPD ¶37,425 (1987).[4] But see King v. Palmer, 778 F.2d 878, 39 EPD ¶35,808, [39 FEP Cases 877] reh'g denied, 39 EPD ¶36,036 [40 FEP Cases 190] (D.C. Cir. 1985).[5]

claim, the plaintiff would have to show that her employer would have or did treat males differently. Id. at 501. Since the plaintiff's male co-workers shared with her the same disadvantage relative to the co-worker who was engaged in the affair with the manager, the plaintiff could not show that she was treated differently than males. Id. On appeal to the Third Circuit, the Commission filed an amicus brief supporting the ruling of the district court on the basis that favoritism toward a female employee because of a consensual romantic relationship with a male supervisor is not sex discrimination against other female employees within the meaning of Title VII. The Court of Appeals summarily affirmed.

[4]In DeCintio, seven male respiratory therapists claimed that they were unlawfully disqualified for a promotion that went to a woman who was engaged in a romantic relationship with the department administrator. The court held that the department administrator's conduct, though unfair, did not violate Title VII. DeCintio, 807 F.2d at 308. The court reasoned that the prohibition of sex discrimination in Title VII refers to discrimination on the basis of one's sex, not on the basis of one's sexual affiliations; the therapists' claims were not cognizable under the Act since they were denied promotion because the administrator preferred his "paramour," rather than because of their status as males. Id. The court distinguished EEOC's Guidelines by stating that they address the granting of employment benefits because of an individual's "submission" to sexual advances or requests, and the word "submission" connotes a lack of consent. Since the department administrator did not force anyone to submit to sexual advances in order to win promotion, his conduct was not within the purview of the Guidelines. Id. at 307-08. Accord, Handley v. Phillips, 715 F.Supp. 657, 675, (M.D. Pa. 1989).

[5]In King, the plaintiff claimed she had been denied a promotion that went to a less qualified co-worker who was engaged in an intimate relationship with the selecting official. Although the issue of whether Title VII applied to preferential treatment was not raised on appeal, the court stated that it agreed with the lower court's conclusion that the case was within the purview of Title VII. King, 778 F.2d at 880. The court ruled in favor of the plaintiff on the basis of its finding that her co-worker was promoted because of the sexual relationship. Id. at 882. In a concurring opinion to the decision denying a suggestion for rehearing en banc, it was emphasized that the issue of whether Title VII applied to the facts of the case was

B. Favoritism Based Upon Coerced Sexual Conduct May Constitute Quid Pro Quo Harassment

If a female employee[6] is coerced into submitting to unwelcome sexual advances in return for a job benefit, other female employees who were qualified for but were denied the benefit may be able to establish that sex was generally made a condition for receiving the benefit.[7] Thus, in order for a woman to have obtained the job benefit at issue, it would have been necessary to grant sexual favors, a condition that would not have been imposed on men. This is substantially the same as a traditional sexual harassment charge alleging that sexual favors were implicitly demanded as a "quid pro quo" in return for job benefits.[8] For example, in Toscano v. Nimmo, 570 F.Supp. 1197, 1199-1201, 32 EPD ¶33,848 [32 FEP Cases 1401] (D. Del. 1983), the court found a violation of Title VII based on the fact that the granting of sexual favors was a condition for promotion. Although the individual who was granted preferential treatment was engaged in a consensual affair with her supervisor, there was evidence that the supervisor made telephone calls to proposition several female employees at home, phoned employees at work to describe his supposed sexual encounters with female em-

not raised on appeal or in the petition for rehearing. 39 EPD ¶36,036.

[6]Although this Policy Guidance uses female pronouns to refer to individuals who are treated favorably because they engage in sexual conduct, it also covers situations in which men are granted favorable treatment based on sexual conduct.

[7]The employer would also be liable for "quid pro quo" harassment with regard to the individual who was coerced into submitting to the advances.

[8]See Section 1604.11(1) of EEOC's Guidelines on Sexual Harassment, which states that a violation will be found when submission to unwelcome sexual conduct is made "either explicitly or implicitly" a term or condition of an individual's employment.

ployees under his supervision, and engaged in suggestive behavior at work.[9]

Many times, a third party female will not be able to establish that sex was generally made a condition for the benefit in question. For example, a supervisor may have been interested in only one woman and, thus, have coerced only her. Nevertheless, in such a case, both women and men who were qualified for but were denied the benefit would have standing to challenge the favoritism on the basis that they were injured as a result of the discrimination leveled against the woman who was coerced. *See* EEOC amicus brief (filed Sept. 30, 1988) in *Clayton v. White Hall School District*, 875 F.2d 676, 50 EPD ¶39,048 [49 FEP Cases 1618] (8th Cir. 1989), in which the Commission argued that a white employee had standing under Title VII to challenge her employer's decision to deny her an employment benefit pursuant to an employment policy which it allegedly enforced for the purpose of denying the same benefit to a black employee; although the plaintiff was not the object of racial discrimination, she was injured as a result of the race discrimination practiced against the black employee.[10] *See also DeCintio v. Westchester County Medical Center*, 807 F.2d at 307-08 (by implication) (male plaintiffs' claims of favoritism rejected not because of lack of standing but because the woman who received the favorable treatment was not coerced into submitting to sexual advances); *EEOC v. T.I.M.E.-D.C. Freight, Inc.*, 659 F.2d 690 n.2, 27 EPD ¶32,202 [27 FEP Cases 10] (5th Cir. 1981) (white plaintiffs could

challenge discrimination against blacks provided that they could establish a personal injury); *Allen v. American Home Foods, Inc.*, 644 F.Supp. 1553, 42 EPD ¶36,911 [42 FEP Cases 407] (N.D. Ind. 1986) (males who lost their jobs due to their employer's discrimination against female coworkers suffered an injury as a result of the discrimination, and therefore had standing to sue under Title VII).

C. Widespread Favoritism May Constitute Hostile Environment Harassment

If favoritism based upon the granting of sexual favors is widespread in a workplace, both male and female colleagues who do not welcome this conduct can establish a hostile work environment in violation of Title VII regardless of whether any objectionable conduct is directed at them and regardless of whether those who were granted favorable treatment willingly bestowed the sexual favors. In these circumstances, a message is implicitly conveyed that the managers view women as "sexual playthings," thereby creating an atmosphere that is demeaning to women. Both men and women who find this offensive can establish a violation if the conduct is "sufficiently severe or pervasive 'to alter the conditions of [their] employment and create an abusive working environment.'" *Vinson*, 477 U.S. at 67, [quoting *Henson v. City of Dundee*, 682 F.2d 897, 904, 29 EPD ¶32,993 [29 FEP Cases 787] (11th Cir. 1982)),.[11] An analogy can be made to a situation in which supervisors in an office regularly

---

[9]*See also DeCintio v. Westchester County Medical Center*, 807 F.2d at 307, in which the court stated that the claim in *Toscano* was premised on the coercive nature of the employer's acts, and therefore that the case lent no support to the contention that a voluntary amorous involvement may form the basis of a Title VII claim.

[10]In *Clayton*, the court ruled that the plaintiff did have standing, but it based that standing on her allegation of a hostile work environment. 875 F.2d at 679.

[11]*See* EEOC's Policy Guidance on Current Issues of Sexual Harassment (10/25/88) at 13-18 for standards governing the determination of whether a work environment is "hostile." That Policy Guidance makes clear that the commission will evaluate the totality of circumstances or a case-by-case basis, employing the objective perspective of a "reasonable person" in the context in which the challenged conduct took place. Some factors that could be considered in determining whether a hostile environment is established are the number of incidents of favoritism, the egregiousness of the incidents, and whether or not other employees in the office were made aware of the conduct.

make racial, ethnic or sexual jokes. Even if the targets of the humor "play along" and in no way display that they object, co-workers of any race, national origin or sex can claim that this conduct, which communicates a bias against protected class members, creates a hostile work environment for them. *See Rogers v. EEOC*, 454 F.2d 234, 4 EPD ¶7597 [4 FEP Cases 92] (5th Cir. 1971), *cert. denied*, 406 U.S. 957, 4 EPD ¶7838 [4 FEP Cases 771] (1972) (discriminatory treatment of medical patients created hostile work environment for plaintiff employee); Commission Decision No. 71-969, CCH EEOC Decisions (1973) ¶6193 (supervisor's habitual use of racial epithet in referring to Black employees created discriminatory work environment for White Charging Party); Compliance Manual Volume II, Section 615.3(a)(3) Examples (1) and (2) (sexual harassment of females may create hostile work environment for other male and female employees).

Managers who engage in widespread sexual favoritism may also communicate a message that the way for a woman to get ahead in the workplace is by engaging in sexual conduct or that sexual solicitations are a prerequisite to their fair treatment.[12] This can form the basis of an implicit "quid pro quo" harassment claim for female employees, as well as a hostile environment claim for both women and men who find this offensive.[13]

---

[12]*See, e.g., Priest v. Rotary*, 634 F.Supp. 571, 39 EPD ¶35,897 [40 FEP Cases 208] (N.D. Cal. 1986), in which the defendant gave preferential treatment to his consensual sexual partner and to those female employees who reacted favorably to his sexual advances and other conduct of a sexual nature, and he disadvantaged those employees, including the plaintiff, who reacted unfavorably to his conduct. The court found a violation of Title VII in part because the defendant's conduct implied that job benefits would be conditioned on an employee's good-natured endurance of his sexually-charged conduct or sexual advances. *Id.* at 581.

[13]In *Miller v. Aluminum Co. of America*, 679 F.Supp. at 501-502, the court rejected a claim that sexual favoritism based on a consensual relationship can create a hostile environment for others in the workplace. The court found that the favoritism itself

The case of *Broderick v. Ruder*, 685 F.Supp. 1269, 46 EPD ¶37,963 [48 FEP Cases 232] (D.D.C. 1988) illustrates how widespread sexual favoritism can be found to violate Title VII. In *Broderick* a staff attorney at the Securities and Exchange Commission alleged that two of her supervisors had engaged in sexual relationships with two secretaries who received promotions, cash awards, and other job benefits. Another of her supervisors allegedly promoted the career of a staff attorney with whom he socialized extensively and to whom he was noticeably attracted. In addition, there were isolated instances of sexual harassment directed at the plaintiff herself, including an incident in which her supervisor became drunk at an office party, untied the plaintiff's sweater, and kissed her. The court found that the conduct of these supervisors "created an atmosphere of hostile work environment" offensive to the plaintiff and several other witnesses. It further stated that the supervisors' conduct in bestowing preferential treatment upon those who submitted to their sexual advances undermined the plaintiff's motivation and work performance and deprived her and other female employees of promotions and job opportunities. *Broderick*, 685 F.Supp. at 1278. While the court in *Broderick* grounded its ruling on the hostile environment theory, it is the Commission's position that these facts could also support an implicit "quid pro quo" harassment claim since the managers, by their conduct, communicated a message to all female employees in the office that job benefits would be awarded to those who participated in

---

did not violate Title VII since it was voluntary, and that "[h]ostile behavior that does not bespeak an unlawful motive cannot support a hostile work environment claim." *Id.* at 502. However, it is the Commission's position that had the sexual favoritism been widespread, the fact that it was exclusively voluntary and consensual would not have defeated a claim that it created a hostile work environment for other people in the workplace. As indicated above in n.11, the question of whether actions complained of are sufficiently widespread or egregious to constitute a hostile environment must be decided case-by-case.

sexual conduct. *See also Spencer v. General Electric*, 697 F.Supp. 204 (E.D. Va. 1988).[14]

Example 1 — Charging Party (CP) alleges that she lost a promotion for which she was qualified because the co-worker who obtained the promotion was engaged in a sexual relationship with their supervisor. EEOC's investigation discloses that the relationship at issue was consensual and that the supervisor had never subjected CP's co-worker or any other employees to unwelcome sexual advances. The Commission would find no violation of Title VII in these circumstances, because men and women were equally disadvantaged by the supervisor's conduct for reasons other than their genders. Even if CP is genuinely offended by the supervisor's conduct, she has no Title VII claim.

Example 2 — Same as above, except the relationship at issue was *not* consensual. Instead, CP's supervisor regularly harassed the co-worker in front of other employees, demanded sexual favors as a condition for her promotion, and then audibly boasted about his "conquest." In these circumstances, CP may be able to establish a violation of Title VII by showing that in order to have obtained the promotion, it would have been necessary to grant sexual favors. In addition, she and other qualified men and women who were denied the promotion would have standing to challenge the favoritism on the basis that they were injured as a result of the discrimination levelled against their co-worker.

Example 3 — Same as Example 1, except CP's supervisor and other management personnel regularly solicited sexual favors from subordinate employees and offered job opportunities to those who complied. Some of those employees willingly consented to the sexual requests and in turn received promotions and awards. Others consented because they recognized that their opportunities for advancement would otherwise be limited. CP, who did not welcome this conduct, was not approached for sexual favors. However, she and other female and male co-workers may be able to establish that the conduct created a hostile work environment. She can also claim that by their conduct, the managers communicated to all female employees that they can obtain job benefits only by acquiescing in sexual conduct.

Date: 1/12/90   Approved: ———————————
                                          Clarence Thomas
                                          Chairman

---

[14]In *Spencer*, the supervisor of an office engaged in virtually daily horseplay of a sexual nature with female subordinates. This behavior included sitting on their laps, touching them in an intimate manner, and making lewd comments. The subordinates joined in and generally found the horseplay funny and inoffensive. With the exception of one incident (which may have been time-barred and was not critical to the court's decision), none of the horseplay was directed at the plaintiff. The supervisor additionally engaged in consensual relations with at least two of his subordinates. The court found that the supervisor's conduct would have interfered with the work performance and would have seriously affected the psychological well-being of a reasonable employee, and on that basis it found a violation of Title VII. 697 F.Supp. at 218. Although *Spencer* did not involve sexual favoritism, the case supports the proposition that pervasive sexual conduct can create a hostile work environment for those who find it offensive even if the targets of the conduct welcome it and even if no sexual conduct is directed at the persons bringing the claim.

EEOC POLICY GUIDANCE ON CURRENT ISSUES OF SEXUAL HARASSMENT

Following is the text of a March 19, 1990, policy guide issued to EEOC field office personnel that defines sexual harassment and establishes employer liability in light of recent court decisions. This policy statement replaces one issued October 17, 1988.

EEOC POLICY GUIDANCE

Subject Matter

This document provides guidance on defining sexual harassment and establishing employer liability in light of recent cases.

Section 703(a)(1) of Title VII, 42 U.S.C. §2000e-2(a) provides:

It shall be an unlawful employment practice for an employer —
... to fail or refuse to hire or to discharge any individual, or otherwise to discriminate against any individual with respect to his compensation, terms, conditions, or privileges of employment, because of such individual's race, color, religion, sex, or national origin[.]

In 1980 the Commission issued guidelines declaring sexual harassment a violation of Section 703 of Title VII, establishing criteria for determining when unwelcome conduct of a sexual nature constitutes sexual harassment, defining the circumstances under which an employer may be held liable, and suggesting affirmative steps an employer should take to prevent sexual harassment. *See* Section 1604.11 of the Guidelines on Discrimination Because of Sex, 29 C.F.R. §1604.11 ("Guidelines") [403:213]. The Commission has applied the Guidelines in its enforcement litigation, and many lower courts have relied on the Guidelines.

The issue of whether sexual harassment violates Title VII reached the Supreme Court in 1986 in *Meritor Savings Bank v. Vinson*, 106 S.Ct. 2399, 40 EPD ¶36,159 [40 FEP Cases 1822] (1986). The Court affirmed the basic premises of the Guidelines as well as the Commission's definition. The purpose of this document is to provide guidance on the following issues in light of the developing law after *Vinson*:

— determining whether sexual conduct is "unwelcome;"
— evaluating evidence of harassment;
— determining whether a work environment is sexually "hostile;"
— holding employers liable for sexual harassment by supervisors; and
— evaluating preventive and remedial action taken in response to claims of sexual harassment.

BACKGROUND

A. Definition

Title VII does not proscribe all conduct of a sexual nature in the workplace. Thus it is crucial to clearly define sexual harassment: only unwelcome sexual conduct that is a term or condition of employment constitutes a violation. 29 C.F.R. §1604.11(a). The EEOC's Guidelines define two types of sexual harassment: "quid pro quo" and "hostile environment." The Guidelines provide that "unwelcome" sexual conduct constitutes sexual harassment when "submission to such conduct is made either explicitly or implicitly a term or condition of an individual's employment," 29 C.F.R. §1604.11(a)(1). "Quid pro quo harassment" occurs when "submission to or rejection of such conduct by an individual is used as the basis for employment decisions affecting such individual," 29 C.F.R. §1604.11(a)(2).[1] The EEOC's

[1]*See, e.g., Miller v. Bank of America*, 600 F.2d 211, 20 EPD ¶30,086 [20 FEP Cases 462] (9th Cir. 1979) (plaintiff discharged when she refused to cooperate with her supervisor's sexual advances); *Barnes v. Costle*, 561 F.2d 983, 14 EPD ¶7755 [15 FEP Cases 345] (D.C. Cir. 1977) (plaintiff's job abolished after

Reprinted from *Fair Employment Practices, Labor Relations Reporter*, The Bureau of National Affairs, Inc., Washington, D.C.

Guidelines also recognize that unwelcome sexual conduct that "unreasonably interfer[es] with an individual's job performance" or creates an "intimidating, hostile, or offensive working environment" can constitute sex discrimination, even if it leads to no tangible or economic job consequences. 29 C.F.R. §1604.11 (a)(3).[2] The Supreme Court's decision in *Vinson* established that both types of sexual harassment are actionable under section 703 of Title VII of the Civil Rights Act of 1964, 42 U.S.C. §2000e-2(a), as forms of sex discrimination.

Although "quid pro quo" and "hostile environment" harassment are theoretically distinct claims, the line between the two is not always clear and the two forms of harassment often occur together. For example, an employee's tangible job conditions are affected when a sexually hostile work environment results in her constructive discharge.[3] Similarly, a supervisor who makes sexual advances toward a subordinate employee may

communicate an implicit threat to adversely affect her job status if she does not comply. "Hostile environment" harassment may acquire characteristics of "quid pro quo" harassment if the offending supervisor abuses his authority over employment decisions to force the victim to endure or participate in the sexual conduct. Sexual harassment may culminate in a retaliatory discharge if a victim tells the harasser or her employer she will no longer submit to the harassment, and is then fired in retaliation for this protest. Under these circumstances it would be appropriate to conclude that both harassment and retaliation in violation of section 704(a) of Title VII have occurred.

Distinguishing between the two types of harassment is necessary when determining the employer's liability (*see infra* Section D). But while categorizing sexual harassment as "quid pro quo," "hostile environment," or both is useful analytically these distinctions should not limit the Commission's investigations,[4] which generally should consider all available evidence and testimony under all possibly applicable theories.[5]

---

she refused to submit to her supervisor's sexual advances); *Williams v. Saxbe*, 413 F.Supp. 665, 11 EPD 10,840 [12 FEP Cases 1093] (D.D.C. 1976), *rev'd and remanded on other grounds sub nom. Williams v. Bell*, 587 F.2d 1240, 17 EPD ¶8605 [17 FEP Cases 1662] (D.C. Cir. 1978), *on remand sub nom. Williams v. Civiletti*, 487 F.Supp. 1387, 23 EPD ¶30,916 [22 FEP Cases 1311] (D.D.C. 1980) (plaintiff reprimanded and eventually terminated for refusing to submit to her supervisor's sexual demands).

[2]*See, e.g., Katz v. Dole*, 709 F.2d 251, 32 EPD ¶33,639 [31 FEP Cases 1521] (4th Cir. 1983) (plaintiff's workplace pervaded with sexual slur, insult, and innuendo and plaintiff subjected to verbal sexual harassment consisting of extremely vulgar and offensive sexually related epithets); *Henson v. City of Dundee*, 682 F.2d 897, 29 EPD ¶32,993 [29 FEP Cases 787] (11th Cir. 1982) (plaintiff's supervisor subjected her to numerous harangues of demeaning sexual inquiries and vulgarities and repeated requests that she have sexual relations with him); *Bundy v. Jackson*, 641 F.2d 934, 24 EPD ¶31,439 [24 FEP Cases 1155] (D.C. Cir. 1981) (plaintiff subjected to sexual propositions by supervisors, and sexual intimidation was "standard operating procedure" in workplace).

[3]To avoid cumbersome use of both masculine and feminine pronouns, this document will refer to harassers as males and victims as females. The Commission recognizes, however, that men may also be victims and women may also be harassers.

[4]For a description of the respective roles of the Commission and other federal agencies in investigating complaints of discrimination in the federal sector, *see* 29 C.F.R. §1613.216. [403:692]

[5]In a subsection entitled "Other related practices," the Guidelines also provide that where an employment opportunity or benefit is granted because of an individual's "submission to the employer's sexual advances or requests for sexual favors," the employer may be liable for unlawful sex discrimination against others who were qualified for but were denied the opportunity or benefit. 29 C.F.R. §1604.11(g). The law is unsettled as to when a Title VII violation can be established in these circumstances. *See DeCintio v. Westchester County Medical Center*, 807 F.2d 304, 42 EPD ¶36,785 [42 FEP Cases 921] (2d Cir. 1986), *cert. denied*, 108 S.Ct. 89, 44 EPD ¶37,425 (1987); *King v. Palmer*, 778 F.2d 878, 39 EPD ¶35,808 [39 FEP Cases 877] (D.C. Cir. 1985), *decision on remand*, 641 F.Supp. 186, 40 EPD ¶36,245 (D.D.C. 1986); *Broderick v. Ruder*, 46 EPD ¶37,963 [48 FEP Cases 232] (D.D.C. 1988); *Miller v. Aluminum Co. of America*, 679 F.Supp. 495, 500-01 [45 FEP Cases 1775] (W.D. Pa.), *aff'd mem.*, No. 88-3099 (3d Cir. 1988). However, the Commission recently analyzed the is-

B. Supreme Court's Decision in Vinson

Meritor Saving Bank v. Vinson posed three questions for the Supreme Court:
(1) Does unwelcome sexual behavior that creates a hostile working environment constitute employment discrimination on the basis of sex;
(2) Can a Title VII violation be shown when the district court found that any sexual relationship that existed between the plaintiff and her supervisor was a "voluntary one"; and
(3) Is an employer strictly liable for an offensive working environment created by a supervisor's sexual advances when the employer does not know of, and could not reasonably have known of, the supervisor's misconduct.

1) Facts — The plaintiff had alleged that her supervisor constantly subjected her to sexual harassment both during and after business hours, on and off the employer's premises; she alleged that he forced her to have sexual intercourse with him on numerous occasions, fondled her in front of other employees, followed her into the women's restroom and exposed himself to her, and even raped her on several occasions. She alleged that she submitted for fear of jeopardizing her employment. She testified, however, that this conduct had ceased almost a year before she first complained in any way, by filing a Title VII suit; her EEOC charge was filed later (*see infra* at n.34). The supervisor and the employer denied all of her allegations and claimed they were fabricated in response to a work dispute.

2) Lower Courts' Decisions — After trial, the district court found the plaintiff was not the victim of sexual harassment and was not required to grant sexual favors as a condition of employ-

ment or promotion. *Vinson v. Taylor*, 22 EPD ¶30,708 [23 FEP Cases 37] (D.D.C. 1980). Without resolving the conflicting testimony, the district court found that if a sexual relationship had existed between plaintiff and her supervisor, it was "a voluntary one ... having nothing to do with her continued employment." The district court nonetheless went on to hold that the employer was not liable for its supervisor's actions because it had no notice of the alleged sexual harassment; although the employer had a policy against discrimination and an internal grievance procedure, the plaintiff had never lodged a complaint.

The court of appeals reversed and remanded, holding the lower court should have considered whether the evidence established a violation under the "hostile environment" theory. *Vinson v. Taylor*, 753 F.2d 141, 36 EPD ¶34,949, [36 FEP Cases 1423] *denial of rehearing en banc*, 760 F.2d 1330, 37 EPD ¶35,232 [37 FEP Cases 1266] (D.C. Cir. 1985). The court ruled that a victim's "voluntary" submission to sexual advances has "no materiality whatsoever" to the proper inquiry: whether "toleration of sexual harassment [was] a condition of her employment." The court further held that an employer is absolutely liable for sexual harassment committed by a supervisory employee, regardless of whether the employer actually knew or reasonably could have known of the misconduct, or would have disapproved of and stopped the misconduct if aware of it.

3) Supreme Court's Opinion — The Supreme Court agreed that the case should be remanded for consideration under the "hostile environment" theory and held that the proper inquiry focuses on the "unwelcomeness" of the conduct rather than the "voluntariness" of the victim's participation. But the Court held that the court of appeals erred in concluding that employers are always automatically liable for sexual harassment by their supervisory employees.

sues in its "Policy Guidance on Employer Liability Under Title VII for Sexual Favoritism" dated January 1990.

a) "Hostile Environment" Violates Title VII — The Court rejected the employer's contention that Title VII prohibits only discrimination that causes "economic" or "tangible" injury: "Title VII affords employees the right to work in an environment free from discriminatory intimidation, ridicule, and insult" whether based on sex, race, religion, or national origin. 106 S.Ct. at 2405. Relying on the EEOC's Guidelines' definition of harassment,[6] the Court held that a plaintiff may establish a violation of Title VII "by proving that discrimination based on sex has created a hostile or abusive work environment." *Id.* The Court quoted the Eleventh Circuit's decision in *Henson v. City of Dundee*, 682 F.2d 897 902 29 EPD ¶32,993 [29 FEP Cases 787] (11th Cir. 1982):

> Sexual harassment which creates a hostile or offensive environment for members of one sex is every bit the arbitrary barrier to sexual equality at the workplace that racial harassment is to racial equality. Surely, a requirement that a man or woman run a gauntlet of sexual abuse in return for the privilege of being allowed to work and make a living can be as demeaning and disconcerting as the harshest of racial epithets.

106 S.Ct. at 2406. The Court further held that for harassment to violate Title VII, it must be "sufficiently severe or pervasive 'to alter the conditions of [the victim's] employment and create an abusive working environment.'" *Id.* (quoting *Henson*, 682 F.2d at 904).

b) Conduct Must Be "Unwelcome" — Citing the EEOC's Guidelines, the Court said the gravamen of a sexual

harassment claim is that the alleged sexual advances were "unwelcome." 106 S.Ct. at 2406. Therefore, "the fact that sex-related conduct was 'voluntary,' in the sense that the complainant was not forced to participate against her will, is not a defense to a sexual harassment suit brought under Title VII .... The correct inquiry is whether [the victim] by her conduct indicated that the alleged sexual advances were unwelcome, not whether her actual participation in sexual intercourse was voluntary." *Id.* Evidence of a complainant's sexually provocative speech or dress may be relevant in determining whether she found particular advances unwelcome, but should be admitted with caution in light of the potential for unfair prejudice, the Court held.

c) Employer Liability Established Under Agency Principles — On the question of employer liability in "hostile environment" cases, the Court agreed with EEOC's position that agency principles should be used for guidance. While declining to issue a "definitive rule on employer liability," the Court did reject both the court of appeals' rule of automatic liability for the actions of supervisors and the employer's position that notice is always required. 106 S.Ct. at 2408-09.

The following sections of this document provide guidance on the issues addressed in *Vinson* and subsequent cases.

GUIDANCE

A. Determining Whether Sexual Conduct Is Unwelcome

Sexual harassment is "unwelcome ... verbal or physical conduct of a sexual nature...." 29 C.F.R. §1604.11(a). Because sexual attraction may often play a role in the day-to-day social exchange between employees, "the distinction between invited, uninvited-but-welcome, offensive-but-tolerated, and flatly rejected" sexual advances may well be difficult to discern. *Barnes v. Costle*, 561 F.2d 983, 999, 14 EPD ¶7755 [15 FEP Cases 345] (D.C. Cir. 1977) (MacKinnon J., con-

---

[6]The Court stated that the guidelines, "'while not controlling upon the courts by reason of their authority, do constitute a body of experience and informed judgment to which courts and litigants may properly resort for guidance.'" *Vinson*, 106 S.Ct. at 2405 (quoting *General Electric Co. v. Gilbert*, 429 U.S. 125, 141–42, 12 EPD ¶11,240 [13 FEP Cases 1657] (1976), quoting in turn *Skidmore v. Swift & Co.*, 323 U.S. 134 (1944)).

curring). But this distinction is essential because sexual conduct becomes unlawful only when it is unwelcome. The Eleventh Circuit provided a general definition of "unwelcome conduct" in *Henson v. City of Dundee*, 682 F.2d at 903: the challenged conduct must be unwelcome "in the sense that the employee did not solicit or incite it, and in the sense that the employee regarded the conduct as undesirable or offensive."

When confronted with conflicting evidence as to welcomeness, the Commission looks "at the record as a whole and at the totality of circumstances...." 29 C.F.R. §1604.11(b), evaluating each situation on a case-by-case basis. When there is some indication of welcomeness or when the credibility of the parties is at issue, the charging party's claim will be considerably strengthened if she made a contemporaneous complaint or protest.[7] Particularly when the alleged harasser may have some reason (e.g., a prior consensual relationship) to believe that the advances will be welcomed, it is important for the victim to communicate that the conduct is unwelcome. Generally, victims are well-advised to assert their right to a workplace free from sexual harassment. This may stop the harassment before it becomes more serious. A contemporaneous complaint or protest may also provide persuasive evidence that the sexual harassment in fact occurred as alleged (*see infra* Section B). Thus, in investigating sexual harassment charges, it is important to develop detailed evidence of the circumstances and nature of any such complaints or protests, whether to the alleged harasser, higher management, co-workers or others.[8]

While a complaint or protest is helpful to a charging party's case, it is not a necessary element of the claim. Indeed, the Commission recognizes that victims may fear repercussions from complaining about the harassment and that such fear may explain a delay in opposing the conduct. If the victim failed to complain or delayed in complaining, the investigation must ascertain why. The relevance of whether the victim has complained varies depending upon "the nature of the sexual advances and the context in which the alleged incidents occurred." 29 C.F.R. §1604.11(b).[9]

Example — Charging Party (CP) alleges that her supervisor subjected her to unwelcome sexual advances that created a hostile work environment. The investigation into her charge discloses that her supervisor began making intermittent sexual advances to her in June, 1987, but she did not complain to management about the harassment. After the harassment continued and worsened, she filed a charge with EEOC in June, 1988. There is no evidence CP welcomed the advances. CP states that she

---

[7]For a complaint to be "contemporaneous," it should be made while the harassment is ongoing or shortly after it has ceased. For example, a victim of "hostile environment" harassment who resigns her job because working conditions have become intolerable would be considered to have made a contemporaneous complaint if she notified the employer of the harassment at the time of her departure or shortly thereafter. The employer has a duty to investigate and, if it finds the allegations true, to take remedial action including offering reinstatement (*see infra* Section E).

[8]Even when unwelcomeness is not at issue, the investigation should develop this evidence in order to aid in making credibility determinations (*see infra* p. 12).

[9]A victim of harassment need not always confront her harasser directly so long as her conduct demonstrates the harasser's behavior is unwelcome. *See, e.g., Lipsett v. University of Puerto Rico*, 864 F.2d 881, 898, 48 EPD ¶38,393 (1st Cir. 1988) ("In some instances a woman may have the responsibility for telling the man directly that his comments or conduct is unwelcome. In other instances, however, a woman's consistent failure to respond to suggestive comments or gestures may be sufficient to communicate that the man's conduct is unwelcome."); Commission Decision No. 84-1, CCH EEOC Decisions ¶6839 (although charging parties did not confront their supervisor directly about his sexual remarks and gestures for fear of losing their jobs, evidence showing that they demonstrated through comments and actions that his conduct was unwelcome was sufficient to support a finding of harassment).

feared that complaining about the harassment would cause her to lose her job. She also states that she initially believed she could resolve the situation herself, but as the harassment became more. frequent and severe, she said she realized that intervention by EEOC was necessary. The investigator determines CP is credible and concludes that the delay in complaining does not undercut CP's claim.

When welcomeness is at issue, the investigation should determine whether the victim's conduct is consistent, or inconsistent, with her assertion that the sexual conduct is unwelcome.[10]

In *Vinson*, the Supreme Court made clear that voluntary submission to sexual conduct will not necessarily defeat a claim of sexual harassment. The correct inquiry "is whether [the employee] *by her conduct* indicated that the alleged sexual advances were unwelcome, not whether her actual participation in sexual intercourse was voluntary." 106 S.Ct. at 2406 (emphasis added). *See also* Commission Decision No. 84-1 ("acquiescence in sexual conduct at the workplace may not mean that the conduct is welcome to the individual").

In some cases the courts and the Commission have considered whether the complainant welcomed the sexual conduct by acting in a sexually aggressive manner, using sexually-oriented language, or soliciting the sexual conduct. Thus, in *Gan v. Kepro Circuit Systems*, 27 EPD ¶32,379 [28 FEP Cases 639] (E.D. Mo. 1982), the plaintiff regularly used vulgar language, initiated sexually-oriented conversations with her co-workers, asked male employees about their marital sex lives and whether they engaged in extramarital affairs, and discussed her own sexual encounters. In rejecting the plaintiff's claim of "hostile environment" harassment, the court found that any propositions or sexual remarks by co-workers were "prompted by her own sexual aggressiveness and her own sexually-explicit conversations." *Id.* at 23,648.[11] And in *Vinson*, the Supreme Court held that testimony about the plaintiff's provocative dress and publicly expressed sexual fantasies is not *per se* inadmissible but the trial court should carefully weigh its relevance against the potential for unfair prejudice. 106 S.Ct. at 2407.

Conversely, occasional use of sexually explicit language does not necessarily negate a claim that sexual conduct was unwelcome. Although a charging party's use of sexual terms or off-color jokes may suggest that sexual comments by others in that situation were not unwelcome, more extreme and abusive or persistent comments or a physical assault

---

[10]Investigators and triers of fact rely on objective evidence, rather than subjective, uncommunicated feelings. For example, in *Ukarish v. Magnesium Electron*, 33 EPD ¶34,087 [31 FEP Cases 1315] (D.N.J. 1983), the court rejected the plaintiff's claim that she was sexually harassed by her co-worker's language and gestures; although she indicated in her personal diary that she did not welcome the banter, she made no objection and indeed appeared to join in "as one of the boys." *Id.* at 32,118. In *Sardigal v. St. Louis National Stockyards Co.*, 41 EPD ¶36,613 [42 FEP Cases 497] (S.D. Ill. 1986), the plaintiff's allegation was found not credible because she visited her alleged harasser at the hospital and at his brother's home, and allowed him to come into her home alone at night after the alleged harassment occurred. Similarly, in the *Vinson* case, the district court noted the plaintiff had twice refused transfers to other offices located away from the alleged harasser. (In a particular charge, the significance of a charging party's refusing an offer to transfer will depend upon her reasons for doing so.)

[11]*See also Ferguson v. E.I. DuPont deNemours and Co.*, 560 F.Supp. 1172, 33 EPD ¶34,131 [31 FEP Cases 795] (D. Del. 1983) ("sexually aggressive conduct and explicit conversation on the part of the plaintiff may bar a cause of action for [hostile environment] sexual harassment"); *Reichman v. Bureau of Affirmative Action*, 536 F.Supp. 1149, 1172, 30 FEP Cases 1644 (M.D. Pa. 1982) (where plaintiff behaved "in a very flirtatious and provocative manner" around the alleged harasser, asked him to have dinner at her house on several occasions despite his repeated refusals, and continued to conduct herself in a similar manner after the alleged harassment, she could not claim the alleged harassment was unwelcome).

will not be excused, nor would "quid pro quo" harrassment be allowed.

Any past conduct of the charging party that is offered to show "welcomeness" must relate to the alleged harasser. In *Swentek v. USAir, Inc.*, 830 F.2d 552, 557, 44 EPD ¶37,457 [44 FEP Cases 1808] (4th Cir. 1987), the Fourth Circuit held the district court wrongly concluded that the plaintiff's own past conduct and use of foul language showed that "she was the kind of person who could not be offended by such comments and therefore welcomed them generally," even though she had told the harasser to leave her alone. Emphasizing that the proper inquiry is "whether plaintiff welcomed the particular conduct in question from the alleged harasser," the court of appeals held that "Plaintiff's use of foul language or sexual innuendo in a consensual setting does not waive 'her legal protections against unwelcome harassment.'" 830 F.2d at 557 (quoting *Katz v. Dole*, 709 F.2d 251, 254 n.3, 32 EPD ¶33,639 [31 FEP Cases 1521] (4th Cir. 1983)). Thus, evidence concerning a charging party's general character and past behavior toward others has limited, if any, probative value and does not substitute for a careful examination of her behavior toward the alleged harasser.

A more difficult situation occurs when an employee first willingly participates in conduct of a sexual nature but then ceases to participate and claims that any continued sexual conduct has created a hostile work environment. Here the employee has the burden of showing that any further sexual conduct is unwelcome, work-related harassment. The employee must clearly notify the alleged harasser that his conduct is no longer welcome.[12]

---

[12]In Commission Decision No. 84-1, CCH Employment Practices Guide ¶6839, the Commission found that active participation in sexual conduct at the workplace, e.g., by "using dirty remarks and telling dirty jokes," may indicate that the sexual advances complained of were not unwelcome. Thus, the Commission found that no harassment occurred with respect to an employee who had joined in the telling of bawdy jokes and the use of vulgar language during

If the conduct still continues, her failure to bring the matter to the attention of higher management or the EEOC is evidence, though not dispositive, that any continued conduct is, in fact, welcome or unrelated to work.[13] In any case, however, her refusal to submit to the sexual conduct cannot be the basis for denying her an employment benefit or opportunity; that would constitute a "quid pro quo" violation.

B. Evaluating Evidence of Harassment

The Commission recognizes that sexual conduct may be private and unacknowledged, with no eyewitnesses. Even sexual conduct that occurs openly in the workplace may appear to be consensual. Thus the resolution of a sexual harassment claim often depends on the credibility of the parties. The investigator should question the charging party and the alleged harasser in detail. The Commission's investigation also should search thoroughly for corroborative evidence of any nature.[14] Supervisory and managerial employees, as well as coworkers, should be asked about their knowledge of the alleged harassment.

---

her first two months on the job, and failed to provide subsequent notice that the conduct was no longer welcome. By actively participating in the conduct, the charging party had created the impression among her co-workers that she welcomed the sort of sexually oriented banter that she later asserted was objectionable. Simply ceasing to participate was insufficient to show the continuing activity was no longer welcome to her. *See also Loftin-Boggs v. City of Meridian*, 633 F.Supp. 1323, 41 FEP Cases 532 (S.D. Miss. 1986) (plaintiff initially participated in and initiated some of the crude language that was prevalent on the job; if she later found such conduct offensive, she should have conveyed this by her own conduct and her reaction to her co-workers' conduct).

[13]However, if the harassing supervisor engages in conduct that is sufficiently pervasive and work-related, it may place the employer on notice that the conduct constitutes harassment.

[14]As the court said in *Henson v. City of Dundee*, 682 F.2d at 912 n.25, "In a case of alleged sexual harassment which involves close questions of credibility and subjective interpretation, the existence of corroborative evidence or the lack thereof is likely to be crucial."

In appropriate cases, the Commission may make a finding of harassment based solely on the credibility of the victim's allegation. As with any other charge of discrimination, a victim's account must be sufficiently detailed and internally consistent so as to be plausible, and lack of corroborative evidence where such evidence logically should exist would undermine the allegation.[15] By the same token, a general denial by the alleged harasser will carry little weight when it is contradicted by other evidence.[16]

Of course, the Commission recognizes that a charging party may not be able to identify witnesses to the alleged conduct itself. But testimony may be obtained from persons who observed the charging party's demeanor immediately after an alleged incident of harassment. Persons with whom she discussed the incident — such as co-workers, a doctor or a counselor — should be interviewed. Other employees should be asked if they noticed changes in charging party's behavior at work or in the alleged harasser's treatment of charging party. As stated earlier, a contemporaneous complaint by the victim would be persuasive evidence both that the conduct occurred and that it was unwelcome (*see supra* Section A). So too is evidence that other employees were sexually harassed by the same person.

The investigator should determine whether the employer was aware of any other instances of harassment and if so what was the response. Where appropriate the Commission will expand the case to include class claims.[17]

Example — Charging Party (CP) alleges that her supervisor made unwelcome sexual advances toward her on frequent occasions while they were alone in his office. The supervisor denies this allegation. No one witnessed the alleged advances. CP's inability to produce eyewitnesses to the harassment does *not* defeat her claim. The resolution will depend on the credibility of her allegations versus that of her supervisor's. Corroborating, credible evidence will establish her claim. For example, three co-workers state that CP looked distraught on several occasions after leaving the supervisor's office, and that she informed them on those occasions that he had sexually propositioned and touched her. In addition, the evidence shows that CP had complained to the general manager of the office about the incidents soon after they occurred. The corroborating witness testimony and her complaint to higher management would be sufficient to establish her claim. Her allegations would be further buttressed if other employees testified that the supervisor propositioned them as well.

If the investigation exhausts all possibilities for obtaining corroborative evi-

---

[15]In *Sardigal v. St. Louis National Stockyards Co.*, 41 EPD ¶36,613 at 44,694 [42 FEP Cases 497] (S.D. Ill. 1986), the plaintiff, a waitress, alleged she was harassed over a period of nine months in a restaurant at noontime, when there was a "constant flow of waitresses or customers" around the area where the offenses allegedly took place. Her allegations were not credited by the district court because no individuals came forward with testimony to support her. It is important to explore all avenues for obtaining corroborative evidence because courts may reject harassment claims due to lack of corroborative evidence. *See Hall v. F.O. Thacker Co.*, 24 FEP Cases 1499, 1503 (N.D. Ga. 1980) (district judge did not credit plaintiff's testimony about sexual advances because it was "virtually uncorroborated"); *Neidhart v. D.H. Holmes Co.*, 21 FEP Cases 452, 457 (E.D. La. 1979), *aff'd mem.*, 624 F.2d 1097 (5th Cir. 1980) (plaintiff's account of sexual harassment rejected because "there is not a scintilla of credible evidence to corroborate [plaintiff's version]").

[16]*See* Commission Decision No. 81-17, CCH EEOC Decisions (1983) ¶6757 (violation of Title VII found where charging party alleged that her supervisor made repeated sexual advances toward her; although the supervisor denied the allegations, statements of other employees supported them).

[17]Class complaints in the federal sector are governed by the requirements of 29 C.F.R. §1613 Subpart F.

dence, but finds none, the Commission may make a cause finding based solely on a reasoned decision to credit the charging party's testimony.[18]

In a "quid pro quo" case, a finding that the employer's asserted reasons for its adverse action against the charging party are pretextual will usually establish a violation.[19] The investigation should determine the validity of the employer's reasons for the charging party's termination. If they are pretextual and if the sexual harassment occurred, then it should be inferred that the charging party was terminated for rejecting the employer's sexual advances, as she claims. Moreover, if the termination occurred because the victim complained, it would be appropriate to find, in addition, a violation of section 704(a).

C. Determining Whether a Work Environment Is "Hostile"

The Supreme Court said in *Vinson* that for sexual harassment to violate Title VII, it must be "sufficiently severe or pervasive 'to alter the conditions of [the victim's] employment and create an abusive working environment.' " 106 S.Ct. at 2406 (quoting *Henson v. City of Dundee*, 682 F.2d at 904. Since "hostile environment" harassment takes a variety of forms, many factors may affect this determination, including: (1) whether the conduct was verbal or physical, or both; (2) how frequently it was repeated; (3) whether the conduct was hostile and patently offensive; (4) whether the alleged harasser was a co-worker or a supervisor; (5) whether others joined in perpetrating the harassment; and (6) whether

---

[18]In Commission Decision No. 82-13, CCH EEOC Decisions (1983) ¶6832, the Commission stated that a "bare assertion" of sexual harassment "cannot stand without some factual support." To the extent this decision suggests a charging party can never prevail based solely on the credibility of her own testimony, that decision is overruled.

[19]*See, e.g., Bundy v. Jackson*, 641 F.2d 934, 953, 24 EPD ¶31,439 [24 FEP Cases 1155] (D.C. Cir. 1981).

the harassment was directed at more than one individual.

In determining whether unwelcome sexual conduct rises to the level of a "hostile environment" in violation of Title VII, the central inquiry is whether the conduct "unreasonably interfer[es] with an individual's work performance" or creates "an intimidating, hostile, or offensive working environment." 29 C.F.R. §1604.11(a)(3). Thus, sexual flirtation or innuendo, even vulgar language that is trivial or merely annoying, would probably not establish a hostile environment.

1) Standard for Evaluating Harassment — In determining whether harassment is sufficiently severe or pervasive to create a hostile environment, the harasser's conduct should be evaluated from the objective standpoint of a "reasonable person." Title VII does not serve "as a vehicle for vindicating the petty slights suffered by the hypersensitive." *Zabkowicz v. West Bend Co.*, 589 F.Supp. 780, 784, 35 EPD ¶34,766 [35 FEP Cases 610] (E.D. Wis. 1984). *See also Ross v. Comsat*, 34 FEP Cases 260, 265 (D. Md. 1984), *rev'd on other grounds*, 759 F.2d 355 (4th Cir. 1985). Thus, if the challenged conduct would not substantially affect the work environment of a reasonable person, no violation should be found.

Example — Charging Party alleges that her co-worker made repeated unwelcome sexual advances toward her. An investigation discloses that the alleged "advances" consisted of invitations to join a group of employees who regularly socialized at dinner after work. The co-worker's invitations, viewed in that context and from the perspective of a reasonable person, would not have created a hostile environment and therefore did not constitute sexual harassment.

A "reasonable person" standard also should be applied to the more basic determination of whether challenged conduct is of a sexual nature. Thus, in the above example, a reasonable person would not consider the co-worker's invitations sexual in nature, and on that basis as well no violation would be found. This objective standard should not be applied in a vacuum, however. Consideration should be given to the context in which the alleged harassment took place. As the Sixth Circuit has stated, the trier of fact must "adopt the perspective of a reasonable person's reaction to a similar environment under similar or like circumstances." *Highlander v. K.F.C. National Management Co.*, 805 F.2d 644, 650, 41 EPD ¶36,675 [42 FEP Cases 654] (6th Cir. 1986).[20]

The reasonable person standard should consider the victim's perspective and not stereotyped notions of acceptable behavior. For example, the Commission believes that a workplace in which sexual slurs, displays of "girlie" pictures, and other offensive conduct abound can constitute a hostile work environment even if many people deem it to be harmless or insignificant. *Cf. Rabidue v. Osceola Refining Co.*, 805 F.2d 611, 626, 41 EPD ¶36,643 [42 FEP Cases 631] (6th Cir. 1986) (Keith, C.J., dissenting), *cert. denied*, 107 S.Ct. 1983, 42 EPD ¶36,984 (1987). *Lipsett v. University of Puerto Rico*, 864 F.2d 881, 898 48 EPD ¶38,393 (1st Cir. 1988).

2) Isolated Instances of Harassment — Unless the conduct is quite severe, a single incident or isolated incidents of offensive sexual conduct or remarks generally do not create an abusive environment. As the Court noted in *Vinson*, "mere utterance of an ethnic or racial epithet which engenders offensive

feelings in an employee would not affect the conditions of employment to a sufficiently significant degree to violate Title VII." 106 S.Ct. at 2406 (quoting *Rogers v. EEOC*, 454 F.2d 234, 4 EPD ¶7597 [4 FEP Cases 92] (5th Cir. 1971), *cert. denied*, 406 U.S. 957, 4 EPD ¶7838 (1972)). A "hostile environment" claim generally requires a showing of a pattern of offensive conduct.[21] In contrast, in "quid pro quo" cases a single sexual advance may constitute harassment if it is linked to the granting or denial of employment benefits.[22]

But a single, unusually severe incident of harassment may be sufficient to constitute a Title VII violation; the more severe the harassment, the less need to show a repetitive series of incidents. This is particularly true when the harassment

---

[20]In *Highlander* and also in *Rabidue v. Osceola Refining Co.*, 805 F.2d 611, 41 EPD ¶36,643 [42 FEP Cases 631] (6th Cir. 1986), *cert. denied*, 107 S.Ct. 1983, 42 EPD ¶36,984 (1987), the Sixth Circuit required an additional showing that the plaintiff suffered some degree of psychological injury. *Highlander*, 805 F.2d at 650; *Rabidue*, 805 F.2d at 620. However, it is the Commission's position that it is sufficient for the charging party to show that the harassment was unwelcome and that it would have substantially affected the work environment of a reasonable person.

[21]*See, e.g., Scott v. Sears, Roebuck and Co.*, 798 F.2d 210, 214, 41 EPD ¶36,439 [41 FEP Cases 805] (7th Cir. 1986) (offensive comments and conduct of co-workers were "too isolated and lacking the repetitive and debilitating effect necessary to maintain a hostile environment claim"); *Moylan v. Maries County*, 792 F.2d 746, 749, 40 EPD ¶36,228 [40 FEP Cases 1788] (8th Cir. 1986) (single incident or isolated incidents of harassment will not be sufficient to establish a violation; the harassment must be sustained and nontrivial); *Downes v. Federal Aviation Administration*, 775 F.2d 288, 293, 38 EPD ¶35,590 [39 FEP CAses 70] (D.C. Cir. 1985) (Title VII does not create a claim of sexual harassment "for each and every crude joke or sexually explicit remark on the job.... [A] pattern of offensive conduct must be proved...."); *Sapp v. City of Warner-Robins*, 655 F.Supp. 1043, 43 FEP Cases 486 (M.D. Ga. 1987) (co-worker's single effort to get the plaintiff to go out with him did not create an abusive working environment); *Freedman v. American Standard*, 41 FEP Cases 471 (D.N.J. 1986) (plaintiff did not suffer a hostile environment from the receipt of an obscene message from her coworkers and a sexual solicitation from one co-worker); *Hollis v. Fleetguard, Inc.*, 44 FEP Cases 1527 (M.D. Tenn. 1987) (plaintiff's co-worker's requests, on four occasions over a four-month period, that she have a sexual affair with him, followed by his coolness toward her and avoidance of her did not constitute a hostile environment; there was no evidence he coerced, pressured, or abused the plaintiff after she rejected his advances).

[22]*See Neville v. Taft Broadcasting Co.*, 42 FEP Cases 1314 (W.D.N.Y. 1987) (one sexual advance, rebuffed by plaintiff, may establish a prima facie case of "quid pro quo" harassment but is not severe enough to create a hostile environment).

is physical.[23] Thus, in *Barrett v. Omaha National Bank*, 584 F.Supp. 22, 35 FEP Cases 585 (D. Neb. 1983), *aff'd*, 726 F.2d 424, 33 EPD ¶34,132 (8th Cir. 1984), one incident constituted actionable sexual harassment. The harasser talked to the plaintiff about sexual activities and touched her in an offensive manner while they were inside a vehicle from which she could not escape.[24]

The Commission will presume that the unwelcome, intentional touching of a charging party's intimate body areas is sufficiently offensive to alter the conditions of her working environment and constitute a violation of Title VII. More so than in the case of verbal advances or remarks, a single unwelcome physical advance can seriously poison the victim's working environment. If an employee's supervisor sexually touches that employee, the Commission normally would find a violation. In such situations, it is the employer's burden to demonstrate that the unwelcome conduct was not sufficiently severe to create a hostile work environment.

When the victim is the target of both verbal and non-intimate physical conduct, the hostility of the environment is exacerbated and a violation is more likely to be found. Similarly, incidents of sexual harassment directed at other employees in addition to the charging party are relevant to a showing of hostile work

environment. *Hall v. Gus Construction Co.*, 842 F.2d 1010, 46 EPD ¶37,905 [46 FEP Cases 573] (8th Cir. 1988); *Hicks v. Gates Rubber Co.*, 833 F.2d 1406, 44 EPD ¶37,542 [45 FEP Cases 608] (10th Cir. 1987); *Jones v. Flagship International*, 793 F.2d 714, 721 n.7, 40 EPD ¶36,392 [41 FEP Cases 358] (5th Cir. 1986), *cert. denied*, 107 S.Ct. 952, 41 EPD ¶36,708 (1987).

3) Non-physical Harassment — When the alleged harassment consists of verbal conduct, the investigation should ascertain the nature, frequency, context, and intended target of the remarks. Questions to be explored might include:

— Did the alleged harasser single out the charging party?

— Did the charging party participate?

— What was the relationship between the charging party and the alleged harasser(s)?

— Were the remarks hostile and derogatory?

No one factor alone determines whether particular conduct violates Title VII. As the Guidelines emphasize, the Commission will evaluate the totality of the circumstances. In general, a woman does not forfeit her right to be free from sexual harassment by choosing to work in an atmosphere that has traditionally included vulgar, anti-female language. However, in *Rabidue v. Osceola Refining Co.*, 805 F.2d 611, 41 EPD ¶36,643 [42 FEP Cases 631] (6th Cir. 1986), *cert. denied*, 107 S.Ct. 1983, 42 EPD ¶36,984 (1987), the Sixth Circuit rejected the plaintiff's claim of harassment in such a situation.[25] One of the factors the court found

---

[23]The principles for establishing employer liability, set forth in Section D below, are to be applied to cases involving physical contact in the same manner that they are applied in other cases.

[24]*See also Gilardi v. Schroeder*, 672 F.Supp. 1043, 45 FEP Cases 283 (N.D. Ill. 1986) (plaintiff who was drugged by employer's owner and raped while unconscious, and then was terminated at insistence of owner's wife, was awarded $113,000 in damages for harassment and intentional infliction of emotional distress); Commission Decision No. 83-1, CCH EEOC Decisions (1983) ¶6834 (violation found where the harasser forcibly grabbed and kissed charging party while they were alone in a storeroom); Commission Decision No. 84-3, CCH Employment Practices Guide ¶6841 (violation found where the harasser slid his hand under the charging party's skirt and squeezed her buttocks).

[25]The alleged harasser, a supervisor of another department who did not supervise plaintiff but worked with her regularly, "was an extremely vulgar and crude individual who customarily made obscene comments about women generally, and, on occasion, directed such obscenities to the plaintiff." 805 F.2d at 615. The plaintiff and other female employees were exposed daily to displays of nude or partially clad women in posters in male employees' offices. 805 F.2d at 623-24 (Keith, J., dissenting in part and concurring in part). Although the employees told manage-

relevant was "the lexicon of obscenity that pervaded the environment of the workplace both before and after the plaintiff's introduction into its environs, coupled with the reasonable expectations of the plaintiff upon voluntarily entering that environment." 805 F.2d at 620. Quoting the district court, the majority noted that in some work environments, "'humor and language are rough hewn and vulgar. Sexual jokes, sexual conversations, and girlie magazines may abound. Title VII was not meant to — or can — change this.'" *Id.* at 620-21. The court also considered the sexual remarks and poster at issue to have a "de minimis effect on the plaintiff's work environment when considered in the context of a society that condones and publicly features and commercially exploits open displays of written and pictorial erotica at the newsstands, on prime-time television, at the cinema, and in other public places." *Id.* at 622.

The Commission believes these factors rarely will be relevant and agrees with the dissent in *Rabidue* that a woman does not assume the risk of harassment by voluntarily entering an abusive, antifemale environment. "Title VII's precise purpose is to prevent such behavior and attitudes from poisoning the work environment of classes protected under the Act." 805 F.2d at 626 (Keith, J., dissenting in part and concurring in part). Thus, in a decision disagreeing with *Rabidue*, a district court found that a hostile environment was established by the presence of pornographic magazines in the workplace and vulgar employee comments concerning them; offensive sexual comments made to and about plaintiff and other female employees by her supervisor; sexually oriented pictures in a company-sponsored movie and slide presentation; sexually oriented pictures and calendars in the workplace; and offensive touching of plaintiff by a co-worker. *Barbetta v. Chemlawn Services*

—————
ment they were disturbed and offended, the employer did not reprimand the supervisor.

Corp., 669 F.Supp. 569, 45 EPD ¶37,568 [44 FEP Cases 1563] (W.D.N.Y. 1987). The court held that the proliferation of pornography and demeaning comments, if sufficiently continuous and pervasive, "may be found to create an atmosphere in which women are viewed as men's sexual playthings rather than as their equal coworkers." *Barbetta*, 669 F.Supp. at 573. The Commission agrees that, depending on the totality of circumstances, such as atmosphere may violate Title VII. *See also Waltman v. International Paper Co.*, 875 F.2d 468, 50 EPD ¶39,106 Commission's position in its amicus brief that evidence of ongoing sexual graffiti in the workplace, not all of which was directed at the plaintiff, was relevant to her claim of harassment. *Bennett v. Corroon & Black Corp.*, 845 F.2d 104, 46 EPD ¶37,955 (5th Cir. 1988) (the posting of obscene cartoons in an office men's room bearing the plaintiff's name and depicting her engaged in crude and deviant sexual activities could create a hostile work environment).

4) Sex-based Harassment — Although the Guidelines specifically address conduct that is sexual in nature, the Commission notes that sex-based harassment — that is, harassment not involving sexual activity or language — may also give rise to Title VII liability (just as in the case of harassment based on race, national origin or religion) if it is "sufficiently patterned or pervasive" and directed at employees because of their sex. *Hicks v. Gates Rubber Co.*, 833 F.2d at 1416; *McKinney v. Dole*, 765 F.2d 1129, 1138, 37 EPD ¶35,339 [38 FEP Cases 364] (D.C. Cir. 1985).

Acts of physical aggression, intimidation, hostility or unequal treatment based on sex may be combined with incidents of sexual harassment to establish the existence of discriminatory terms and conditions of employment. *Hall v. Gus Construction Co.*, 842 F.2d at 1014; *Hicks v. Gates Rubber Co.*, 833 F.2d at 1416.

5) Constructive Discharge — Claims of "hostile environment" sexual harassment often are coupled with claims of constructive discharge. If constructive discharge due to a hostile environment is proven, the claim will also become one of "quid pro quo" harassment.[26] It is the position of the Commission and a majority of courts that an employer is liable for constructive discharge when it imposes intolerable working conditions in violation of Title VII when those conditions foreseeably would compel a reasonable employee to quit, whether or not the employer specifically intended to force the victim's resignation. *See Derr v. Gulf Oil Corp.*, 796 F.2d 340, 343-44, 41 EPD ¶36,468 [41 FEP Cases 166] (10th Cir. 1986); *Goss v. Exxon Office Systems Co.*, 747 F.2d 885, 888, 35 EPD ¶34,768 [36 FEP Cases 344] (3d Cir. 1984); *Nolan v. Cleland*, 686 F.2d 806, 812-15, 30 EPD ¶33,029 [29 FEP Cases 1732] (9th Cir. 1982); *Held v. Gulf Oil Co.*, 684 F.2d 427, 432, 29 EPD ¶32,968 [29 FEP Cases 837] (6th Cir. 1982); *Clark v. Marsh*, 665 F.2d 1168, 1175 n.8, 26 EPD ¶32,082 (D.C. Cir. 1981); *Bourque v. Powell Electrical Manufacturing Co.*, 617 F.2d 61, 65, 23 EPD ¶30,891 [22 FEP Cases 1191] (5th Cir. 1980); Commission Decision 84-1, CCH EEOC Decision ¶6839. However, the Fourth Circuit requires proof that the employer imposed the intolerable conditions with the intent of forcing the victim to leave. *See EEOC v. Federal Reserve Bank of Richmond*, 698 F.2d 633, 672, 30 EPD ¶33,269 (4th Cir. 1983). But this case is not a sexual harassment case and the Commission believes it is distinguishable because specific intent is not as likely to be present in "hostile environment" cases.

---

[26]However, while an employee's failure to utilize effective grievance procedures will not shield an employer from liability for "quid pro quo" harassment, such failure may defeat a claim of constructive discharge. *See* discussion of impact of grievance procedures later in this section, and section D(2)(c)(2), below.

An important factor to consider is whether the employer had an effective internal grievance procedure. (*See* Section E, *Preventive and Remedial Action*). The Commission argued in its *Vinson* brief that if an employee knows that effective avenues of complaint and redress are available, then the availability of such avenues itself becomes a part of the work environment and overcomes, to the degree it is effective, the hostility of the work environment. As Justice Marshall noted in his opinion in *Vinson*, "Where a complainant without good reason bypassed an internal complaint procedure she knew to be effective, a court may be reluctant to find constructive termination...." 106 S.Ct. at 2411 (Marshall, J., concurring in part and dissenting a part). Similarly, the court of appeals in *Dornhecker v. Malibu Grand Prix Corp.*, 828 F.2d 307, 44 EPD ¶37,557 [44 FEP Cases 1604] (5th Cir. 1987), held the plaintiff was not constructively discharged after an incident of harassment by a co-worker because she quit immediately, even though the employer told her she would not have to work with him again, and she did not give the employer a fair opportunity to demonstrate it could curb the harasser's conduct.

D. Employer Liability for Harassment by Supervisors

In *Vinson*, The Supreme Court agreed with the Commission's position that "Congress wanted courts to look to agency principles for guidance" in determining an employer's liability for sexual conduct by a supervisor:

While such common-law principles may not be transferable in all their particulars to Title VII, Congress' decision to define "employer" to include any "agent" of an employer, 42 U.S.C. §2000e(b), surely evinces an intent to place some limits on the acts of employees for which employers under Title VII are to be held responsible. 106 S.Ct. at 2408. Thus, while declining to issue a "definitive rule on employer liability," the Court did make it clear that employers are not "automatically liable" for the acts of their supervisors. For the same reason, the Court said, "absence of notice to an employer does not necessarily insulate that employer from liability." *Id.*

As the Commission argued in *Vinson,* reliance on agency principles is consistent with the Commission's Guidelines, which provide in section 1604.11(c) that:

> ... an employer ... is responsible for its acts and those of its agents and supervisory employees with respect to sexual harassment regardless of whether the specific acts complained of were authorized or even forbidden by the employer and regardless of whether the employer knew or should have known of their occurrence. The Commission will examine the circumstances of the particular employment relationship and the job functions performed by the individual in determining whether an individual acts in either a supervisory or agency capacity.

Citing the last sentence of this provision, the Court in *Vinson* indicated that the Guidelines further supported the application of agency principles. 106 S.Ct. at 2408.

1) Application of Agency Principles — "Quid Pro Quo" Cases — An employer will always be held responsible for acts of "quid pro quo" harassment. A supervisor in such circumstances has made or threatened to make a decision affecting the victim's employment status, and he therefore has exercised authority delegated to him by his employer. Although the question of employer liability for "quid pro quo" harassment was not at issue in *Vinson,* the Court's decision noted with apparent approval the position taken by the Commission in its brief that:

> where a supervisor exercises the authority actually delegated to him by his employer, by making

or threatening to make decisions affecting the employment status of his subordinates, such actions are properly imputed to the employer whose delegation of authority empowered the supervisor to undertake them.

106 S.Ct. at 2407-08 (citing Brief for the United States and Equal Employment Opportunity Commission as *Amicus Curiae* at 22).[27] *See also Sparks v. Pilot Freight Carriers, Inc.,* 830 F.2d 1554, 44 EPD ¶37,493 [45 FEP Cases 160] (11th Cir. 1987) (adopting EEOC position quoted in *Vinson* opinion); *Lipsett,* 864 F.2d at 901 (adopting, for Title IX of the Education Amendments, the *Vinson* standard that an employer is absolutely liable for acts of quid pro quo harassment "whether [it] knew, should have known, or approved of the supervisor's actions"). Thus, applying agency principles, the court in *Schroeder v. Schock,* 42 FEP Cases 1112 (D. Kans. 1986), held an employer liable for "quid pro quo" harassment by a supervisor who had authority to recommend plaintiff's discharge. The employer maintained the supervisor's acts were beyond the scope of his employment since the sexual advances were made at a restaurant after work hours. The court held that because the supervisor was acting within the scope of his authority when making or recommending employment decisions, his conduct

---

[27]This well-settled principle is the basis for employer liability for supervisors' discriminatory employment decisions that violate Title VII. 106 S.Ct. at 2408; *see, e.g., Anderson v. Methodist Evangelical Hospital, Inc.,* 464 F.2d 723, 725, 4 EPD ¶7901 [4 FEP Cases 987] (6th Cir. 1972) (racially motivated discharge "by a person in authority at a lower level of management" is attributable to employer despite upper management's "exemplary" record in race relations); *Tidwell v. American Oil Co.,* 332 F.Supp. 424, 436, 4 EPD ¶7544 [3 FEP Cases 1007] (D. Utah 1971) (upper level management's lack of knowledge irrelevant where supervisor illegally discharged employee for refusing to disqualify black applicant discriminatorily); *Flowers v. Crouch-Walker Corp.,* 552 F.2d 1277, 1282, 14 EPD ¶7510 [14 FEP Cases 1265] (7th Cir. 1977) ("The defendant is liable as principal for any violation of Title VII ... by [a supervisor] in his authorized capacity as supervisor.")

may fairly be imputed to the employer. The supervisor was using his authority to hire, fire, and promote to extort sexual consideration from an employee, even though the sexual advance itself occurred away from work.

2) Application of Agency Principles — "Hostile Environment" Cases

a) Vinson — In its *Vinson* brief the commission argued that the employer should be liable for the creation of a hostile environment by a supervisor when the employer knew or had reason to know of the sexual misconduct. Ways by which actual or constructive knowledge could be demonstrated include: by a complaint to management or an EEOC charge; by the pervasiveness of the harassment; or by evidence the employer had "deliberately turned its back on the problem" of sexual harassment by failing to establish a policy against it and a grievance mechanism to redress it. The brief argued that an employer should be liable "if there is no reasonably available avenue by which victims of sexual harassment can make their complaints known to appropriate officials who are in a position to do something about those complaints." Brief for the United States and Equal Employment Opportunity Commission as *Amicus Curiae* at 25. Under that circumstance, an employer would be deemed to know of any harassment that occurred in its workplace.

While the *Vinson* decision quoted the Commission's brief at length, it neither endorsed nor rejected its position.[28] 106 S.Ct. at 2407-08. The Court did state, however, that "the mere existence of a grievance procedure and a policy against discrimination, coupled with [the victim's] failure to invoke the procedure" are "plainly relevant" but "not necessarily dispositive." *Id.* at 2408-09. The Court further stated that the employer's argu-

ment that the victim's failure to complain insulated it from liability "might be substantially stronger if its procedures were better calculated to encourage victims of harassment to come forward." *Id.* at 2409.

The Commission, therefore, interprets *Vinson* to require a careful examination in "hostile environment" cases of whether the harassing supervisor was acting in an "agency capacity" (29 C.F.R. §1604.11(c)). Whether the employer had an appropriate and effective complaint procedure and whether the victim used it are important factors to consider, as discussed below.

(b) Direct Liability — The initial inquiry should be whether the employer knew or should have known of the alleged sexual harassment. If actual or constructive knowledge exists, and if the employer failed to take immediate and appropriate corrective action, the employer would be directly liable.[29] Most commonly an employer acquires actual knowledge through first-hand observation, by the victim's internal complaint to other supervisors or managers, or by a charge of discrimination.

---

[28]The Court observed that the Commission's position was "in some tension" with the first sentence of section 1604.11(c) of the Guidelines but was consistent with the final sentence of that section. (*See supra* at 21).

[29]*Barrett v. Omaha National Bank*, 584 F.Supp. 22, 30-31 [35 FEP Cases 593] (D. Neb. 1983), *aff'd*, 726 F.2d 424, 33 EPD ¶34,132 (8th Cir. 1984); *Ferguson v. duPont Corp.*, 560 F.Supp. 1172, 1199 (D. Del. 1983); Commission Decision No. 83-1, CCH EEOC Decisions (1983) ¶6834. "[A]n employer who has reason to know that one of his employees is being harassed in the workplace by others on ground of race, sex, religion, or national origin, and does nothing about it, is blameworthy." *Hunter v. Allis-Chalmers Corp.*, 797 F.2d 1417, 1422, 41 EPD ¶36,417 [41 FEP Cases 721] (7th Cir. 1986).

This is the theory under which employers are liable for harassment by co-workers, which was at issue in *Hunter v. Allis-Chalmers.* Section 1604.11(d) provides:

With respect to conduct between fellow employees, an employer is responsible for acts of sexual harassment in the workplace where the employer (or its agents or supervisory employees) knows or should have known of the conduct, unless it can show that it took immediate and appropriate corrective action.

Section E(2) of this paper discusses what constitutes "immediate and appropriate corrective action," and is applicable to cases of harassment by co-workers as well as supervisors.

An employer is liable when it "knew, or *upon reasonably diligent inquiry should have known*," of the harassment. *Yates v. Avco Corp.*, 819 F.2d 630, 636, 43 EPD ¶37,086 [43 FEP Caes 1595] (6th Cir. 1987) (emphasis added) (supervisor harassed two women "on a daily basis in the course of his supervision of them" and the employer's grievance procedure did not function effectively). Thus, evidence of the pervasiveness of the harassment may give rise to an inference of knowledge or establish constructive knowledge. *Henson v. City of Dundee*, 682 F.2d 897, 905, 29 EPD ¶32,993 [29 FEP Caes 787] (11th Cir. 1982); *Taylor v. Jones*, 653 F.2d 1193, 1197-99, 26 EPD ¶31,923 [28 FEP Cases 1024] (8th Cir. 1981). Employers usually will be deemed to know of sexual harassment that is openly practiced in the workplace or well-known among employees. This often may be the case when there is more than one harasser or victim. *Lipsett*, 864 F.2d at 906 (employer liable where it should have known of concerted harassment of plaintiff and other female medical residents by more senior male residents).

The victim can of course put the employer on notice by filing a charge of discrimination. As the Commission stated in its *Vinson* brief, the filing of a charge triggers a duty to investigate and remedy any ongoing illegal activity. It is important to emphasize that an employee can always file an EEOC charge without first utilizing an internal complaint or grievance procedure[30] and may wish to pursue both avenues simultaneously because an internal grievance does not prevent the Title VII charge-filing time period from expiring.[31] Nor does the filing of an EEOC charge allow an employer to cease

action on an internal grievance[32] or ignore evidence of ongoing harassment.[33] Indeed, employers should take prompt remedial action upon learning of evidence of sexual harassment (or any other form of unlawful discrimination), whether from an EEOC charge or an internal complaint. If the employer takes immediate and appropriate action to correct the harassment and prevent its recurrence, and the Commission determines that no further action is warranted, normally the Commission would administratively close the case.

(c) Imputed Liability — The investigation should determine whether the alleged harassing supervisor was acting in an "agency capacity" (29 C.F.R. §1604.11(c)).[34] This requires a determination whether the supervisor was acting within the scope of his employment (*see* Restatement (Second) of Agency, §219(1) (1958)), or whether his actions can be imputed to the employer under some exception to the "scope of employ-

---

[30]Sexual harassment claims are no different from other types of discrimination claims in this regard. *See Alexander v. Gardner-Denver Co.*, 415 U.S. 36, 52, 7 EPD ¶9148 [7 FEP Cases 81] (1974).

[31]*See I.U.O.E. v. Robbins & Myers, Inc.*, 429 U.S. 229, 236, 12 EPD ¶11,256 [13 FEP Cases 1813] (1976).

[32]The Commission has filed suit in such circumstances, alleging that termination of grievance processing because a charge has been filed constitutes unlawful retaliation in violation of §704(a). *See EEOC v. Board of Governors of State Colleges & Universities*, 706 F.Supp. 1378, 50 EPD ¶39,035 [50 FEP Cases 126] (D. Ill. 1989) (denying EEOC's motion for summary judgment on ground that ADEA's retaliation provision is not violated if termination of grievance proceedings was done in good faith).

[33]*See Brooms v. Regal Tube Co.*, 44 FEP Cases 1119 (N.D. Ill. 1987), *aff'd in relevant part*, 881 F.2d 412 (7th Cir. 1989).

[34]The fact that an EEOC charge puts the employer on notice of sexual harassment means that the question of imputed employer liability under agency principles often will become of secondary importance. It figured critically in the *Vinson* case because the plaintiff never filed an EEOC charge before filing her Title VII lawsuit. Without having given any prior notice of the sexual harassment to anyone, she waited to file her lawsuit until almost a year after she admitted it had ceased. The sexual harassment was alleged to have taken place mostly in private, and she produced no witnesses either to the alleged harassment or to its adverse effects on her. Her case did not include a constructive discharge claim, and the district court found no "quid pro quo" harassment.

ment" rule (*Id.* at §219(2)). The following principles should be considered, and applied where appropriate in "hostile environment" sexual harassment cases.

1. Scope of Employment. — A supervisor's actions are generally viewed as being within the scope of his employment if they represent the exercise of authority actually vested in him. It will rarely be the case that an employer will have authorized a supervisor to engage in sexual harassment. *See Fields v. Horizon House, Inc.*, No. 86-4343 (E.D. Pa. 1987) (available on Lexis, Genfed library, Dist. file). *Cf. Hunter v. Allis-Chalmers Corp.*, 797 F.2d 1417, 1421-22, 41 EPD ¶36,417 [41 FEP Cases 721] (7th Cir. 1986) (co-worker racial harassment case). However, if the employer becomes aware of work-related sexual misconduct and does nothing to stop it, the employer, by acquiescing, has brought the supervisor's actions within the scope of his employment.

2. Apparent Authority — An employer is also liable for a supervisor's actions if these actions represent the exercise of authority that third parties reasonably believe him to possess by virtue of his employer's conduct. This is called "apparent authority." See Restatement (Second) of Agency, §§7, 8; 219(2)(d) (1958). The Commission believes that in the absence of a strong, widely disseminated, and consistently enforced employer policy against sexual harassment, and an effective complaint procedure, employees could reasonably believe that a harassing supervisor's actions will be ignored, tolerated, or even condoned by upper management. This apparent authority of supervisors arises from their power over their employees, including the power to make or substantially influence hiring, firing, promotion and compensation decisions. A supervisor's capacity to create a hostile environment is enhanced by the degree of authority conferred on him by the employer, and he may rely upon apparent authority to force an employee to endure a harassing environment for

fear of retaliation. If the employer has not provided an effective avenue to complain, then the supervisor has unchecked, final control over the victim and it is reasonable to impute his abuse of this power to the employer.[35] The Commission generally will find an employer liable for "hostile environment" sexual harassment by a supervisor when the employer failed to establish an explicit policy against sexual harassment and did not have a reasonably available avenue by which victims of sexual harassment could complain to someone with authority to investigate and remedy the problem. (*See* Section E.) *See also EEOC v. Hacienda Hotel*, 881 F.2d 1504, 51 EPD ¶39,250 [50 FEP Cases 877] (9th Cir. 1989) (finding employer liable for sexual harassment despite plaintiff's failure to pursue internal remedies where the employer's anti-discrimination policy did not specifically proscribe sexual harassment and its internal procedures required initial resort to the supervisor accused of engaging in or condoning harassment).

But an employer can divest its supervisors of this apparent authority by implementing a strong policy against sexual harassment and maintaining an effective complaint procedure. When employees know that recourse is available, they cannot reasonably believe that a harassing work environment is authorized or condoned by the employer.[36] If an employee failed to use an effective, available complaint procedure, the employer may

[35]*See also Fields v. Horizon House, supra* (an employer might be charged with constructive notice of a supervisor's harassment if the supervisor is vested with unbridled authority to retaliate against an employee).

[36]It is important to reemphasize, however, that no matter what the employer's policy, the employer is always liable for any supervisory actions that affect the victim's employment status, such as hiring, firing, promotion or pay. *See supra* at 21-22. Moreover, this discussion of apparent authority recognizes the unique nature of "hostile environment" sexual harassment claims and therefore is limited to such cases.

be able to prove the absence of apparent authority and thus the lack of an agency relationship, unless liability attaches under some other theory.[37] Thus, even when an employee failed to use an effective grievance procedure, the employer will be liable if it obtained notice through other means (such as the filing of a charge or by the pervasiveness of the harassment) and did not take immediate and appropriate corrective action.

Example — Charging Party (CP) alleges that her supervisor made repeated sexual advances toward her that created a hostile work environment. The investigation into her charge discloses that CP had maintained an intermittent romantic relationship with the supervisor over a period of three years preceding the filing of the charge in September of 1986. CP's employer was aware of this relationship and its consensual nature. CP asserts, however, that on frequent occasions since January of 1986 she had clearly stated to the supervisor that their relationship was over and his advances were no longer welcome. The supervisor nevertheless persisted in making sexual advances toward CP, berating her for refusing to resume their sexual relationship. His conduct did not put the employer on notice that any unwelcome harassment was occurring. The employer has a well-communicated policy against sexual harassment and a complaint procedure designed to facilitate the resolution of sexual harassment complaints and ensure against re-

taliation. This procedure has worked well in the past. CP did not use it, however, or otherwise complain to higher management. Even if CP's allegations are true, the Commission would probably not find her employer liable for the alleged harassment since she failed to use the complaint procedure or inform higher management that the advances had become unwelcome. If CP resigned because of the alleged harassment, she would not be able to establish a constructive discharge since she failed to complain.

In the preceding example, if the employer, upon obtaining notice of the charge, failed to take immediate and appropriate corrective action to stop any ongoing harassment, then the employer will be unable to prove that the supervisor lacked apparent authority for his conduct, and if the allegations of harassment are true, then the employer will be found liable. Or if the supervisor terminated the charging party because she refused to submit to his advances, the employer would be liable for "quid pro quo" harassment.

3. Other Theories — A closely rated theory is agency by estoppel. *See* Restatement (Second) of Agency at §8B. An employer is liable when he intentionally or carelessly causes an employee to mistakenly believe the supervisor is acting for the employer, or knows of the misapprehension and fails to correct it. For example, an employer who fails to respond appropriately to past known incidents of harassment would cause its employees to reasonably believe that any further incidents are authorized and will be tolerated.

Liability also may be imputed if the employer was "negligent or reckless" in supervising the alleged harasser. *See* Restatement (Second) of Agency §219(2)(6); *Hicks v. Gates Rubber Co.*, 833 F.2d 1406, 1418, 44 EPD ¶37,542 [45 FEP Cases 608] (10th Cir. 1987). "Under this standard,

---

[37]*Cf. Fields v. Horizon House* ("Apparent authority is created by and flows from the acts of the principal, not from the personal beliefs of the third party."). Moreover, as noted above, an employee would find it difficult to establish a constructive discharge in this situation because she could not show she had no alternative but to resign. Failure to complain also might undermine a later assertion that the conduct occurred or was unwelcome.

liability would be imposed if the employer had actual or constructive knowledge of the sexual harassment but failed to take remedial action." *Fields v. Horizon House, Inc.*, No. 86-4343 (E.D. Pa. 1987). This is essentially the same as holding the employer directly liable for its failure to act.

An employer cannot avoid liability by delegating to another person a duty imposed by statute. Restatement (Second) of Agency at §492 (1958), Introductory Note, p.435 ("liability follows if the person to whom the performance is delegated acts improperly with respect to it"). An employer who assigns the performance of a non-delegable duty to an employee remains liable for injuries resulting from the failure of the employee to carry out that duty. Restatement, ¶¶214 and 219. Title VII imposes on employers a duty to provide their employees with a workplace free of sexual harassment. An employer who entrusts that duty to an employee is liable for injuries caused by the employee's breach of the duty. *See, e.g., Brooms v. Regal Tube Co.*, 44 FEP Cases 1119 (N.D. Ill. 1987) (employer liable for sexual harassment committed by the management official to whom it had delegated the responsibility to devise and enforce its policy against sexual harassment), *aff'd on other ground*, 881 F.2d 412, 240-21 (7th Cir. 1989).

Finally, an employer also may be liable if the supervisor "was aided in accomplishing the tort by the existence of the agency relation," Restatement (Second) of Agency §219(2)(d). *See Sparks v. Pilot Freight Carriers, Inc.*, 830 F.2d 1554, 44 EPD ¶37,493 [45 FEP Cases 160] (11th Cir. 1987); *Hicks v. Gates Rubber Co.*, 833 F.2d at 1418. For example, in *Sparks v. Pilot Freight Carriers*, the court found that the supervisor had used his supervisory authority to facilitate his harassment of the plaintiff by "repeatedly reminding [her] that he could fire her should she fail to comply with his advances." 830 F.2d at 1560. This case illus-

trates how the two types of sexual harassment can merge. When a supervisor creates a hostile environment through the aid of work-related threats or intimidation, the employer is liable under both the "quid pro quo" and "hostile environment" theories.

E. Preventive and Remedial Action

1) Preventive Action — The EEOC's Guidelines encourage employers to:

> take all steps necessary to prevent sexual harassment from occurring, such as affirmatively raising the subject, expressing strong disapproval, developing appropriate sanctions, informing employees of their rights to raise and how to raise the issue of harassment under Title VII, and developing methods to sensitize all concerned.

23 C.F.R. §1604.11(f). An effective preventive program should include an explicit policy against sexual harassment that is clearly and regularly communicated to employees and effectively implemented. The employer should affirmatively raise the subject with all supervisory and non-supervisory employees, express strong disapproval, and explain the sanctions for harassment. The employer should also have a procedure for resolving sexual harassment complaints. The procedure should be designed to "encourage victims of harassment to come forward" and should not require a victim to complain first to the offending supervisor. *See Vinson*, 106 S.Ct. at 2408. It should ensure confidentiality as much as possible and provide effective remedies, including protection of victims and witnesses against retaliation.

2) Remedial Action — Since Title VII "affords employees the right to work in an environment free from discriminatory intimidation, ridicule, and insult" *(Vinson*, 106 S.Ct. at 2405), an employer is liable for failing to remedy known hostile or offensive work environments. *See, e.g., Garziano v. E.I. DuPont deNemours & Co.*, 818 F.2d 380, 43 EPD ¶37,171 [43 FEP Cases 1790] (5th Cir. 1987) (*Vinson* holds employers have an "affirmative duty to eradicate 'hostile or offensive' work environments"); *Bundy v. Jackson*, 641 F.2d 934, 947, 24 EPD ¶31,439 [24 FEP Cases 1155] (D.C. Cir. 1981) (employer violated Title VII by failing to investigate and correct sexual harassment despite notice); *Tompkins v. Public Service Electric & Gas Co.*, 568 F.2d 1044, 1049, 15 EPD 7954 [16 FEP Cases 22] (3rd Cir. 1977) (same); *Henson v. City of Dundee*, 682 F.2d 897, 905, 15 EPD ¶32,993 [29 FEP Cases 787] (11th Cir. 1982) (same); *Munford v. James T. Barnes & Co.*, 441 F.Supp. 459, 466, 16 EPD ¶8233 [17 FEP Cases 107] (E.D. Mich. 1977) (employer has an affirmative duty to investigate complaints of sexual harassment and to deal appropriately with the offending personnel; "failure to investigate gives tacit support to the discrimination because the absence of sanctions encourages abusive behavior").[38]

When an employer receives a complaint or otherwise learns of alleged sexual harassment in the workplace, the employer should investigate promptly and thoroughly. The employer should take immediate and appropriate corrective action by doing whatever is necessary to end the harassment, make the victim whole by restoring lost employment benefits or opportunities, and prevent the misconduct from recurring. Disciplinary action against the offending supervisor or employee, ranging from reprimand to discharge, may be necessary. Generally,

---

[38]The employer's affirmative duty was first enunciated in cases of harassment based on race or national origin. *See, e.g., United States v. City of Buffalo*, 457 F.Supp. 612, 632-35, 18 EPD ¶8899 [19 FEP Cases 776] (W.D.N.Y. 1978), *modified in part*, 633 F.2d 643, 24 EPD ¶31,333 [24 FEP Cases 313] (2d Cir. 1980) (employer violated Title VII by failing to issue strong policy directive against racial slurs and harassment of black police officers, to conduct, full investigations, and to take appropriate disciplinary action); *EEOC v. Murphy Motor Freight Lines, Inc.*, 488 F.Supp. 381, 385-86, 22 EPD ¶30,888 [22 FEP Cases 892] (D. Minn. 1980) (defendant violated Title VII because supervisors knew or should have known of co-workers' harassment of black employees, but took inadequate steps to eliminate it).

the corrective action should reflect the severity of the conduct. *See Waltman v. International Paper Co.* 875 F.2d at 479 (appropriateness of remedial action will depend on the severity and persistence of the harassment and the effectiveness of any initial remedial steps). *Dornhecker v. Malibu Grand Prix Corp.*, 828 F.2d 307, 309-10, 44 EPD ¶37,557 [44 FEP Cases 1604] (5th Cir. 1987) (the employer's remedy may be "assessed proportionately to the seriousness of the offense"). The employer should make follow-up inquiries to ensure the harassment has not resumed and the victim has not suffered retaliation.

Recent court decisions illustrate appropriate and inappropriate responses by employers. In *Barrett v. Omaha National Bank*, 726 F.2d 424, 33 EPD ¶34,132 [35 FEP Cases 593] (8th Cir. 1984), the victim informed her employer that her co-worker had talked to her about sexual activities and touched her in an offensive manner. Within four days of receiving this information, the employer investigated the charges, reprimanded the guilty employee, placed him on probation, and warned him that further misconduct would result in discharge. A second co-worker who had witnessed the harassment was also reprimanded for not intervening on the victim's behalf or reporting the conduct. The court ruled that the employer's response constituted immediate and appropriate corrective action, and on this basis found the employer not liable.

In contrast, in *Yates v. Avco Corp.*, 819 F.2d 630, 43 EPD ¶37,086 [43 FEP Cases 1595] (6th Cir. 1987), the court found the employer's policy against sexual harassment failed to function effectively. The victim's first-level supervisor had responsibility for reporting and correcting harassment at the company, yet he was the harasser. The employer told the victims not to go to the EEOC. While giving the accused harasser administrative leave pending investigation, the employer made the plaintiffs take sick leave, which was never credited back to them and was recorded in their personnel files as excessive absenteeism without indicating they were absent because of sexual harassment. Similarly, in *Zabkowicz v. West Bend Co.*, 589 F.Supp. 780, 35 EPD ¶34,766 [35 FEP Cases 610] (E.D. Wis. 1984), co-workers harassed the plaintiff over a period of nearly four years in a manner the court described as "malevolent" and "outrageous." Despite the plaintiff's numerous complaints, her supervisor took no remedial action other than to hold occasional meetings at which he reminded employees of the company's policy against offensive conduct. The supervisor never conducted an investigation or disciplined any employees until the plaintiff filed an EEOC charge, at which time one of the offending co-workers was discharged and three others were suspended. The court held the employer liable because it failed to take immediate and appropriate corrective action.[39]

---

[39]*See also Delgado v. Lehman*, 665 F.Supp. 460, 44 EPD ¶37,517 [43 FEP Cases 593] (E.D. Va. 1987) (employer failed to conduct follow-up inquiry to determine if hostile environment had dissipated); *Salazar v. Church's Fried Chicken, Inc.*, 44 FEP Cases 472

When an employer asserts it has taken remedial action, the Commission will investigate to determine whether the action was appropriate and, more important, effective. The EEOC investigator should, of course, conduct an independent investigation of the harassment claim, and the Commission will reach its own conclusion as to whether the law has been violated. If the Commission finds that the harassment has been eliminated, all victims made whole, and preventive measures instituted, the Commission normally will administratively close the charge because of the employer's prompt remedial action.[40]

Date 3/19/90

Approved:

/s/R. Gaull Silberman
Vice Chairman

(S.D. Tex. 1987) (employer's policy inadequate because plaintiff, as a part-time teenage employee, could have concluded a complaint would be futile because the alleged harasser was the roommate of her store manager); *Brooms v. Regal Tube Co.*, 44 FEP Cases 1119 (N.D. Ill. 1987) (employer liable when a verbal reprimand proved ineffective and employer took no further action when informed of the harasser's persistence).

[40]For appropriate procedures, see §§4.4(e) and 15 of Volume I of the Compliance Manual.

SAMPLE ANTIHARASSMENT POLICY

The ABC Company is committed to maintaining a work environment that is free of discrimination. In keeping with this commitment, we will not tolerate harassment of ABC employees by anyone, including any supervisor, co-worker, vendor, client, or customer of ABC.

Harassment consists of unwelcome conduct, whether verbal, physical, or visual, that is based upon a person's protected status, such as sex, color, race, ancestry, religion, national origin, age, physical handicap, medical condition, disability, marital status, veteran status, citizenship status, or other protected group status. The Company will not tolerate harassing conduct that affects tangible job benefits, that interferes unreasonably with an individual's work performance, or that creates an intimidating, hostile, or offensive working environment.

Sexual harassment deserves special mention. Unwelcome sexual advances, requests for sexual favors, and other physical, verbal, or visual conduct based on sex constitute sexual harassment when (1) submission to the conduct is an explicit or implicit term or condition of employment, (2) submission to or rejection of the conduct is used as the basis for an employment decision, or (3) the conduct has the purpose or effect of unreasonably interfering with an individual's work performance or creating an intimidating, hostile, or offensive working environment. Sexual harassment may include explicit sexual propositions, sexual innuendo, suggestive comments, sexually oriented "kidding" or "teasing," "practical jokes," jokes about gender-specific traits, foul or obscene language or gestures, display of foul or obscene printed or visual material, and physical contact such as patting, pinching, or brushing against another's body.

All ABC employees are responsible to help assure that we avoid harassment. If you feel that you have experienced or witnessed harassment, you are to notify immediately Mr. _____ or Ms. _____ in the Department of Human Resources. The Company forbids retaliation against anyone for reporting sexual harassment, assisting in making a sexual harassment complaint, or cooperating in a sexual harassment investigation.

The Company's policy is to investigate all such complaints thoroughly and promptly. To the fullest extent practicable, the Company will keep complaints and the terms of their resolution confidential. If an investigation confirms that harassment has occurred, the Company will take corrective action, including such discipline, up to and including immediate termination of employment, as is appropriate.

THE CIVIL RIGHTS ACT OF 1991

In November 1991 Congress approved and President Bush signed the Civil Rights Act of 1991. The Act amended Title VII of the Civil Rights Act of 1964, the Civil Rights Act of 1866 (as codified in 42 U.S.C. §1981), the Attorney's Fees Awards Act of 1976, the Americans with Disabilities Act of 1990, and the Age Discrimination in Employment Act of 1967. A full summary and analysis of the Act appears in Daily Labor Report (BNA) Special Supplement No. 218. The discussion below focuses on the changes that will affect sexual harassment litigation.

I. COMPENSATORY AND PUNITIVE DAMAGES

Section 102(a) of the Act adds a new section after 42 U.S.C. §1981 to provide that in cases of "intentional discrimination" unlawful under Title VII, a party may recover compensatory and punitive damages in addition to back pay, interest on back pay, and any other relief already authorized by §706(g) of Title VII.

Section 102(b)(1) of the Act provides that punitive damages are available upon proof that "the respondent engaged in a discriminatory practice or discriminatory practices with malice or with reckless indifference to the federally protected rights of an aggrieved individual."

Section 102(b)(3) of the Act indicates that compensatory damages may be awarded for "future pecuniary losses, emotional pain, suffering, inconvenience, mental anguish, loss of enjoyment of life, and other nonpecuniary losses."

II. CAP ON TOTAL COMPENSATORY AND PUNITIVE DAMAGES

Section 102(b)(3) of the Act provides that the sum total of compensatory and punitive damages is subject to a cap that varies with the size of the respondent, as follows:

Number of Employees	Cap on Total Damages
15–100	$50,000
101–200	$100,000
201–500	$200,000
more than 500	$300,000

III. TRIAL BY JURY

Section 102(c) of the Act provides that when compensatory or punitive damages are sought, any party can demand a jury trial. The court is forbidden to inform the jury about the cap on damage awards.

IV. EXPERT FEES

Section 113(b) of the Act amends Title VII to provide that an award of reasonable attorney's fees may include an award of expert fees.

V. ARBITRATION

Section 118 of the Act provides:

Where appropriate and to the extent authorized by law, the use of alternative means of dispute resolution, including settlement negotiations, conciliation, facilitation, mediation, factfinding, minitrials, and arbitration, is encouraged to resolve disputes arising under the Acts or provisions of Federal law amended by this title.

VI. RACIAL HARASSMENT

Section 101 of the Act amends 42 U.S.C. §1981 by providing that the right to "make and enforce contracts" includes "the enjoyment of all benefits, privileges, terms, and conditions of the contractual relationship." This amendment is intended to overrule the holding in *Patterson v. McLean Credit Union* that §1981 applied to the hiring and perhaps to the promotion process and did not prohibit racial harassment on the job.

VII. MIXED MOTIVE CASES

Section 107 of the Act amends Title VII to provide that where the plaintiff proves that a prohibited factor motivated an employment action, and where the employer proves that the same action would have been taken even absent the discriminatory motive, a violation of Title VII has been proven, with the employer's proof going to the issue of remedy rather than to liability. This change overrules a portion of *Price Waterhouse v. Hopkins.*

VIII. EFFECTIVE DATE

Section 402 of the Act states that absent specific provisions to the contrary, the Act takes effect upon enactment. The effect on pending cases is not specified.

AUDITING AN ANTISEXUAL HARASSMENT POLICY

The following *Questionnaire* and *Analysis* are designed to monitor the scope of a company's antisexual harassment policy and to determine if a company's educational programs, internal complaint procedures, and remedial action measures are sufficient to help create a positive working environment for all employees and help limit exposure to workplace liability stemming from sexual harassment.

QUESTIONNAIRE
(some questions may have more than one answer)

	Yes	No

Policy Considerations

1. Does your firm state specifically and emphatically in its employment handbook or other policy notices that it is committed to maintaining a workplace free of sexual harassment?

2. Does your policy define as "prohibited acts" such actions as: improper suggestions, pornographic objects or pictures, graphic or descriptive comments or discussions about an individual's body or physical appearance,

---

Reproduced with permission from *Employment–Labor Law Audit*, Laurdan Associates, Inc.; published by The Bureau of National Affairs, Inc.

	Yes	No

degrading verbal comments, and offensive
sexual flirtations?

3. Have you made all employees fully aware
    of your company's policy and procedures
    dealing with sexual harassment?

4. Have you established and promulgated a
    policy concerning disciplinary actions that
    may be taken against policy violators?

5. Has your firm established a separate and
    specific grievance or complaint procedure for
    employees victimized by harassment?

6. Is someone other than an employee's
    supervisor available to receive and investigate
    sexual harassment complaints?

7. Has your policy been reviewed by your labor
    counsel?

8. Does your policy make clear that sexual
    harassment investigations will be conducted
    on a confidential basis?

9. Does your policy make clear that a sexual
    harassment complainant will not be retaliated
    against for filing a complaint?

Education and Training

10. Do you hold routine training programs for
    supervisors, managers, and employees on
    sexual harassment and your firm's policies?

Reproduced with permission from *Employment–Labor Law Audit*, Laurdan Associates, Inc.;
published by The Bureau of National Affairs, Inc.

	Yes	No

11. Do you record the dates on which these training sessions take place and keep attendance records? ____ ____

12. Have you surveyed your employees to learn of their concerns about sexual harassment; to discuss their perceptions, experiences, and problems; and to obtain their thoughts on developing, implementing, and maintaining a sexual harassment-free environment? ____ ____

Investigating Process

13. Which individuals are interviewed during the investigation process:
    a. the complainant? ____ ____
    b. the alleged harasser? ____ ____
    c. witnesses? ____ ____
    d. other complainants? ____ ____

14. Who in your organization normally conducts the investigation:
    a. personnel? ____ ____
    b. the employee's supervisor? ____ ____
    c. top management? ____ ____
    d. an external or independent investigator? ____ ____

15. To whom are the results of the investigation communicated:
    a. the complainant? ____ ____
    b. the alleged harasser? ____ ____
    c. personnel? ____ ____
    d. other employees and supervisors? ____ ____
    e. top management? ____ ____
    f. general public? ____ ____

Yes   No

Remedying Sexual Harassment

16. Are complaints of sexual harassment acted
    upon immediately and investigated fully?   ____   ____

17. How are violators of your sexual harassment
    policy disciplined:
    a. counselled?   ____   ____
    b. transferred?   ____   ____
    c. suspended?   ____   ____
    d. demoted?   ____   ____
    e. terminated?   ____   ____
    f. no action is taken?   ____   ____

18. What factors influence the type of discipline
    that is administered:
    a. weight of evidence?   ____   ____
    b. nature of the sexual harassment?   ____   ____
    c. position of the individual harassed?   ____   ____
    d. position of the harasser?   ____   ____
    e. whether or not the complainant
        has an attorney?   ____   ____
    f. whether or not the complainant
        has notified the EEOC?   ____   ____
    g. whether or not the complainant
        has notified the press?   ____   ____
    h. other factors?   ____   ____

Lawsuits and Other Claims of Sexual Harassment

19. Has your company experienced one or more
    sexual harassment-related claims, EEO
    charges, or lawsuits?   ____   ____

20. Have you calculated the cost to your organ-
    ization of sexual harassment in terms of:
    a. awards and settlement?   ____   ____

	Yes	No
b. legal fees?	____	____
c. administrative costs?	____	____
d. public relations costs?	____	____
e. turnover?	____	____
f. sick leave and personal time off?	____	____
g. absenteeism and tardiness?	____	____
h. lower productivity?	____	____

Standards of Workplace Conduct

21. Do you allow employees to display lewd or indecent pictures or other materials depicting men or women as sex objects?   ____   ____

22. Do you require uniforms to be worn that are sexually provocative?   ____   ____

23. Do you allow sexually connotative remarks, sex related jokes, or "off color" stories to be routinely told in front of mixed audiences?   ____   ____

24. Do you allow a sexually charged atmosphere to permeate the workplace environment?   ____   ____

ANALYSIS

Questions 1 and 2

One of the first items that an EEO investigator will examine as part of a sexual harassment investigation is your sexual harassment policy. As EEOC guidelines make clear, investigators will look for a separate policy specifically setting forth your commitment to a workplace free from any traces of sexual harassment or a sexually charged environment. Simply having a general EEO, nondiscrimination policy is not sufficient. As the guidelines clearly state, a policy tailored specifically to defining, prohibiting, investigating, and remedying sexual harassment is required. In some states, the absence of such

Reproduced with permission from *Employment–Labor Law Audit*, Laurdan Associates, Inc.; published by The Bureau of National Affairs, Inc.

a policy is a "per se" violation. In any event, you will be in a better position to defend a sexual harassment charge if a formal policy has been implemented.

Any written policy regarding sexual harassment should be broadly drafted to ensure that the full scope of prohibited sexual harassment activity is included.

Question 3

The EEOC's guidelines emphasize the need to communicate your sexual harassment policy to all supervisors and all employees. These communications may include supervisory and employee meetings or the distribution of your sexual harassment policy, either separately or as part of the employee handbook, or as a poster placed in common areas of the workplace. Because management officials, from the president to front line supervisors, are responsible for communicating, administering, enforcing, and adhering to the policy, separate meetings should be held for your management team. Records should be kept documenting when and where these educational sessions were conducted, who was present, and what was discussed. Maintaining these records will go a long way toward defending your position should a sexual harassment complaint be filed against your company. The EEOC will look at your commitment to implementing and enforcing your policy in this area.

Question 4

Employees should be informed that violations of the company's sexual harassment policy will be considered a serious violation of company rules and will be dealt with accordingly. Although there is no requirement that certain violations automatically give rise to specific forms of disciplinary action, you must emphasize that all violations will be dealt with swiftly. The punishment should be tailored to the offense, after consideration of all relevant factors. Questions 17 and 18 identify some disciplinary options, and some of the factors used in meting out discipline.

Questions 5 to 7

An internal system to facilitate employee complaints of sexual harassment should be established. The existence of this complaint procedure should be set forth in your sexual harassment policy and employees should be encouraged to utilize it if the occasion demands. The complaint procedure should give an employee the option of bypassing his or her immediate supervisor,

Reproduced with permission from *Employment–Labor Law Audit*, Laurdan Associates, Inc.; published by The Bureau of National Affairs, Inc.

or any other member of management, if that supervisor or manager is the subject of the complaint or is involved in any way with the complainant's difficulty. Remember, employees should be encouraged to resolve their problems internally, rather than seeking outside intervention. Indeed, it is far less costly and time consuming to handle employee problems of this nature "in house," than it is if the EEOC or local civil rights agency gets involved. In many instances, the complaining party will also be better served by a quick and effective resolution of the matter through informal channels. Once developed, you should have your policy reviewed by labor counsel to ensure that the policy conforms as closely as possible to the EEOC guidelines and evolving case law on the subject.

Questions 8 and 9

Once a complaint is brought to your attention, you have a duty to investigate the matter thoroughly and expeditiously. Such an investigation naturally requires tact, sensitivity, and an appreciation of the seriousness of the allegations for all concerned. Therefore, any investigation must be limited to designated individuals who have had some training in performing this function. Interviews should be handled privately and confidentially. Reports dealing with the investigation should be revealed only to those with a need to know. The investigation should be conducted only by individuals designated as part of the investigation team. All information obtained as a result of the investigation should be dealt with in the strictest confidence. All parties to the investigation should be assured that their participation is appreciated, and that they will not be retaliated against in any way because of their participation and cooperation in the investigation. (For a fuller treatment of these considerations, see the discussion pertaining to questions 13–15.)

Questions 10 to 12

The threat of sexual harassment in the workplace is a constant one. Therefore, you must alert supervisors to watch for signs of sexual harassment and remind them of the importance of their role in maintaining a harassment-free workplace. In addition to conducting regular training sessions, you should record the dates of these sessions and list those in attendance, so that this information is available in the event of an EEOC investigation.

It is untrue that the less said about sexual harassment the better. The causes, forms of harassment, and injury caused by sexual harassment need to be discussed. When everyone in your organization is aware of the illegality

---

Reproduced with permission from *Employment–Labor Law Audit*, Laurdan Associates, Inc.; published by The Bureau of National Affairs, Inc.

of sexual harassment, the harm caused by it, and your strong policy against it, it is less likely to flourish.

Questions 13 to 15

An important step in implementing an effective sexual harassment policy is conducting a thorough investigation of all claims that keeps allegations confidential to the extent practical. You will be better able to protect your interests and those of your employees if an incident of sexual harassment is thoroughly and immediately investigated rather than ignored. All identified or likely witnesses, in addition to the parties involved, should be interviewed if necessary, to determine if they have any knowledge of the alleged harassment. Although there are seldom witnesses to sexual harassment, other employees may have noticed a change in the victim's behavior following the incident, or the victim may have discussed the harassment with other employees. In addition, a thorough investigation is also a good source for discovering if other employees have experienced sexual harassment.

An investigation is also important in determining if the alleged conduct was unwelcome. Your company's liability is generally limited to unwelcome advances or conduct. Thus, even if the employee participated in the activity, you may still be liable if the employee demonstrated in other ways that the advance or conduct was unwelcome. An investigation may reveal whether the employee had ever manifested any objections to the activity.

The person chosen to conduct the investigation should demonstrate that you wish to encourage victims of sexual harassment to come forward. The investigator should be capable of acting impartially and you should stress in your sexual harassment policy that employees will not be subject to retaliation for filing a complaint or for cooperating in an investigation. The investigator should also have the authority to remedy or effectively recommend the remedy of any violations that he or she discovers. If the employee's supervisor normally conducts the investigation, the employee should be given the name of an alternative person to contact if the complaint involves the supervisor. If the results of the investigation are disclosed, the identity of the parties should not be revealed in order to preserve their confidentiality.

A prompt investigation followed by corrective action will greatly reduce the likelihood of your being held liable for the sexual harassment. If the sexual harassment relates to the work environment, a prompt investigation will also reduce the chance that knowledge of the harassment will be imputed to you. If the sexual harassment resulted in the loss of a promotion, discharge, or otherwise affects the victim's employment status, you can reduce your liability and promote positive employee relations by investigating the incident and remedying the problem.

Questions 16 to 18

Under Title VII of the Civil Rights Act of 1964, as amended, an employee is guaranteed the right to a work environment free of hostile or offensive behavior. You should implement a separate, preventive program to discourage sexual harassment, and the policy should be clearly and regularly communicated to employees. If sexual harassment does occur, you should take prompt corrective action and ensure that your disciplinary policy is strictly enforced. Your failure to act promptly once you know or should have known that sexual harassment exists may be interpreted as approval of the harassing employee's illegal actions. If, however, you act quickly to remedy the incident, you will generally not be held liable under Title VII.

The remedy should include whatever actions are necessary to end the harassment and restore lost benefits or opportunities to the victim. The proper disciplinary action will vary from a reprimand to discharge based on the severity of the misconduct. Disciplinary measures should be strictly and consistently enforced against all employees. You should also check with the harassed employee after the matter is resolved to ensure that the harassment has not reoccurred, and the he/she has not suffered any retaliation. Although a victim is not required to exhaust the internal grievance procedure available to him or her before filing a complaint with the EEOC, the commission will normally close any charges if the matter has been satisfactorily resolved. In addition, an employee is less likely to resort to the EEOC or a state agency, which is ultimately more expensive for the employer, if the internal grievance policy is considered fair and effective.

Questions 19 and 20

An employee may use other instances of sexual harassment, especially other incidents involving the person accused of sexual harassment, to corroborate his or her complaint. If the complaint charges a hostile work environment, an employee may also use evidence of other claims against you to establish that sexual harassment was so pervasive in the workplace that you must have had knowledge of it. Thus a poor "track record" can increase the likelihood that you will incur liability in the future.

The lack of an effective sexual harassment policy can be expensive. Costly settlements and legal fees are only some of the possible financial

Reproduced with permission from *Employment–Labor Law Audit*, Laurdan Associates, Inc.; published by The Bureau of National Affairs, Inc.

repercussions. Sexual harassment also results in many other hidden costs, including lost productivity. NOTE: Some experts assert that most employers do not know the real cost of sexual harassment. As a result, total management commitment is lacking. The better able you are to show your management team the P&L impact of sexual harassment, the greater the commitment you will receive from them in ensuring compliance. Thus, establishing a strategy that emphasizes prevention, calculates and promulgates the real cost of sexual harassment, and implements a grievance procedure that produces fair results is the most cost-effective method of dealing with sexual harassment.

Questions 21 to 24

Even if an employee does not experience any financial detriment from sexual harassment, you may still be liable if the work environment is hostile or offensive. Title VII protects an employee from having to endure an offensive environment in order to earn a living. However, you will not be liable simply because one employee is more sensitive to certain behavior than another. Instead, you will be liable if a reasonable person in similar circumstances would find the work environment to be hostile, intimidating, or offensive.

A hostile working environment typically is one that unreasonably interferes with the employee's ability to do his or her job. Single incidents are normally not sufficient to establish a hostile environment, although a particularly abusive incident may be sufficient to establish a violation. If the harassment consists solely of verbal conduct, the abusiveness of the work environment will depend on the nature, frequency, context, and the intended target of the comments. In some instances, the requirement to wear revealing uniforms or other similar employment practices may be enough to constitute an abusive working environment. In workplaces where some vulgar language or actions has traditionally been tolerated, the totality of the circumstances might possibly be considered in determining whether the environment exceeds acceptable, non-hostile levels of behavior; but some courts have held that the existence of a traditionally vulgar workplace is immaterial.

TABLE OF CASES

INDEX

293

ABOUT THE AUTHORS

Barbara Lindemann is an attorney with Seyfarth, Shaw, Fairweather & Geraldson in Los Angeles, the largest labor law firm in the United States, where she represents management in employment matters. She is an honor graduate of Yale Law School where she was a member of the Board of Editors of the *Yale Law Journal*. She is a former Police Commissioner of the City of Los Angeles and served with the Equal Employment Opportunity Commission from 1965–1977 both in Washington, D.C., and as Regional Counsel to the Los Angeles office. She is a member of the U.S. Trade Representative's Service Policy Advisory Committee, having been appointed under both the Reagan and Bush administrations. She also serves on the California Commission for Economic Development's Advisory Council on Asia. A nationally prominent civil rights lawyer, she is co-author of *Employment Discrimination Law*, the official publication of the American Bar Association that is widely regarded by scholars and judges to be the "Bible" in its field. She is also co-author of the highly acclaimed legal treatise *Sexual Harassment in Employment Law*.

David D. Kadue is a partner in the Los Angeles office of Seyfarth, Shaw, Fairweather & Geraldson, where he has specialized in employment law counseling and litigation since 1983. He received his B.A. degree, with honors, from Yale University in 1975 and his J.D. degree, with honors, from the University of Minnesota Law School in 1978. He served as notes & comments editor on the *Minnesota Law Review*. Upon graduation

301

from law school, he served for one year as an instructor at the University of Miami Law School in Coral Gables, Florida, and for the next two years as a law clerk, first to Circuit Judge Roy L. Stephenson of the United States Court of Appeals for the Eighth Circuit and then to Circuit Judge George E. MacKinnon of the United States Court of Appeals for the D.C. Circuit. He then joined the federal employment law practice of Seyfarth, Shaw, Fairweather & Geraldson in Washington, D.C., and continued with that practice upon his move to Los Angeles in 1983. In addition to his writings on sexual harassment, including co-authoring *Sexual Harassment in Employment Law*, he has published several law journal articles on federal civil procedure, employment discrimination law, and the Americans With Disabilities Act of 1990.